MEDITATIONS

FOR ALL THE DAYS OF THE YEAR

VOLUME IV

MEDITATIONS

FOR ALL THE DAYS OF THE YEAR

VOLUME IV

*From the Sixth Sunday after Pentecost
to the Seventeenth Sunday after Pentecost*

"Indeed this was the Son of God." - *St. Matthew 27:54*

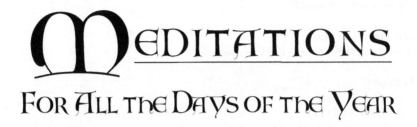

MEDITATIONS

FOR ALL THE DAYS OF THE YEAR

**FOR THE USE OF PRIESTS, RELIGIOUS
AND THE FAITHFUL.**

BY
REV. M. HAMON, S.S.,

Pastor of St. Sulpice, Paris, Author of "Life of St. Francis de Sales" and "Life of Cardinal Cheverus."

From the Twenty-third Revised and Enlarged Edition
BY
MRS. ANNE R. BENNETT,
(née GLADSTONE.)

WITH A METHOD OF USING THESE MEDITATIONS,
BY VERY REV. A. MAGNIEN, S.S., D.D.

VOLUME IV

*From the Sixth Sunday after Pentecost
to the Seventeenth Sunday after Pentecost*

Originally published by:

NEW YORK, CINCINNATI, CHICAGO:
Benzinger Brothers
Printers to the Holy Apostolic See

Reprinted by Valora Media
Cover and layout by: Kenneth R. Henderson

Nihil Obstat

D. J. McMAHON, D.D.,

Censor Librorum
Imprimatur

MICHAEL AUGUSTINE,

Archbishop of New York

NEW YORK, July 14, 1894.

PREFACE

To aid Christian souls better to know God with His infinite perfections and His adorable mysteries; better to love and serve Him, better to know themselves, their faults and their duties; better to reform themselves and to make progress in virtue: such is the end we have proposed to ourselves in writing this work. In this futile and frivolous age, in which hardly any one occupies himself with aught except external events, there are very few souls who seriously reflect upon these great and holy things; very few who carefully meditate every morning how much God deserves to be loved and served, how they can serve Him during the present day, and what they will do for His glory, for their own salvation, and their personal sanctification. As a remedy for this evil, we have believed it will be useful to make the very important exercise of meditation easy for souls of goodwill, by putting into their hands not a literary work which addresses itself to their minds, but a course of meditations which addresses itself to their hearts, and which should be read calmly, attentively, with reflection, with the object of entering into themselves and being awakened to a better life. May the reader thoroughly understand our design, meditate deeply and get to the bottom of each phrase, if we may so speak, penetrate himself with it and apply it to himself, by comparing what he is with what he ought to be, and deducing practical consequences for the reformation of his life, not in the distant future, but on the very same day. In the composition of his work, we have followed, step by step, if we can so say, the Roman liturgy, which has so admirably collected together the whole of religion within the course of the ecclesiastical year, and under the direction of such a sure guide we have meditated: first, upon the mysteries which are the basis of Christian virtues; second, the Christian virtues themselves, which are the edifice to be built upon this basis; third, the feasts of the most celebrated among the saints, whose life is virtue itself in action; and we have endeavored to present here these great subjects in a manner which will be equally suitable to the clergy and the faithful, so that our work may be useful to a greater number. The reader must not be astonished sometimes to meet with the same truth or the same virtue presented for meditation under different aspects. The soul needs to have the same truth often repeated to it, otherwise the impression would be effaced, until it became for us as though it had never been; it needs to reproach itself often with certain faults, otherwise it would lose sight of them, and would no longer take any care to correct them; lastly, it needs to be often raised up, because it often falls; hence our repetitions are anything but idle repetitions.

He must not be astonished, either, on the preceding evening, to find there the summary of the morrow s meditation. It is very important, in order to succeed properly in meditation, to fix precisely the subject on the preceding evening, and to arrive at the meditation of it already penetrated with what is about to occupy him. Hence, at the head of every meditation we have placed: First, an indication of the points of the meditation; Second, the enunciation of the resolutions which should be the practical consequence of it. We have added afterwards what St. Francis de Sales calls a spiritual nosegay; that is to say, a good thought which will be the sum total as it were of the meditation, and of which the perfume, embalming our heart during the whole day, recalls to us our morning meditation.

We have also placed at the beginning of each volume the usual morning and evening prayers, so that there may be no need to have recourse to another book to fulfill the daily duties of every Christian. Lastly, we have added to this third edition: First, several new meditations; second, a more careful and complete index; third, a plan of meditations for an eight day retreat; fourth, self examinations inserted in the greater part of the meditations; fifth, various developments op several subjects of meditation. May God, in His love for souls, deign to bless this new work and make it serve to His glory and to the sanctification of the elect!

&ℭ Contents ℭ&

SAINTS DAYS

MORNING PRAYERS

In the name of the Father, + and of the Son, and of the Holy Ghost. Amen.

Place Yourself in the Presence of God, and adore His holy Name.

Most holy and adorable Trinity, one God in three Persons, I believe that Thou art here present: I adore Thee with the deepest humility, and render to Thee, with my whole heart, the homage which is due to Thy sovereign majesty.

ACT OF FAITH

O my God, I firmly believe that Thou art one God in three divine Persons. Father, Son, and Holy Ghost; I believe that Thy divine Son became man, and died for our sins, and that He will come to judge the living and the dead. I believe these and all the truths which the holy Catholic Church teaches, because Thou hast revealed them, who canst neither deceive nor be deceived.

ACT OF HOPE

O my God, relying on Thy infinite goodness and promises, I hope to obtain pardon of my sins, the help of Thy grace, and life everlasting, through the merits of Jesus Christ, my Lord and Redeemer.

ACT OF LOVE

O my God, I love Thee above all things, with my whole heart and soul, because Thou art all-good and worthy of all love. I love my neighbor as myself for the love of Thee. I forgive all who have injured me, and ask pardon of all whom I have injured.

THANK GOD FOR ALL FAVORS AND OFFER YOURSELF TO HIM

O my God, I most humbly thank Thee for all the favors Thou hast bestowed upon me up to the present moment. I give Thee thanks from the bottom of my heart that Thou hast created me after Thine own image and likeness, that Thou hast redeemed me by the precious blood of Thy dear Son, and that Thou hast preserved me and brought me safe to the beginning of another day. I offer to Thee, O Lord, my whole being, and in particular all my thoughts, words, actions, and sufferings of this day. I consecrate them all to the glory of Thy name, beseeching Thee that through the infinite merits of Jesus Christ my Savior they may all find acceptance in Thy sight. May Thy divine love animate them, and may they all tend to Thy greater glory.

RESOLVE TO AVOID SIN AND TO PRACTICE VIRTUE

Adorable Jesus, my Savior and Master, model of all perfection, I resolve and will endeavor this day to imitate Thy example, to be, like Thee, mild, humble, chaste, zealous, charitable, and resigned. I will redouble my efforts that I may not fall this day into any of those sins which I have heretofore committed (here name any besetting sin), and which I sincerely desire to forsake.

ASK GOD FOR THE NECESSARY GRACES

O my God, Thou knowest my poverty and weakness, and that I am unable to do anything good without Thee; deny me not, O God, the help of Thy grace: proportion it to my necessities; give me strength to avoid anything evil which Thou forbiddest and to practice the good which Thou hast commanded; and enable me to bear patiently all the trials which it may please Thee to send me.

THE LORD'S PRAYER

Latin

Pater noster, qui es in caelis, sanctificetur nomen tuum. Adveniat regnum tuum. Fiat voluntas tua, sicut in caelo et in terra. Panem nostrum quotidianum da nobis hodie, et dimitte nobis debita nostra sicut et nos dimittimus debitoribus nostris. Et ne nos inducas in tentationem, sed libera nos a malo. Amen.

English

Our Father, who art in heaven, hallowed be Thy name. Thy kingdom come. Thy will be done on earth as it is in heaven. Give us this day our daily bread and forgive us our trespasses as we forgive those who trespass against us. And lead us not into temptation, but deliver us from evil. Amen.

THE HAIL MARY

Latin

Ave Maria, gratia plena, Dominus tecum. Benedicta tu in mulieribus, et benedictus fructus ventris tui, Jesus. Sancta Maria, Mater Dei, ora pro nobis peccatoribus, nunc, et in hora mortis nostrae. Amen.

English

Hail Mary, full of grace, the Lord is with thee. Blessed art thou amongst women and blessed is the fruit of thy womb, Jesus. Holy Mary, Mother of God, pray for us sinners, now, and in the hour of our death. Amen.

THE APOSTLE'S CREED

Latin

Credo in Deum Patrem omnipotentem, Creatorem caeli et terrae. Et in Iesum Christum, Filium eius unicum, Dominum nostrum, qui conceptus est de Spiritu Sancto, natus ex Maria Virgine, passus sub Pontio Pilato, crucifixus, mortuus, et sepultus, descendit ad infernos, tertia die resurrexit a mortuis, ascendit ad caelos, sedet ad dexteram Dei Patris omnipotentis, inde venturus est iudicare vivos et mortuos. Credo in Spiritum Sanctum, sanctam Ecclesiam catholicam, sanctorum communionem, remissionem peccatorum, carnis resurrectionem et vitam aeternam. Amen.

English

I believe in God, the Father almighty, Creator of heaven and earth. I believe in Jesus Christ, His only Son, our Lord. He was conceived by the power of the Holy Spirit and born of the Virgin Mary. He suffered under Pontius Pilate, was crucified, died, and was buried. He descended to the dead. On the third day He rose again. He ascended into heaven and sits at the right hand of God, the Father Almighty. From thence He shall come to judge the living and the dead. I believe in the Holy Spirit, the holy catholic Church, the communion of saints, the forgiveness of sins, the resurrection of the body, and the life everlasting. Amen.

ASK THE PRAYERS OF THE BLESSED VIRGIN, YOUR GUARDIAN ANGEL, AND YOUR PATRON SAINT.

Holy Virgin Mother of God, my Mother and Patroness, I place myself under thy protection, I throw myself with confidence into the arms of thy compassion. Be to me, O Mother of mercy, my refuge in distress, my consolation under suffering, my advocate with thy adorable Son, now and at the hour of my death.

> Angel of God, my guardian dear,
> To whom His love commits me here,
> Ever this day be at my side,
> To light and guard, to rule and guide. Amen.

O great Saint whose name I bear, protect me, pray for me that like thee I may serve God faithfully on earth, and glorify Him eternally with thee in heaven. Amen.

LITANY OF THE MOST HOLY NAME OF JESUS

O Lord Jesus Christ, who hast said: Ask, and ye shall receive; seek, and ye shall find; knock, and it shall be opened unto you; grant, we beseech Thee, unto us who ask, the gift of Thy most divine love, that we may ever love Thee with all our hearts, and in all our words and actions, and never cease from showing forth Thy praise.

Latin	*English*
Kyrie eleison.	Lord, have mercy on us.
Christe eleison.	Christ, have mercy on us.
Kyrie eleison.	Lord, have mercy on us.
Jesu aucli nos.	Jesus, hear us.
Jesu exaudi nos.	Jesus, graciously hear us.
Pater de coelis Deus,	God the Father of heaven,
...Miserere nobis	...Have mercy on us.
Fill, Redemptor mundi, Deus,	God the Son, Redeemer of the world,
Spiritus Sancte Deus,	God the Holy Ghost,
Sancta Trinitas, unus Deus,	Holy Trinity, one God,
Jesu, Fili Dei vivi,	Jesus, Son of the living God,
Jesu, splendor Patris,	Jesus, splendor of the Father,
Jesu, candor lucis aeternx,	Jesus, brightness of eternal light,
Jesu, rex gloriae,	Jesus, king of glory,
Jesu, sol justitiae,	Jesus, sun of justice,
Jesu, fili Mariae Virginis,	Jesus, son of the Virgin Mary,
Jesu amabilis,	Jesus, most amiable,
Jesu admirabilis,	Jesus, most admirable,

Jesu, Deus fords,	Jesus, mighty God,
Jesu, pater futuri saeculi,	Jesus, father of the world to come,
Jesu, magni consilii angele,	Jesus, angel of the great council,
Jesu potentissime,	Jesus, most powerful,
Jesu patientissime,	Jesus, most patient,
Jesu obedientissime,	Jesus, most obedient,
Jesu, mitis et humilis corde,	Jesus, meek and humble of heart,
Jesu, amator castitatis,	Jesus, lover of chastity,
Jesu, amator noster,	Jesus, lover of us,
Jesu, Deus pacis,	Jesus, God of peace,
Jesu, auctor vitae,	Jesus, author of life,
Jesu, exemplar virtutum,	Jesus, model of virtues,
Jesu, zelator animarum,	Jesus, zealous for souls,
Jesu, Deus noster,	Jesus, our God,
Jesu, refugium nostrum,	Jesus, our refuge,
Jesu, pater pauperum,	Jesus, father of the poor,
Jesu, thesaurus fidelium,	Jesus, treasure of the faithful,
Jesu, bone pastor,	Jesus, good shepherd,
Jesu, lux vera,	Jesus, true light,
Jesu, sapientia aeterna,	Jesus, eternal wisdom,
Jesu, bonitas infinita,	Jesus, infinite goodness,
Jesu, via et vita nostra,	Jesus, our way and our life,
Jesu, gaudium angelorum,	Jesus, joy of angels,
Jesu, rex patriarcharum,	Jesus, king of patriarchs,
Jesu, magister apostolorum,	Jesus, master of apostles,
Jesu, doctor evangelistarurn,	Jesus, teacher lists,
Jesu, fortitude martyrum,	Jesus, strength of martyrs,
Jesu, lumen confessorum,	Jesus, light of confessors,
Jesu, puritas virginum,	Jesus, purity of virgins,
Jesu, corona sanctorum omnium,	Jesus, crown of all saints,
Propitius esto,	Be merciful,
Parce nobis,Jesu.	Spare us, O Jesus,
Propitius esto,	Be merciful,
Exaudi nos, Jesu.	Graciously hear us, O Jesus.
Ab omni malo,	From all evil,
Ab omni peccato,	From all sin,
Ab ira tua,	From Thy wrath,
Ab insidiis diaboli,	From the snares of the devil,
A spiritu fornicationis,	From the spirit of fornication,

A morte perpetua,
A neglectu inspirationumtuarum,
Per mysterium sanctse incamationis tuae,
Pet nativitatem tuam,
Per infantiam tuam,
Per divinissimam vitam tuam,
Per labores tuos,
Per agoniam et passionem tuam,
Per crucem et derelictionem tuam,
Per languores tuos,
Per mortem et sepulturam tuam,
Per resurrectionem tuam,
Per ascensionem tuam,
Per gaudia tua,
Per gloriam tuam,
Agnus Dei, qui tollis peccata mundi,
Parce nobis, Jesu.
Agnus Dei, qui tollis peccata mundi,
Exaudi nos, Jesu.
Agnus Dei, qui tollis peccata mundi,
Miserere nobis, Jesu.
Jesu audi nos.
Jesu, exaudi nos.

Oremus.
Domine Jesu Christe, qui dixisti: Petite, et accipietis; qiiaerite, et invenietis ; pul sate, et aperietur vobis, quaesumus ; da nobis peteu tibus divinissimi tui amoris affectum, ut te toto corde, ore et opere diligamus, et a tua nunquam laude cessemus. Sancti Nominis tui, Domine, timorem pariter et amorem fac nos habere per petuum, quia nunquam tua gubernatione destituis quos in soliditate tuae dilectionis instituis. Qui vivis et reg. uas, etc. Amen.

From everlasting death,
From the neglect of Thy inspirations,
Through the mystery of Thy holy incarnation,
Through Thy nativity,
Through Thine infancy,
Through Thy most divine life,
Through Thy labors,
Through Thine agony and passion,
Through Thy cross and dereliction,
Through Thy faintness and weariness,
Through Thy death and burial,
Through Thy resurrection,
Through Thine ascension,
Through Thy joys,
Through Thy glory,
Lamb of God, who takes away the sins of the world
Spare us, O Jesus.
Lamb of God, who takest away the sins of the world.
Graciously hear us, O Jesus.
Lamb of God, who takest away the sins of the world,
Have mercy on us, O Jesus*
Jesus, hear us.
Jesus, graciously hear us

Let us pray.
Make us, O Lord, to have a perpetual fear and love of Thy holy Name; for Thou never failest to govern those whom Thou dost solidly establish in Thy love. Who livest and reignest, etc. Amen.

THE ANGELUS DOMINI

Latin

V. Angelus Domini nuntiavit Mariae.
R. Et concepit de Spiritu Sancto.

> Ave Maria, gratia plena; Dominus tecum: benedicta tu in mulieribus, et benedictus fructus ventris tui Iesus. * Sancta Maria, Mater Dei ora pro nobis peccatoribus, nunc et in hora mortis nostrae. Amen.

V. Ecce ancilla Domini,
R. Fiat mihi secundum verbum tuum.

> Ave Maria, gratia plena; Dominus tecum: benedicta tu in mulieribus, et benedictus fructus ventris tui Iesus. * Sancta Maria, Mater Dei ora pro nobis peccatoribus, nunc et in hora mortis nostrae. Amen.

V. Et Verbum caro factum est,
R. Et habitavit in nobis.

> Ave Maria, gratia plena; Dominus tecum: benedicta tu in mulieribus, et benedictus fructus ventris tui Iesus.* Sancta Maria, Mater Dei ora pro nobis peccatoribus, nunc et in hora mortis nostrae. Amen.

V. Ora pro nobis, sancta Dei Genetrix,
R. Ut digni efficiamur promissionibus Christi.

> Oremus. Gratiam tuam, quaesumus, Domine, mentibus nostris infunde; ut qui, Angelo nuntiante, Christi Filii tui incarnationem cognovimus, per passionem eius et crucem ad resurrectionis gloriam perducamur. Per eumdem Christum Dominum nostrum.

R. Amen.

English

V. The angel of the Lord declared unto Mary.
R. And she conceived of the Holy Spirit.

Hail Mary, full of grace; the Lord is with Thee: blessed art thou among women, and blessed is the fruit of thy womb, Jesus.* Holy Mary, Mother of God, prayer for us sinners, now and at the hour of our death.

V. Behold the handmaid of the Lord,
R. Be it done to me according to Thy word.

Hail Mary, full of grace; the Lord is with Thee: blessed art thou among women, and blessed is the fruit of thy womb, Jesus.* Holy Mary, Mother of God, prayer for us sinners, now and at the hour of our death.

V. And the Word was made flesh,
R. And dwelt among us.

Hail Mary, full of grace; the Lord is with Thee: blessed art thou among women, and blessed is the fruit of thy womb, Jesus.* Holy Mary, Mother of God, prayer for us sinners, now and at the hour of our death.

V. Pray for us, O holy Mother of God,
R. That we may be made worthy of the promises of Christ.

Let us pray.

Pour forth, we beseech Thee, Lord, Thy grace into our hearts; that, as we have known the Incarnation of Christ, Thy Son, by the message of an angel, so by His Passion and Cross we may be brought to the glory of the Resurrection. Through the same Christ our Lord.

R. Amen.

EVENING PRAYERS

In the name of the Father, + and of the Son, and of the Holy Ghost. Amen.

Come, O Holy Ghost, fill the hearts of Thy faithful, and kindle in them the fire of Thy love.

Place Yourself in the Presence of God and Humbly Adore Him.

O my God, I present myself before Thee at the end of another day, to offer Thee anew the homage of my heart. I humbly adore Thee, my Creator, my Redeemer, and my Judge! I believe in Thee, because Thou art Truth itself; I hope in Thee, because Thou art faithful to Thy promises; I love Thee with my whole heart, because Thou art infinitely worthy of being loved; and for Thy sake I love my neighbor as myself.

RETURN THANKS TO GOD FOR ALL HIS MERCIES.

Enable me, O my God, to return Thee thanks as I ought for all Thine inestimable blessings and favors. Thou hast thought of me and loved me from all eternity; Thou hast formed me out of nothing; Thou hast delivered up Thy beloved Son to the ignominious death of the cross for my redemption; Thou hast made me a member of Thy holy Church; Thou hast preserved me from falling into the abyss of eternal misery, when my sins had provoked Thee to punish me; Thou hast graciously continued to spare me, even though I have not ceased to offend Thee. What return, O my God, can I make for Thy innumerable blessings, and particularly for the favors of this day? O all ye saints and angels, unite with me in praising the God of mercies, who is so bountiful to so unworthy a creature.

Our Father. Hail Mary. I believe.

ASK OF GOD LIGHT TO DISCOVER THE SINS COMMITTED THIS DAY.

O my God, sovereign judge of men, who desirest not the death of a sinner, but that he should be converted and saved, enlighten my mind, that I may know the sins which I have this day committed in thought, word, or deed, and give me the grace of true contrition.

O my God, I heartily repent and am grieved that I have offended Thee, because Thou art infinitely good and sin is infinitely displeasing to Thee. I humbly ask of Thee mercy and pardon, through the infinite merits of Jesus Christ. I resolve, by the assistance of Thy grace, to do penance for my sins, and I will endeavor never more to offend Thee.

THE CONFITEOR

Latin

Confiteor Deo omnipotenti, et vobis fratres, quia peccavi nimis cogitatione, verbo opere et omissione: mea culpa, mea culpa, mea maxima culpa. Ideo precor beatam Mariam semper Virginem, omnes angelos et Sanctos, et vobis fratres, orare pro me ad Dominum Deum nostrum. Amen.

Misereatur nostril Omnipotens Deus, et dimissis peccatis nobis, perducat nos ad vitam aeternam. Amen.

Indulgentiam, + absolutionem, et remissionem peccatorum nostrorum, tribuat nobis omnipotens et misericors Dominus. Amen.

English

I confess to almighty God, and to you my brothers and sisters, that I have sinned through my own fault, in my thoughts and in my words, in what I have done and what I have failed to do. I ask blessed Mary ever Virgin, all the angels and saints, and you my brothers and sisters, to pray for me to the Lord our God. Amen.

May Almighty God have mercy upon us, and forgive us our sins, and bring us unto life everlasting. Amen.

May the Almighty and merciful Lord grant us pardon, + absolution, and remission of our sins. Amen.

PRAY FOR THE CHURCH OF CHRIST

O God, hear my prayers on behalf of our Holy Father Pope N., our Bishops, our clergy, and for all that are in authority over us. Bless, I beseech Thee, the whole Catholic Church, and convert all heretics and unbelievers.

PRAY FOR THE LIVING AND FOR THE FAITHFUL DEPARTED

Pour down Thy blessings, O Lord, upon all my friends, relations, and acquaintances, and upon my enemies, if I have any. Help the poor and sick, and those who are in their last agony. O God of mercy and goodness, have compassion on the souls of the faithful in purgatory; put an end to their sufferings, and grant to them eternal light, rest, and happiness. Amen.

COMMEND YOURSELF TO GOD, TO THE BLESSED VIRGIN, AND THE SAINTS

Bless, O Lord, the repose I am about to take, that, my bodily strength being renewed, I may be the better enabled to serve Thee.

O blessed Virgin Mary, Mother of mercy, pray for me that I may be preserved this night from all evil, whether of body or soul. Blessed St. Joseph, and all ye saints and angels of Paradise, especially my guardian angel and my chosen patron, watch over me. I commend myself to your protection now and always. Amen.

LITANY OF LORETTO

Latin	*English*
Kyrie, eleison.	Lord, have mercy.
Christe, eleison.	Christ, have mercy.
Kyrie, eleison.	Lord, have mercy.
Christe, audi nos.	Christ, hear us.
Christe, exaudi nos.	Christ, graciously hear us.
Pater de caelis, Deus,	God the Father of heaven,
...miserere nobis.	...have mercy upon us.
Fili, Redemptor mundi, Deus,	God the Son, Redeemer of the world,
Spiritus Sancte, Deus,	God the Holy Spirit,
Sancta Trinitas, unus Deus,	Holy Trinity, one God,
Sancta Maria,	Holy Mary,
...ora pro nobis.	...pray for us.
Sancta Dei Genetrix,	Holy Mother of God,
Sancta Virgo virginum,	Holy Virgin of virgins,
Mater Christi,	Mother of Christ,
Mater divinae gratiae,	Mother of divine grace,

Mater purissima,	Mother most pure,
Mater castissima,	Mother most chaste,
Mater inviolata,	Mother inviolate,
Mater intemerata,	Mother undefiled,
Mater amabilis,	Mother most amiable,
Mater admirabilis,	Mother most admirable,
Mater boni consilii,	Mother of good counsel,
Mater Creatoris,	Mother of our Creator,
Mater Salvatoris,	Mother of our Savior,
Virgo prudentissima,	Virgin most prudent,
Virgo veneranda,	Virgin most venerable,
Virgo praedicanda,	Virgin most renowned,
Virgo potens,	Virgin most powerful,
Virgo clemens,	Virgin most merciful,
Virgo fidelis,	Virgin most faithful,
Speculum iustitiae,	Mirror of justice,
Sedes sapientiae,	Seat of wisdom,
Causa nostrae laetitiae,	Cause of our joy,
Vas spirituale,	Spiritual vessel,
Vas honorabile,	Vessel of honor,
Vas insigne devotionis,	Singular vessel of devotion,
Rosa mystica,	Mystical rose,
Turris Davidica,	Tower of David,
Turris eburnea,	Tower of ivory,
Domus aurea,	House of gold,
Foederis arca,	Ark of the covenant,
Ianua caeli,	Gate of heaven,
Stella matutina,	Morning star,
Salus infirmorum,	Health of the sick,
Refugium peccatorum,	Refuge of sinners,
Consolatrix afflictorum,	Comfort of the afflicted,
Auxilium Christianorum,	Help of Christians,
Regina Angelorum,	Queen of angels,
Regina Patriarcharum,	Queen of patriarchs,
Regina Prophetarum,	Queen of prophets,
Regina Apostolorum,.	Queen of apostles,
Regina Martyrum,	Queen of martyrs,
Regina Confessorum,	Queen of confessors,
Regina Virginum,	Queen of virgins,

Regina Sanctorum omnium,
Regina sine labe originali concepta,
Regina in caelum assumpta,
Regina sacratissimi Rosarii,
Regina pacis,
Agnus Dei, qui tollis peccata mundi,
parce nobis, Domine.
Agnus Dei, qui tollis peccata mundi,
exaudi nos, Domine.
Agnus Dei, qui tollis peccata mundi,
miserere nobis.

V. Ora pro nobis, sancta Dei Genetrix.
R. Ut digni efficiamur promissionibus
Christi.

Oremus.

Concede nos famulos tuos,
quaesumus, Domine Deus,
perpetua mentis et corporis
sanitate gaudere, et gloriosae
beatae Mariae simper Virginis
intercessione, a praesenti liberari
tristitia, et aeterna perfrui laetitia.
Per Christum Dominum nostrum.

R. Amen.

Queen of all saints,
Queen conceived without original
sin,
Queen assumed into heaven,
Queen of the most holy Rosary,
Queen of peace,
Lamb of God, who take away the
sins of the world,
spare us, O Lord.
Lamb of God, who take away the
sins of the world,
spare us, O Lord.
Lamb of God, who take away the
sins of the world,
have mercy upon us.

R. Pray for us, O holy Mother of
God.
V. That we may be made worthy of
the promises of Christ.

Let us pray.

Grant, we beseech Thee, O Lord
God, unto us Thy servants, that
we may rejoice in continual
health of mind and body; and,
by the glorious intercession of
blessed Mary ever Virgin, may be
delivered from present sadness,
and enter into the joy of Thine
eternal gladness. Through Christ
our Lord.

R. Amen

Meditations

For All the Days of the Year

VOLUME IV

*From the Sixth Sunday after Pentecost
to the Seventeenth Sunday after Pentecost*

THE GOSPEL ACCORDING TO ST. MARK, 8:1-9

"At that time, when there was a great multitude with Jesus, and had nothing to eat, calling His disciples together, He saith to them: I have compassion on the multitude, for behold they have now been with Me three days, and have nothing to eat; and if I shall send them away fasting to their homes, they will faint in the way, for some of them came from afar. And His disciples answered Him: From whence can anyone fill them here with bread, in the wilderness? And He asked them: How many loaves have ye? Who said: Seven. And He commanded the multitude to sit down upon the ground. And taking the seven loaves, giving thanks, He broke, and gave to His disciples for to set before them: and they set them before the people. And they had a few little fishes, and He blessed them, and commanded them to be set before them. And they did eat, and were filled; and they took up that which was left of the fragments, seven baskets; and they that had eaten were about four thousand; and He sent them away."

SUMMARY OF TOMORROW'S MEDITATION

e will meditate tomorrow upon the gospel of the day, and we shall learn from it: First, to abandon ourselves to Providence; Second, to cooperate with Providence. We will then make the resolution: First, to see, adore, and bless Providence in all the events of life; Second, never to allow ourselves to give way to discouragement or anxiety, still less to murmurs in the midst of reverses and contrarieties. We will retain as our spiritual nosegay the words of Our Lord in the gospel of the day, which recall to us the tenderness of Providence towards us: "I have compassion on the multitude." (Mark 8:2)

MEDITATION FOR THE MORNING

Let us adore Our Lord followed in the desert by the crowd, who, persuaded that nothing will be wanting to them when they are following Him, rest the care of providing them with food upon the omnipotent and good providence of their divine Saviour. Let us admire the manner in which He justifies the confidence of these good people, is touched with compassion for their needs, and comes to their succor by means of the multiplication of bread. Let us render to Him all our homage with this object in view.

FIRST POINT

✝ *On Abandonment to Providence*

Let us consider that nothing is done in the universe without God willing or permitting it. He alone rules everything with infinite wisdom, with a strength which nothing can resist, and with a more than paternal goodness, to such a point that not even a hair falls from our head without His permission (Luke 21:18). "Thy providence, Father, governeth it," says the Book of Wisdom (Wis. 14:3); and to appreciate without reference to Providence the events which take place here below, the revolutions which occur in families, in towns, and in states, in the Church, and throughout the whole universe, would be to judge of events like a pagan. In addition to this general providence, God has a special providence which He exercises towards those who love Him. He watches over them with particular tenderness and attention, as over His favorite friends, His cherished children, and He shows Himself to be rich in goodness and mercy towards them (Rom. 10:12). Whence it follows, that not to abandon our selves with full confidence to His providence is to misunderstand His power, which can do all things; His goodness, which wills all kinds of good on our behalf; His wisdom, whose lights are always infinite; His ends, which are always most holy, and His means for attaining them, which are always most admirable. Often His reasons are unknown to us, His designs escape our short-sightedness; but what we cannot comprehend here below we shall understand in heaven (John 13:7); in heaven, where we shall sing that God has done all things well (Mark 7:37). Meantime, let us live in a state of abandonment and confidence. This abandonment will be a source of peace and consolation for us. Persuaded that God watches over us, we shall be at rest; and, looking upon ourselves as beloved children in the arms of the best of fathers, we shall say: Why distress and trouble myself? Why afflict myself? Even when human means fail, and men are opposed to me, I will rejoice as for an opportunity which enables me more perfectly to practice holy abandonment to Providence and confidence in its goodness. Even when I may have sinned, I will always have confidence, because God is the Father of the repentant prodigal and has promised pardon to the publican who humbles himself. Consequently, I ought always to confide in God, without being troubled or allowing myself to be cast down.

SECOND POINT

✝ *On Cooperation with Providence*

God does not wish that our abandonment to His Providence should be idle. He desires that we should give Him our concurrence, that we should be His helps and His arms (1 Cor. 3:9). In what has respect to us personally, He desires that we should do everything which depends upon us, awaiting success not from our own efforts, but from His goodness, which alone can enable us to succeed; and as regards our neighbor, He desires us to be good, charitable, compassionate, the worthy agents of His love in doing good to men. Happy are those who, entering into these designs of God, endeavor to do their neighbor all the good they can, and to show themselves in everything like to Jesus Christ, full of compassion for human misery, full of kindness towards all to whom they can render any service! They will at the last day enjoy the happiness of hearing from the mouth of the Judge these sweet words, "Come, ye blessed of My Father; I was hungry, and you gave Me to eat, I was thirsty, and you gave Me to drink." (Matt 25:34, 35). Do we thus cooperate with Divine Providence, whether as regards ourselves or our neighbor? What reproaches have we not to address to ourselves on this subject! *Resolutions and spiritual nosegay as above.*

SIXTH MONDAY AFTER PENTECOST

SUMMARY OF TOMORROW'S MEDITATION

e will meditate tomorrow on a third principle of the Christian life, which is always to tend in everything to what is most perfect, and we shall see: First, how entirely this principle is founded upon reason; Second, how imprudent it would be to adopt the opposite principle in practice. We will then make the resolution: First, always to choose between the two ways of performing an action the one which seems to be the most agreeable to God; Second, to maintain ourselves always in the disposition to embrace in all things what is most perfect. Our spiritual nosegay shall be the words of St. Paul: In every action I seek the most perfect manner of performing it. (Phil. 3:13)

MEDITATION FOR THE MORNING

Let us adore Our Lord inviting us by His apostle always to aspire to a higher degree of virtue (1 Cor. 12:31). Let us thank Him for so useful a lesson; let us ask Him to enable us to understand it and to put it into practice.

FIRST POINT

✝ *Reasons for Aspiring in all Things towards what is most Perfect*

First; God Himself has told us so in His great commandment: "Thou shalt love the Lord thy God with thy whole heart, with thy whole soul, and with thy whole strength." (Deut. 6:5) Evidently this commandment will only have its perfect accomplishment in heaven, because here below the infirmity of our nature and the needs of life will not permit us to have our mind and heart solely occupied with God and continually absorbed in Him. Now, why has God given us a command which surpasses our strength, if it be not to say to us: Never stop at certain limits, as though you had done enough, but constantly aspire towards always doing better; and after you have done it repeat to yourself: it is not good enough, I must do much better. It is in this sense that it is written that the just man always aspires to rise higher still (Ps. Ixxxiii?: 6); he tends ceaselessly towards a more lofty justice (Philipp. 3:13), and encourages himself to take his flight upwards to a more perfect life, saying to himself every morning: I desire to live better today than I lived yesterday; and at the beginning of every action: I wish to perform this better than I did the one which preceded it. Second; we find in human infirmity another reason of this principle, namely that with regard to virtue we always fall short of what we had proposed to ourselves; whence it follows, that if we only propose to ourselves to observe the moderate degree of virtue necessary to our salvation we shall never reach it. In order to attain what is moderate we must aim at what is most perfect; that is the condition of our salvation. Third; the practice of aspiring to what is most perfect will make us think of the saints, the true models of the perfect life to which we aspire; this remembrance, showing us clearly how great is the distance between the saints and ourselves, and thereby filling us with holy shame, will animate us to imitate them, whilst we say to ourselves: Behold, these are my ancestors, my fathers, and my brothers (Tob. 8:5). I ought to render myself worthy of such parentage; what they have done, why should not I also do? (St. Augustine.) And thus will be accomplished the words of Job: He shall look at men who are worth more than himself, and shall say: I am a sinner (Job 33:27). Do we follow these rules of conduct, and are we always aspiring to do better and better?

SECOND POINT

✝ *How Imprudent it would be to Adopt in Practice the Principle of Contenting ourselves with Mediocrity and not aim at what is most Perfect*

Unhappily, Christians are not rare who, filled with a presumptuous security in regard to the stationary point at which they live, think they do enough for their salvation and do not feel the least anxiety respecting it. Why should I disquiet myself? They say; I do not commit any serious faults, I do not act like such and such persons, whose scandalous and ill-regulated lives provoke public remark. It is true that I am not fervent, but a great amount of fervor is not necessary; I am not perfect, but perfection is the portion of cloisters and of hermits; I observe the essential points of the law, and I leave to others who are ceaselessly engaged in making progress these pious solicitudes. There is nothing more dangerous for salvation than such dispositions as these. In this deplorable state, we neglect the reformation of our faults and the practice of virtues; we confess from habit, but without ever becoming any better. We live by routine, without hardly ever thinking seriously of our salvation. We are wholly under the empire of the tepidity which is so supremely displeasing to God that He already begins to eject it (Apoc. 3:16), and that He curses it (Jer. 43:10). We are the apathetic and indolent servant who impresses on all his actions the seal of his idleness; the bad son who is not afraid of displeasing his father as long as he does not drive him away from his home, and who does not understand how to do anything from love. Now whilst our dispositions are such as these we have no right to calculate upon our salvation. Let us examine ourselves as to whether we are not in this state. Let us thoroughly understand that perfection is not intended only for the cloister, but that on every Christian the precept is obligatory: "Be you therefore perfect as also your heavenly Father is perfect," (Matt. 5:48) that is to say, that we ought always to tend to perfection and always be endeavoring to lead a better life. *Resolutions and spiritual nosegay as above.*

Sixth Tuesday after Pentecost

SUMMARY OF TOMORROW'S MEDIATION

e will meditate tomorrow upon a fourth principle of the Christian life, which is that in what concerns the service of God we ought to make great account of even little things, and we shall see that we ought: First, greatly to esteem even the slightest acts of virtue; Second, to avoid, with the greatest care, even the smallest faults. We will then make the resolution: First, willingly to perform any good work, and every act of virtue, even though it may be but very slight, and to keep ourselves on our guard against even the most trifling faults; Second, to have a horror of the false maxim that an elevated mind does not occupy itself with small details, and is contented to serve God in great things. Our spiritual nosegay shall be the words of St. Bernard: "We begin by little faults before falling into great ones." (De Vila ord. et mor. inform.).

MEDITATION FOR THE MORNING

Let us adore Our Lord teaching us to esteem small things by means of His beautiful answer to the Pharisees, who, whilst violating justice and charity, were faithful in paying the tax for the commonest little vegetables. It was a duty to be faithful to these small observances, He said to them, but at the same time it was necessary to be exact in regard to more serious obligations (Matt. 23:23). Let us thank Him for this lesson and ask of Him grace to profit by it.

FIRST POINT

✝ *We ought to Hold the Smallest Acts of Virtue in Great Esteem*

First, faith shows us that the least acts of virtue are of great value, because whatever is worthy of heaven is of great price, because it is always a great thing to please God even in little things, because, in the service of this Sovereign Lord, little attentions are the sign of great love; because if when we fear God we neglect nothing, as the Holy Spirit says (Eccles. 7:19), with much greater reason we may say that nothing is little which is done with great love, as well as that nothing is great which is done with but little love; God not appreciating things according to the more or less degree of intrinsic greatness which they possess, but according to the more or less love with which they are performed. A man gathers a flower in a garden and innocently inhales its perfume, another man abstains from it and sacrifices to God the slight pleasure he would have derived from it; there is as much distance between the one action and the other as there is between heaven and earth, between a natural and a supernatural action. Second, opportunities for doing great things are rare. If we desire to be faithful to God only in great things, we shall be so but rarely, because the life of man is composed of hardly anything more than a number of little things. We may even say that we shall never be faithful, because a creature as little as is man cannot call anything great of what he does for so lofty a Majesty. Now we are obliged to serve God always and at every moment, since He is always our Master. Third, the more things are little, the easier they are, and the easier they are, the more inexcusable we are to refuse them to God, to whom we owe everything, to Jesus Christ His Son, who has done so much and suffered so much for us. "If the prophet," said the servants of Naaman to their master, "had commanded thee to do something difficult, thou wouldst have done it; wherefore, then, when he asks of thee so easy a thing as to wash thyself seven times in the Jordan, wilt thou not do it?" Let us apply these words to ourselves. Salvation is so serious a thing that in order to obtain it we must perform the most difficult things. Therefore, with much greater reason, we ought to perform things which are the most easy. God has done and suffered so much for us that in order to please Him we ought lovingly to embrace the greatest sacrifices. Therefore to refuse Him a little sacrifice, a little act of virtue, is baseness, ingratitude, and an indignity. Ah, Lord, if when there is a question of pleasing Thee I find easy things difficult, it is a sad proof that I have very little love for Thee. Let us here examine ourselves, let us humble ourselves, and let us resolve to make great account of the smallest acts of virtue that we have an opportunity of accomplishing.

SECOND POINT

✝ *We ought to Avoid with the Greatest Care even the Slightest Faults*

It is wrong to say of certain faults: It is only a little sin. There are venial faults, but there are no little sins. We cannot call that a small thing which offends an infinite Majesty, which is a want of respect for His greatness, a piece of ingratitude for His blessings, disobedience to His commands, rebellion against His will, a diminution of His exterior glory, an indifference towards His love. We cannot call that little which is an evil that God can never cease to hate any more than He can cease to be God; an evil so great that it surpasses all imaginable evils, even the death of all men, even the ruin of the universe; an evil so great that hell itself would be a lesser evil, because it would not be allowed to deliver all the damned, if one were able to do so, by one venial sin. We cannot call that little which is an evil punished by God in the next life by purgatory, and which He has often punished in this life by terrible chastisements. What, lastly, shall we say? We cannot call that little which is an evil that compromises our salvation. Now this is what little faults do; they cool the friendship of God towards us, they diminish His graces, they render our faith tepid, they take from us those spiritual tastes which are the supports of our weakness; they soften our will and fashion it little by little to evil, they stifle remorse, dissipate watchfulness, and thereby lead to the great falls which are almost always the consequence of a series of relaxations. No one becomes all at once either a great sinner or a great saint (St. Bernard, De Vitce ord. et mor. inform.); we fall to the bottom of the abyss only by degrees, so that whoever remains standing on the first step, without descending farther, will not fall; whence it follows that to fly is the strongest guarantee of perseverance; we commence with little faults before falling into greater. What illusions do we not entertain in regard to this question! *Resolutions and spiritual nosegay as above.*

SUMMARY OF TOMORROW'S MEDITATION

fter having meditated upon the preliminary principles of the Christian life, we will now meditate upon the Christian life itself, and we shall see: First, that the perfection of our ordinary actions forms the whole foundation of the Christian life; Second, that nothing is more consoling than this doctrine. We will then make the resolution: First, to endeavor to perform all our actions well from morning till night, without neglecting any one of them; Second, to be on our guard against the illusion of those who go elsewhere in search of sanctity. We will retain as our spiritual nosegay the words which the people applied to Our Lord: "He hath done all things well." (Mark 7:37)

MEDITATION FOR THE MORNING

Let us adore God, who in the creation and the government of the universe does all that He performs in a perfect manner, because He does it with number, weight, and measure (Wis. 11:21). He performs great works and He performs little ones, but in both the one and the other He always acts with supreme perfection (St. Augustine). Let us admire this perfection God exhibits in performing all that He does perfectly well, and let us profit, like the saints, by the lesson He therein gives us.

FIRST POINT

✝ *The Whole Perfection of the Christian Life Consists in the Perfection of our Ordinary Actions*

In point of fact, the foundation of the rule of all holiness lies in the will of God alone, which alone forms the value and the merit of all our works. Independent of this holy will, the greatest actions count for nothing; with it, the least actions acquire a high degree of merit, and we may even say that the soul which in all things sees, loves, and follows this most adorable will has reached the perfect life. Now what is the will of God in regard to us? It evidently consists in the perfection of our ordinary actions: every day and of every moment, since what is extraordinary is essentially rare; Second, because the great interests of order and of happiness, whether in society or in the family, whether in the Church or in the State, which clearly enter into the will of God, cannot be safely preserved except by means of the fidelity of each individual in fulfilling the duties of his position; Third, because Jesus Christ and the saints placed their holiness in the perfection of the ordinary actions proper to their state and position. What did Jesus Christ do during thirty years? Nothing remarkable in the opinion of the world, nothing even but what was common and almost contemptible in the eyes of man. From morning until night He occupied Himself with the little employments assigned to Him by Mary and Joseph (Luke ii. 51); these were the duties of His state and of His condition. But He performed these little employments most perfectly, both as regarded the exterior action and the interior dispositions through which He acted; and by doing that alone He practiced a holiness which was the object of the complaisance of God His Father. After Jesus Christ, nothing more holy under heaven has been seen than Mary and Joseph; and yet their holiness consisted only in performing perfectly the common and simple actions belonging to their state; and what millions of saints we shall see at the last day whose life has been obscure, hidden, unknown to the world, and who sanctified themselves without doing anything brilliant, but by performing in a perfect manner the humble and modest actions which entered into the duties of their state. They may have passed unperceived upon earth, but at the great day of judgment they will shine with incomparable splendor, which will make all the assembled people comprehend that all holiness really consists in the perfection of ordinary actions. Are we thoroughly convinced of the truth of this maxim of the spiritual life?

SECOND POINT

✝ *There is Nothing more Consoling than this Doctrine*

What, in fact, is more consoling than to be able to say: In order to become holy, I need not go very far to seek what I must do; my perfection is near to me, and in me; it consists in the duties of my position and of my state being properly fulfilled; in my daily exercises being well performed; a perfection which, apart from these exercises and which would not help me to fulfill these obligations, would be a religion ill understood and badly regulated, a religion that God would not recognize, that even the world would reprove, might inspire me with pride, and expose me to commit a thousand faults; whilst perfection in ordinary life is approved by God and man, it edifies, it gives a credit to virtue, it preserves order and the rule; it does not swell the soul with pride, it is not subject to vanity, and at the same time it is very meritorious, because of the difficulties which must be overcome and the violence we must do our selves constantly to keep up the practice of it. Let us beg of God to enable us thoroughly to understand and practice this rule of conduct. *Resolutions and spiritual nosegay as above.*

SUMMARY OF TOMORROW'S MEDITATION

 e will meditate tomorrow upon the manner of performing our ordinary actions well, and we shall see that we must perform them: First, in a state of grace and with sustained application in their right performance; Second, with exactitude and fervor. Our resolution shall be: First, to preserve ourselves always in a state of grace; Second, to infuse into all our actions exactness and fervor, or a great desire to perform them perfectly. Our spiritual nosegay shall be the words of the Imitation: "Give yourself up entirely to what you art doing."

MEDITATION FOR THE MORNING

Let us adore Our Lord Jesus Christ performing so perfectly each one of His ordinary actions that God the Father was well pleased (Luke 2:22), and that the people, beholding His actions, uttered the admiring- exclamation: "He hath done all things well." (Mark 7:37) Let us unite ourselves with the complaisance of the Father and with the praises of the people; and let us congratulate our Divine Savior on the perfection with which He does all things.

FIRST POINT

✝ *Of the State of Grace and of Sustained Application in the Right Performance of all that we do*

It is an elementary truth that unless we are in a state of grace all our actions are but dead works, and that, however excellent they may be, they have no merit in regard to salvation. "If I should distribute all my goods to feed the poor," says St. Paul, "and have not charity, it profits me nothing." (1 Cor. 8:3) It is true that venial sins do not take away life from our actions, but they diminish the merit of them; imperfections affect in a more or less degree their goodness before God. Hence we may conclude that we must avoid everything which may in the slightest degree diminish the state of grace in which we are, consequently all that would distract us from endeavoring to do in a perfect manner all that we have to perform, for if we act from routine and without reflection, without aiming at the best manner of performing our actions, without desiring to take the trouble to ensure their success; if we divide our attention instead of thinking solely on what we are doing, occupying ourselves with other thoughts under the pretext that they are not evil, or that we have a mind large enough to occupy ourselves with several things at one and the same time, our actions will necessarily be bad, or at any rate defective. It is even not anything great to be inspired with this spirit of application on certain days when we are touched by God; the essential thing is to have it in all our actions one day as well as another, to walk always with an equal step, without ever giving way to relaxation or giving the lie to ourselves. Let us examine if such be our conduct. Are there not, on the contrary, in our daily life continual alternatives of good and evil, without there being anything sustained or persevering in it?

SECOND POINT

✝ *On the Exactitude Accompanied by Fervor with which we must do Everything*

To perform our actions with exactitude means not to omit any of them voluntarily; not to retrench from any one of them the smallest portions of which it is composed; to do them at the fixed hour assigned to them, in a suitable place, and in the manner in which they ought to be performed. Want of exactitude in these things is an imperfection which diminishes the value of our actions; it is a transgression of the will of God, which extends itself to everything, even to the smallest details. With this exactitude must be associated fervor, that is to say, a great desire to perform all our actions well and an energetic resolve not to neglect anything in the way of duty, notwithstanding the dislikes and repugnances, the coldness and the dryness we may experience. The absence of taste and of pleasure in what we do ought never to discourage us or incline us to give way to relaxation. Far from being an evil, this want of taste renders our fervor more solid and more meritorious. Let us here again examine ourselves: have we infused into our actions the exactitude and the fervor upon which we have been meditating? Alas! what cowardice, what omissions and variations have marked our conduct! *Resolutions and spiritual nosegay as above.*

SIXTH FRIDAY AFTER PENTECOST

SUMMARY OF TOMORROW'S MEDITATION

e will meditate tomorrow upon the third condition which the perfection of our ordinary actions requires, that is to say, the purity of intention by which we propose to ourselves, in all that we do, solely to please God; and we shall see: First, the necessity of this purity of intention; Second, its advantages. We will then make the resolution: First, always to keep the eye of our intention steadfastly fixed upon the good pleasure of God, and to embrace this good pleasure with a love full of gladness; Second, constantly to reject all other intentions which we might be tempted to mingle with our acts. Our spiritual nosegay shall be the words of St. Paul: "Whatever you do in word or in work, all things do ye in the name of the Lord Jesus Christ, giving thanks to God the Father by Him." (Coloss. 3:17)

MEDITATION FOR THE MORNING

Let us adore Jesus Christ performing all actions for the glory and the good pleasure of His Father. He never did anything except with this object (John 8:29), and it was to that all His thoughts, all His words, and all His actions tended. (Ibid.) How greatly does this purity of intention merit our praises, our admiration, and our reverence!

FIRST POINT

✝ *The Necessity of Purity of Intention*

It is the essential and principal condition for the goodness of our works. This purity of intention is what the foundation is to the building, the root to the tree, the soul to the body; take away the foundation and the building crumbles; cut the root and the tree dies; without the soul, the body is nothing more than a corpse. It is the same with our actions. Without purity of intention, we may do what we will, we only amass ruins; the basis which supports the edifice is wanting; our works are but as dry branches, where the sap which makes them live circulates no longer; they are dead works; the intention, which is their soul and their life, is wanting to them. What God considers in our actions is not so much the exterior and the substance of the acts as the intention with which we act. (1 Kings 16:7) As He is our first principle, He also is essentially the last end to which we ought to refer everything; as everything comes from Him through His love, so all ought to be referred back to Him by ours. Otherwise He takes no account of even our best works, even if they were to be heroic actions; and if we were to ask Him to recompense us for them, He would justly reply: I recompense only what is done for Me; go and ask your reward from those for whom you have labored. This is a truth worthy of our most serious meditation. We apparently fulfill all our duties, we even perform many good works, but if, in all these things, carried away by frivolity and dissipation, we act without having a view to God, from habit and routine, our natural temperament and our inclinations, from interest, from human respect, from ostentation, from purely natural reasons, such as necessity and propriety, it will all count as nothing in the sight of God. Yet, and it is painful to think it is so, is it not of acts thus performed that nearly my whole life is composed? I seek and I find myself in everything. I seldom so forget myself as to have only God in view. Alas, the purity of my intentions is often a secret which is hidden from myself, and if I could see all the impurity that is mingled with it, I should be confounded, and, as it were, annihilated. O God! What then is my life? It is a life of sterility and of time wasted: I am the useless servant of the gospel, if I am not the guilty and prevaricating servant.

SECOND POINT

✝ *The Advantages of Purity of Intention*

First, purity of intention enables us to perform all things well. When we say to ourselves, inspired by a lively sentiment of faith, It is for God I am doing this, we come to the conclusion that we must do it most perfectly, otherwise it would be unworthy of God. We are as careful as it is possible for us to be when we take in hand any piece of work destined for kings and the great ones of the earth; with how much stronger reason ought we not then perfectly to perform what is done for God? Second, purity of intention enables us to gain heaven cheaply. Through it, the most common actions, even eating and drinking, are worthy of heaven; and in order to be saved I have only to perform my actions with a view to God and from a desire to please Him; there is no action, however little it may be, which, when it is referred to God, is not attended with a certain degree of merit. If I have not the talents which others possess, if I cannot perform the splendid actions which distinguish such men, I can be as great in the sight of God as are the greatest saints and acquire the same merits; I can, by the uprightness and purity of my intentions, raise to so high a degree even the most humble of my actions that, whilst leading a common life, I shall surpass in merit even the apostles, if God sees in my heart a more ardent desire to please Him; so true it is that all the beauty, all the merits, and all the greatness of a soul come from within (Ps. 44:14). O wisdom and sweetness of Providence! How worthy of condemnation I should be if, having such easy means at my command to enrich myself for heaven, I should remain poor, devoid of all spiritual graces, and reduced to presenting myself with empty hands before Thee, O my God. Let us here examine ourselves. Do we not act from pride, to attract to ourselves the applause and esteem of the world, from love of ourselves, to satisfy our senses, to follow our inclinations? Do we not act from purely natural ends, eating only to live, amusing ourselves solely for the sake of amusement; do we not often act without having any intention, mechanically and from habit? *Resolutions and spiritual nosegay as above.*

SUMMARY OF TOMORROW'S MEDITATION

e will meditate tomorrow on two means for performing all our actions in a very perfect manner; it is to perform them: First, as in the presence of God; Second, with a view to Jesus Christ. We will then make the resolution: First, to recall to ourselves as often as possible the presence of God, in order that we may thereby be excited to perform everything in a very perfect manner; Second, to apply ourselves to perform all our actions in imitation of, through dependence upon, and in union with Jesus Christ, begging Him to fill us with His spirit and His dispositions. We will retain as our spiritual nosegay the words of God to Abraham: "Walk before Me and be perfect". (Gen. 17:1)

MEDITATION FOR THE MORNING

Let us adore God, who destined all the faithful to be perfect images of His Son (Rom. 8:29), and with this end in view giving Him to us to be the model and the soul of all our actions. Let us bless Him for having called us to imitate the life and the actions of a God; (Tertullian, Orat. adv. Marc., lib. 2:27) there cannot be a more beautiful or happy vocation.

FIRST POINT

✝ *To Perform all our Actions as in the Presence of God, the first Means whereby to Please Him*

A Pagan philosopher once said: If you desire to be virtuous, live as though you were always in the presence of a personage of great merit and of great virtue; do nothing and say nothing except what you would do and say before him (Seneca, Ep. 23). How much more efficacious, in order to lead us to do all things well, is a lively faith in the presence of God, who not only sees our actions but also our thoughts and our most secret intentions! If we had this faith, what care should we not then exercise over our actions, over our procedures, our eyes, our words, over what we think of, love, and desire, in order that nothing should be mingled therein which would be unworthy of the sight of God, whose eyes are upon us. "Let the just feast and rejoice before God." (Ps. 67:4) Let them eat, let them drink, let them take recreation; it is right to do so, provided that all be done as in the presence of God, and in a manner which does not in any way wound His eyes. "We ought always to pray and not to faint," (Luke 18:1) says Jesus Christ. We must sing the praises of

God all day long, the Psalmist says; (Ps. 80:8) that is to say, that we must do everything in the best possible manner, as in the sight of God; for that is the continual prayer and the uninterrupted praise of God of which it is written in Ecclesiasticus: "He that keepeth the law, multiplieth offerings." (Ecclus. 35:1) Happy is he who always walks thus in the presence of God! He does everything well and is perfect. What point have we reached in this holy practice? If we do so many things badly, if we allow so many regrettable words to escape us, is it not because we live a life of frivolity and forgetfulness of God?

SECOND POINT

✝ *To do all Things with a View to Jesus Christ, the Second Means whereby to perform them well*

One of the most excellent means for doing all things well is to perform them in imitation, through dependence upon, and in union with Jesus Christ. First, in imitation, by placing this divine Model of the elect often before our eyes; by observing His characteristics in order to impress them upon our hearts and give them expression in our acts; by considering, not only how He acted, how He spoke, how He behaved, how He treated God His Father with honor, His neighbor with charity, the world with indifference, and how He treated Himself with contempt, but also what were His interior dispositions of humility, of mortification, of recollection, of love, and of sacrifice; studying to retrace in ourselves a faithful copy of an exterior which was so admirable, and an interior which was so divine. Second, through dependence on Our Lord; that is to say, by abandoning ourselves into His hands, as an instrument in the hands of the workman, as members who have no life or movement except through the influence of their head, and allowing ourselves to be led by the inspiration of His grace rather than by our own mind and our own will. Third, lastly we must act in union with Him, binding our actions with His by desire and by prayer, in order that the infinite value of His may cover the defects and the baseness of ours. It is thus that the angels and saints in heaven unite in all the praises which this perfect Worshipper renders to His Father (Apoc. 7:9,12). It is thus that the Church offers all her prayers through Our Lord Jesus Christ. Is it thus that we act? *Resolutions and spiritual nosegay as above.*

Seventh Sunday after Pentecost

THE GOSPEL ACCORDING TO ST. MATTHEW, 7:15-21

"At that time, Jesus said to His disciples: Beware of false prophets who come to you in the clothing of sheep, but invariably they are ravening wolves.

By their fruits you shall know them. Do men gather grapes of thorns or figs of thistles? Even so every good tree bringeth forth good fruit, and the evil tree bringeth forth evil fruit. A good tree cannot bring forth evil fruit, neither can an evil tree bring forth good fruit. Every tree that bringeth not forth good fruit shall be cut down and shall be cast into the fire. Wherefore by their fruits you shall know them, not everyone that saith to Me: "Lord, Lord, shall enter into the kingdom of heaven: but he that doth the will of My Father who is in heaven, he shall enter into the kingdom of heaven."

SUMMARY OF TOMORROW'S MEDITATION

 e will listen tomorrow to Jesus Christ revealing to us in the gospel: First, the necessity of good works under the symbol of the tree which ought to bear good fruit; Second, the characteristics which these good works ought to have in order that they may be saving. We will then make the resolution: First, joyfully to seize all opportunities for doing good works which we may meet with during the day, even to obliging our neighbor in little things, as well as in great; to say a pleasant word and to behave kindly to the poor, the unhappy, and servants; Second, carefully to fulfill all the duties of our position, which are the primary good works to which we ought to apply ourselves. Our spiritual nosegay shall be the words of the gospel: "Every good tree bringeth forth good fruit." (Matt. 7:7)

MEDITATION FOR THE MORNING

Let us adore Jesus Christ revealing to us in the gospel of the day one of the truths which are most important in regard to our salvation, that is to say, that we cannot be saved except on condition of sanctifying our life upon earth by good works (Matt. 7:19). Let us thank Him for so precious a lesson and ask of Him grace thoroughly to profit by it.

FIRST POINT

✝ *The Necessity of Good Works for our Salvation*
Each one of us is like a tree planted by the hand of God in the field of the Church, in a ground of benediction, cultivated with care, watered with profusion. If neither this careful culture nor the fruitful dew of heaven makes us produce good works, we fall under the anathema pronounced by the Apostle: "The earth that drinketh in the rain which cometh often upon it and bringeth forth thorns and briars, is reprobate, and very near unto a curse;" (Heb. 6:7,8) an anathema which is only the reproduction of the words of our gospel: "Every tree that bringeth not forth good fruit shall be cut down and shall be cast into

the fire."(Matt. 7:19) The reasons for this sentence are numerous, First, he who neglects to perform good works does not love God. Love is an active passion which turns the heart towards its object and makes it act for it. (St. Gregory) If I do nothing for God, it is a proof that I do not love Him; if I do but little, it is a proof that I do not love Him much. Second, he who neglects good works does not love his neighbor; when we love any one we give him succor by means of works of mercy. Third, he who neglects good works does not love himself, because being wholly taken up with the things of this world, which so quickly passes away, where we live for so short a time, we are not occupied with preparing a happy destiny for ourselves throughout eternity. We class ourselves amongst the useless servants, of whom it as written that they shall be cast into the exterior darkness, instead of being of the number of those righteous whom one of the Fathers calls "the riches of eternity," because by means of their good works they send before them into heaven treasures of merit. Let us here examine our conscience and listen to its reproaches.

SECOND POINT

✝ *The Characteristics which Good Works ought to Possess in order to be Saving*

First, they must be wholly good; for, if they are defective in one single particular, whether because of the time at which they are done, or the manner of performing them, or on account of the intention which accompanies them, it is enough to deprive them of their value or diminish the merit of them. God loves order and desires to have it in all things; He is not pleased with any diversion from it. Let us examine as to whether our good works have this primary characteristic, or whether, spite of the great number of them which we have performed, we are still very poor. Second, they must be done in the order of the will of God; He alone, says Jesus Christ in the gospel of the day, who does the will of My heavenly Father shall enter into the kingdom of heaven. Therefore all that turns us away from the duties of our state, all that is inspired by caprice or some human object, does not count amongst good works. The only good works are those which God commands or which He counsels, or which He gives us an opportunity of doing. Third, it is not enough to apply ourselves to good works only when we have a taste for them; we must continue them even when we feel disgust for them. "Be thou faithful until death." (Apoc. 2:10) Let us again examine our selves on this subject. *Resolutions and spiritual nosegay as above.*

SEVENTh MONDAY AFTER PENTECOST

SUMMARY OF TOMORROW'S MEDITATION

e will meditate tomorrow upon two other means for performing our actions well. The first is, not to think, whilst we are acting, of anything except of what we are performing; secondly, not to have any thoughts except those which belong to the present day. We will then make the resolution: First, to concentrate upon the action with which we are occupied the whole of our mind and of our attention, that we may perform it as well as possible; Second, to propose to ourselves every day that we will live in a holy manner until the evening. Our spiritual nosegay shall be the words of an ancient: "He who thinks of many things at once performs each of them less well."

MEDITATION FOR THE MORNING

Let us adore Our Lord teaching us different ways of performing our actions well. Our good Father never forgets anything that may be useful to us. He loves us; He wills that we should render ourselves worthy of His love, and, in order that we may become so, He teaches us the means whereby we may please Him. Let us thank Him for so much kindness.

FIRST POINT

✝ *Whilst Acting to Think only of what we are Doing*

One of the greatest obstacles to the perfection of our ordinary actions is, when we are doing one thing to think of another, so that our mind, being distracted, only half attends to what has to be done. We are uneasy and troubled, one thing gets mixed up with another, and so we do nothing as it ought to be and as it might be done. The remedy for this evil is to attend only and entirely to what we are about, as though we had nothing else to do. "All things have their season." the Holy Spirit says (Eccles. 3:1) "Be not solicitous for tomorrow. For the morrow will be solicitous for itself; sufficient for the day is the evil thereof." (Matt. 7:34) During prayer do not let us think upon worldly matters or on the anxieties attendant upon our position. When we are occupied with our affairs, let us give our entire attention to them and give to them the whole of our care. Wherefore go back to the past? It is a thing which is consummated, and we cannot change it. Wherefore anticipate the future? We are ignorant of what it will be; we do not even know whether we shall see it. It is a great evil to distract our attention from the employments in which we are at the moment engaged and to give it to what we shall have to do later, often even to imaginations and reveries which will never be realized. It is to kill the present by the future, the reality by phantoms; it is the way in which never to do anything well. Wisdom, on the contrary, tells us to send the thought of things to come to the time when we shall have to do them, and not to be afraid that later on we shall forget the good idea which has presented itself to our minds during the action with which we are occupied. God, who is a friend of order, will bless the postponement of the inopportune thought, and will make it return in due season with an added profit because of our having left it on one side that we may thereby please Him. We shall gain instead of losing by it. The knowledge, says St. Basil, with which we do not occupy ourselves for the sake of virtue, is better acquired afterwards through virtue. Let us here examine ourselves. What vitiated prayers and actions have been ours for want of following these rules!

SECOND POINT

✝ *Not to Occupy ourselves with Anything Beyond the Present Day*

We are so weak that perhaps courage would fail us if we could behold at one glance the fifty or sixty years to be spent in perfect restraint, in a perpetual attention to ourselves, in the privation of the comforts of life, and in the renunciation of our wills and our desires; whilst, on the contrary, courage will be easy to us if, instead of beholding all this at once, we see things in detail, and say to ourselves: This is not a question of calculating upon long years; what would be the good of it I, who do not know if I shall live until tomorrow? It has to do solely with the present day. If I live until tomorrow I shall see what I have to do. Now, from the present moment until this evening, would it be possible for me to find it too hard to live well, to inconvenience myself and mortify myself? A day is so soon over: a day compared with eternity. Oh, it is nothing; and how unreasonable I should be if I did not employ it in a holy manner! Strengthened by this thought, I set myself to work and I spend the day in a holy manner. The next day I begin again without ever looking beyond the present day. By means of this innocent stratagem, everything in virtue becomes easy, and we arrive at perfection. Let us propose to ourselves to employ this means constantly. *Resolutions and spiritual nosegay as above.*

SUMMARY OF TOMORROW'S MEDITATION

e will meditate tomorrow upon another means whereby to perform our actions well, which is to perform each one of them as though it were to be the last of our life; and we shall see: First, that nothing is wiser; Second, that nothing is more useful. We will then make the resolution: First, following the advice of St. Bernard, to ask ourselves at the commencement of each action; If thou wert destined to die after this action, wouldst thou do it, and how wouldst thou do it? Second, always to keep ourselves in the state in which we should desire to be found at our death. Our spiritual nosegay shall be the words of St. Bernard: "If thou hadst to die in a few moments wouldst thou do this?"

MEDITATION FOR THE MORNING

Let us adore Jesus Christ inviting us in the gospel to be at any moment ready to die. Blessed is that servant, He says, whom when his Lord shall come He shall find doing his duty (Matt. 24:46). Let us thank Him for counsel so important, and let us ask of Him grace to profit by it.

FIRST POINT

✝ *How Wise it is to Perform each Action as though it were Destined to be the Last of our Life*

Nothing is more uncertain than the moment of death. Death will come, says Jesus Christ, at an hour when you think not; it will seize you suddenly, like a thief in the night (1 Thess. 5:2). Now in this state of uncertainty, what does wisdom say to us if it be not that we ought at every moment to live and act as though we ought to die the moment afterwards? "Happy and prudent is he who, at every moment of his life, endeavors to be such as he would desire to be found at his death" (I. Imit. 23:4). If the father of a family could but know at what hour the thieves would come, he would watch for that hour, says Jesus Christ, in order to prevent them from entering into his house; but because he is ignorant of it, he is continually on his guard. In the same way, O my God, Thou hast hidden from us the hour of our death, in order to urge us to spend each day as though it were our last and to perform each action as though it were our final one. There is no question of deferring from one day to another; there is no question of saying: I will live better when I have terminated such or such an affair which absorbs my attention, when I have done with these embarrassments; I must this very day live and act as though I had to die to-night, because perhaps it will so happen. Perhaps also, as I know, it may not be so, but in a matter so serious as is that of our salvation, wisdom does not allow us to reassure ourselves by a chance and thereby to risk our eternity. Every day, said Job, I expect the moment of my death; Thou wilt call me, O Lord, and I will answer Thee (Job 14:14,15). St. Francis Borgia went farther still: he recommended his religious to place themselves twenty four times a day in the position of a man who was about to die, and to perform everything as being obliged to render an account to God of it the next moment Do we imitate the saints in this practice?

SECOND POINT

✝ *How Useful it is to Perform each Action as though it were destined to be our Last.*

It is an infallible means of doing all things well. With what fervor should we not pray if we knew that we were saying our last prayer, after which we should no longer have any time in which to ask pardon of God and implore His mercy; with what perfection should we not make our confession if we knew it was the last, and the communion after which we should have to yield up our soul. If an angel of God had come to tell us in the morning that we were to die the same night, how we should sanctify the day, how holy would be all our actions, how irreproachable our words, how pious our thoughts, how pure our desires, how well employed all our moments would be! This is why the author of the Imitation says to us: "You ought to conduct yourselves in regard to all your actions and all your thoughts as though you were going to die immediately afterwards; " and he adds: "Think in the morning that perhaps you will not see the evening, and at night that perhaps you will not see the next morning." (Imit. 23:1-3) This practice is still a means of knowing the state of our soul and seeing what there is in it which needs correction. Let us ask ourselves: If I had to die today, what is it which would trouble my conscience? Should I do the action I am now performing, and should I do it in the way in which I am performing it? If in answer to these questions conscience replies by pointing out some defects to us, let us promptly obey its dictates; if we find nothing to trouble us, let us be encouraged and have confidence. The steward whose accounts are in order is not afraid of his master's visit. *Resolutions and spiritual nosegay as above.*

SUMMARY OF TOMORROW'S MEDITATION

e will meditate tomorrow upon two other means for performing all things well; the first is the thought of the last judgment; the second is the thought of a happy or a miserable eternity. We will then make the resolution: First, often to ask ourselves, during the day, what God will say at the last day of this action, of this prayer, of this conversation, of the employment of this present day, of this confession, of this communion; Second, often to say, as a means of encouraging ourselves to do good and to avoid evil: O heaven, how desirable Thou art! O hell, how terrible! Our spiritual nosegay shall be the words of St. Paul: "After this the judgment." (Heb. 9:27)

MEDITATION FOR THE MORNING

Let us adore Jesus Christ declaring to us, in the gospel, that on the judgment-day we shall have to render to Him an account of all our actions, of all our speeches, even of our idle words (Matt. 12:36), that is to say, of those which are not justified by any reasonable motive, and that this judgment will be followed by eternal torment in the case of some, and by a blissful eternity for others (Matt. 25:46). Let us thank Him for a warning so well adapted to make us perform everything in a holy manner.

FIRST POINT

✝ *The Thought of the Last Judgment an All-powerful Motive for Doing Everything Well*

Who, in fact, would not do all things well if he said to himself, The action I am performing will be severely examined in the presence of God, as regards itself, all its circumstances, the intention which caused me to perform it, and the more or less zeal with which I did it? From the most common act up to the highest; from the most obscure which is known to myself alone, up to the most brilliant which is known to the public, all will be submitted to the judgment (Heb. 9:27) Shall I not then be in the position of the faithless steward, when his master said to him, Give an account of thy stewardship (Luke 16:2), or in that of the King of Babylon, to whom it was said, Thou hast been weighed in the balance; the weight of the evil has weighed down the good (Dan. 5:27), thy kingdom shall be taken from thee? (Ibid. 28) Oh, if this thought were but to accompany each one of our actions, how holy every one of them would be! Let us think seriously upon it. If we thus judge ourselves, we shall not be judged. (1 Cor. 11:31)

SECOND POINT

✝ *The Thought of a Blessed or a Miserable Eternity another Motive for Doing all Things Well*

It is very true that God offers His paradise to us at a very cheap rate, since He promises it to even our smallest and commonest actions. Oh, how well suited is the thought of such happiness to encourage us and animate us to do all things well. If in order to acquire the rewards given by the world, rewards which are so full of vanity, so uncertain, so unable to make us happy, we give ourselves so much trouble and anxiety, what ought we not to do for the recompenses bestowed by Heaven, so solid as they are, so sure, so delightful, and which nothing can take from us (John 16: 22). In the same degree as the thought of heaven is well suited to endowing us with courage to do all things well, the thought of hell is all-powerful in animating us to do well; for, in presence of the sacrifices and the acts of renunciation which are imposed upon us by the perfection of our ordinary actions, we have only to say to ourselves: What is it in comparison with hell, where, if I am not a saint, I shall burn forever? There is no temptation which can resist this question. We read in the lives of the Fathers of the desert that a young religious, being wearied of the cavern in which he had constituted himself a hermit, went to speak of his troubles to a holy old man. "My son," he replied to him, "you never can have meditated on what hell is, from which you are preserved by your solitude, for what comparison can there be between the one and the other? "Do we make use of these serious thoughts for the purpose of encouraging ourselves to fly from what is evil and to practice what is good? *Resolutions and spiritual nosegay as above.*

Seventh Thursday after Pentecost

SUMMARY OF TOMORROW'S MEDITATION

e will consider tomorrow in our meditation that to love is the means for doing all things well: First, because love inspires us with the desire and the will to do so; Second, because it gives us courage; Third, because it enables us to find joy and merit in it. Our resolution shall be: First, to perform everything through love, saying joyfully to God whilst performing each one of our actions: All for Thy love, all to please Thee, O my God! Second, to excite ourselves to what is most perfect through the thought that that is what is most agreeable to God Our spiritual nosegay shall be the words of St. Augustine: "Do that with which love inspires you."

MEDITATION FOR THE MORNING

Let us adore God teaching us by the mouth of St. Paul that the whole of religion consists in love, and that love is the secret of doing all things well (Rom. 13:10). Let us thank Him for so kind and precious a lesson.

FIRST POINT

✝ *Love Inspires us with the Desire and the Will to do all Things Well*

The more we love, the more we have it at heart to please God, whom we love. The one is the necessary effect of the other, and the exact measure of it. If we really love God, we will aspire after nothing else from morning to night except to please Him that is to say, to do all things well, since it is only thereby that we can please Him. The soul which does not love except in a half hearted kind of way is inspired with nothing more than a miserably weak inclination to perform its actions well, and therefore does nothing well; it drags itself painfully along in the service of God, falls and rises again, makes a false step and falls once more, makes resolutions and executes none of them. But the soul which loves derives from its love a great desire to do all things most perfectly, in order to please all the more the God whom it loves, and this desire, dilating the heart, makes it turn in the way of the commandments and of the perfect life. In proportion as it acts, this desire increases; practice increases it, even as wood cast upon the fire augments the flame, and there results from it a continually more ardent desire to do everything in the best possible manner, in order to please the God whom we love always more and more.

SECOND POINT

✝ *Love Gives Courage to do all Things Well*

Nothing costs us aught when we love, says St. Augustine; or, if it does give us any trouble, it makes us love even the trouble. Nothing is stronger than love, says the author of the Imitation. He who loves springs across all difficulties, flies, and triumphs (Imit. 5:3,4). Fatigue does not exhaust him, or discomfort stop him, or fear disconcert him. In vain nature shudders at the severity of the morals of the Gospel; he treads nature under foot and passes on. In vain the world attempts to hinder him by its sarcasm and its railings, or to attract him by the temptation of its honors and its pleasures; he treads the world under foot and passes on. In vain self-will, with its inconstancies and its caprices; temper, with its outbursts and its impatience; idleness, with its distastes, all seem to conspire together to hinder him from doing well; he treads all underfoot and passes on. Let us here examine our conscience; if we do not possess this great courage, it is because we do not love; let us love God with our whole heart, and nothing will be difficult to us.

THIRD POINT

✝ *Love Makes us Find Joy and Merit in the Good we do*

The happiness of pleasing God by doing all things well is a foretaste of paradise. All for Thy love, all to please Thee, the soul which loves God says to Him; and it is content it triumphs. All for Thy love, all in order to please Thee, it repeats to itself on performing its next action, and its joy is redoubled, its happiness multiplied. If it meets with crosses on its path and where are they not to be found? With love, all its troubles are softened; its crosses lose their severity, its thorns their points.(Imit. 5:3) We see in the cross a present sent us by God, who does not afflict us excepting because He loves us, and who sees in this cross a means of salvation for us; from that time we bless it, and we kiss His hand, which is always good, even when it strikes us. Then to the joy of doing well love adds merit, for the motive of love marvelously raises the merit of our actions; and in heaven there will be an immense difference between actions performed through love and those which will have had faith or hope as their motive. Oh, how good it is, then, to do everything from love! Is it thus that we act? *Resolutions and spiritual nosegay as above.*

Seventh Friday after Pentecost

SUMMARY OF TOMORROW'S MEDITATION

 fter having meditated upon our actions in general, we will meditate tomorrow: First, upon the importance of a rule of life which assigns to each action its own particular season and manner; Second, on the manner of making and of observing this rule. We will then make the resolution: First, to trace out for ourselves this rule of life if we have not already done so; Second, to observe it with punctuality and love even in its smallest details. We will retain as our spiritual nosegay these words of the saints: "He who lives according to rule lives according to God." (St Gregory of Nyssa)

MEDITATION FOR THE MORNING

Let us adore Our Lord Jesus Christ always keeping engraved, in the middle of His heart, the most holy will of His Father as the only rule of all His actions, whether small or great. Never once did He follow His own will; at every moment His Father's will was the law of His conduct.(John 8:29) How adorable He is in this life of loving submission to the divine good pleasure! Let us render to Him all our homage with this object in view.

FIRST POINT

✝ *The Importance of a Rule of Life*

A Christian who lives without rule lives at the bidding of his caprices or his changing, vacillating will, or at the bidding of circumstances, which carry him away as by a whirlwind. There is no order in the employment of his time; there is no ingredient of faith in his actions. It is not God whom he serves; it is his own will or his own humor that rules over all that he does. Hence exercises of piety omitted, abridged, or badly performed; hence numerous duties neglected, so much time lost, so many moments badly employed. With a rule, the exact contrary happens. The rule, which directs everything, constantly recalls the mind to God, and renders the soul recollected, and the beautiful order which distinguishes all the exterior actions is reflected within. The soul is always master of itself, and we do everything well, small things as well as great. As each duty has its time marked out for it, not only do we not omit any, but we perform it with greater ease, because we follow a path which is traced out; with more perfection, because obedience raises and ennobles all we do; with greater merit, because the continual submission of our will is very meritorious in the sight of God; with more constancy, because our rule necessarily prevents omissions and maintains everything in order. We are then entirely and solely given up to the present action, time is always well employed, and we are able to perform labors which a man who has no rule of life cannot comprehend. When we behold the numerous books written by our great doctors, or the prodigious works performed by certain men, we ask ourselves how they were able to do so many things. The secret of the mystery is, that everything was regulated in regard to the employment of their time, and that a rule multiplies time. When we have a spirit of order, and we know how to arrange all our moments, we are able to find time for everything, said the holy Bishop of Amiens, M. de la Motte. A rule gives a spirit of order, and a spirit of order accelerates all kinds of affairs. Let us here examine our conscience. Has not our life been ill-regulated? Sometimes we have been idle, as though we had nothing to do; sometimes we have been hurried on by an uneasy ardor, which embroils and confounds everything together, as if we should never be able to reach the end of anything; we are always undecided as to what must be done, and for the most part employed in what we ought not to be doing at that moment. The reason is that we have no rule, or that we do not attend to it.

SECOND POINT

✝ On the Manner of Making and Observing the Rule

Every good rule of life ought to be in harmony with our position, in such a manner that no duty of our state ought to suffer from it, and that no one should have to complain of us. It ought to embrace the plan of the day, of the week, of the month, of the year, and should settle in so proper a manner exercises of piety, frequentation of the sacraments, family duties, the employment of free moments, that every one around us, instead of finding anything to cavil at in it, should be obliged to admire the beautiful order which would be its result. The rule being thus made, we must observe its smallest details as well as the most important, with the purity of intention which aims only at pleasing God; with the courage which is able to do itself violence in order to bend the will to it; with the joy which makes it a pleasure for us to immolate ourselves wholly to God; with the promptitude which never defers the execution of it for a moment; with the exactitude which never allows caprice to be mingled with it; and always with the discretion which enables us to derogate from it, with a good grace, every time that charity, propriety, or the duties of our position require us to do so. Is it thus that we observe our rule? *Resolutions and spiritual nosegay as above.*

SEVENTH SATURDAY AFTER PENTECOST

SUMMARY OF TOMORROW'S MEDITATION

e will enter tomorrow into the details of the particular actions prescribed by our rule. We will commence by the action of rising, which is the first of the day, and we shall see: First, the importance of performing it well; Second, the manner of doing it well. We will then make the resolution: First, to rise everyday at a fixed hour, and to do so promptly; Second, to accompany this action with modesty, a spirit of piety, and, above all, of preparation of the subject of our meditation. We will retain as our spiritual nosegay the words of St. John Climachus: "Give to the Lord the first-fruits of your day, for it will belong entirely to him to whom you give its first moments." (Gr. 26. No 103)

MEDITATION FOR THE MORNING

Let us adore Our Lord Jesus Christ subjecting Himself to all the weaknesses of mankind; He slept, He awoke, He arose, He dressed Himself as we do; but He performed all these actions in an admirable manner, issuing from His sleep with the same love which, on the day of His incarnation, made Him quit the repose He was enjoying in the bosom of His Father that He might come upon earth and labor for our salvation. Let us bless Him for having taught us by His example how to begin the day in a holy manner.

FIRST POINT

✝ *The Importance of Performing the Action of Rising in a Christian Manner*

Consecrate to God the first-fruits of the day, says St. John Climachus, for it will be given entirely to him who will have first taken possession of it. If, from the moment when we awake, we give ourselves to God with our whole heart, it will be easy for us to keep ourselves all day long in this disposition. Let our first thought, our first word, our first action, be given to God. Our first thought, by representing Him to ourselves as being close beside us, He who has watched over us during the night, and who offers us His assistance during the day; our first words, by pronouncing the names of Jesus, Mary, Joseph; our first action, by making the sign of the cross; our first sentiments, by rendering Him our homage of adoration, of love, and of gratitude, and by offering to Him the whole of our day with the intention of never living any more for a single instant except for Him in Jesus Christ. (Rom. 6:2) The soul which is thus firmly established in these holy dispositions will find it easy to maintain itself in them. If, on the contrary, we begin the day with wandering thoughts, with forgetfulness of God, with ministering to our own comforts, love for our caprices and for our fancies, idleness, cowardice, it will be all the more difficult for us to change these bad dispositions, because, even during the whole day, we shall not think either of our deplorable state or of the duty of reforming ourselves. And wherefore, then, should we refuse to God the first-fruits of the day, when we know that they are especially dear to Him? It would be an injustice, seeing that these first moments belong to Him (Num. 21:29); it would be ingratitude after the blessing of our preservation during the night; it would be blindness, since on this first action depend all the others, and because, therefore, our greatest interests are concerned in performing it well. Have we before now reflected seriously upon the importance of performing this action well?

SECOND POINT

✝ *On the Way of Performing the Act of Rising in a Holy Manner*

Three virtues ought to sanctify this first action of the day: obedience, modesty, and piety. Obedience wills that we should rise at the precise hour fixed by our rule, without conceding anything to idleness or reveries, and that we should spend the smallest time possible in dressing ourselves; for it is a waste of time to employ more of it than is strictly necessary in this action. Modesty wills, on its side, that we should avoid as much as possible too much thought about our clothing, too much delicacy as regards the care of our body, all affectation of excessive cleanliness, as well as too little attention in regard to it, proposing to ourselves, as a model, the perfect decency which Jesus, Mary, and Joseph observed in this act. Lastly, religion ought to occupy our interior with pious and holy thoughts. You shall keep My words in your heart, God said to His people, and you shall meditate upon them at your rising. (Deut. 6:7) It is the moment for saying to the Lord: "Thanks, my God, for having preserved me during the night; thanks for having granted me another day in which to labor for my salvation; thanks for having given me these garments to clothe me, when so many others have hardly anything but rags. This clothing, O my God, at the same time that it excites my gratitude, fills me with confusion; it recalls to mind the sin which placed me lower than even the animals, who have no need to clothe themselves; this clothing is the sorrowful memorial of my lost innocence; it is the remains and the spoils of animals. What humiliation for mankind to be obliged to have recourse to them! O Jesus, be Thou my garment, as Thy apostle says (Rom. 13:14); that is to say, give me in all things Thy sentiments, Thy manner of thinking, of speaking, and of acting, and may I imitate Thee so closely that Thy sacred person may seem to cover mine. With this object in view, O Lord, I am going to dispose myself to make a good meditation." Then we recall to ourselves the subject on which we are about to meditate, and we occupy ourselves with it until we begin it. Is it thus that we habitually perform the act of rising? *Resolutions and spiritual nosegay as above.*

Eighth Sunday after Pentecost

THE GOSPEL ACCORDING TO ST. LUKE, 16:1-9

"At that time Jesus spoke to His disciples this parable: There was a certain rich man who had a steward; and the same was accused unto him, that he had wasted his goods. And he called him, and said to him: How is it that I hear this of thee? Give an account of thy stewardship, for now thou canst be steward no longer. And the steward said within himself: What shall I do, because my lord taketh away from me the stewardship? To dig I am not able; to beg I am ashamed. I know what I will do, that when I shall be removed from the stewardship they may receive me into their houses. Therefore, calling together every one of his lord's debtors, he said to the first: How much dost thou owe my lord? But he said: A hundred barrels of oil. And he said to him: Take thy bill, and sit down quickly, and write fifty. Then he said to another: And how much dost thou owe? Who said; A hundred quarters of wheat. He said to him: Take thy bill, and write eighty. And the lord commended the unjust steward, forasmuch as he had done wisely; for the children of this world are wiser in their generation than the children of light. And I say to you: Make unto you friends of the mammon of iniquity, that when you shall fail, they may receive you into everlasting dwellings."

SUMMARY OF TOMORROW'S MEDITATION

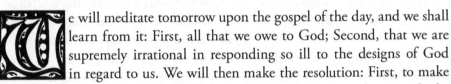 e will meditate tomorrow upon the gospel of the day, and we shall learn from it: First, all that we owe to God; Second, that we are supremely irrational in responding so ill to the designs of God in regard to us. We will then make the resolution: First, to make use of all that we have and of all that we are only in accordance with the good pleasure of God; Second, to infuse into the service of God and our own salvation at least as much zeal as the world infuses into its search after riches, honors, and pleasures. Our spiritual nosegay shall be these two sentences of the gospel: "Give an account of thy stewardship. The children of this world are wiser in their generation than the children of light." (Luke 16:2)

MEDITATION FOR THE MORNING

Let us adore God under the semblance of the rich man of whom the gospel of the day speaks. God is eminently rich, not only because He possesses in Himself an infinity of perfections which are the most splendid riches, but also because He is the infinite Master of all things, of all the riches of nature, of all the riches of grace, of the inestimable riches of glory; and He might still create thousands of worlds richer and more magnificent, without the riches which are in Him being either exhausted or diminished. Let us rejoice that God is so rich, and let us deem ourselves happy to belong to such a Master. When we love, we delight in everything which honors the person beloved.

FIRST POINT

✝ *We Owe ourselves Entirely to God*

All that we have and all that we are belongs absolutely and essentially to God, since, as He is our Creator and our Preserver, He is essentially our sovereign Master. In communicating to us His gifts, He does not thereby intend to give up His right to them; He keeps the ownership of them for Himself, and confides to us only their steward ship and management, with the charge of administering them, not according to our liking and caprices, but according to His will. We are only servants or agents to whom does not belong even the bread they eat or the water they drink, and He has the right to drive us away or to punish us if we do not administrate His possessions in the way He desires we should do. This principle being laid down, it follows that if God has given us riches, it is on condition that after having provided for our necessities we should employ what remains for the needs of the poor; if He has imparted to us mental gifts, or certain personal advantages, or certain natural or supernatural privileges; if at every moment He adds to our existence the blessing of another moment, it is on condition that we shall make use of all these things according to His good pleasure, not disposing of anything from caprice, from love of the world and our own comfort, from vanity or sensuality; and all these requirements belong to Him by right. At every moment He may say to us, as He certainly will one day say, "Give an account of thy stewardship." What have you done with all My possessions? What have you done with the wealth of which I confided to you the stewardship? Did you give the portion which was due of it to the poor, taking for yourself only what was necessary? What have you done with your intelligence? Have you applied it to things which were useful and in the order of your duties, or have you not paralyzed it through idleness, perverted it by bad books, evil thoughts, sinful conversations, or given it up to the service of self-love and of pride? What have you done with your body? Have you not made it a slave to vanity, an idol of sensuality? What have you done with your time? Have you economized every particle of it? What have you done with My graces? Have you not been unfaithful to them? Give Me an account of the evils you have done, and of the good you ought to have done and have not done, and of the good you have done badly by mingling with it negligence, cowardice, self-love, for it is not enough to do what is right; you must also do it well (Wis. 6:11).

SECOND POINT

✝ *We are Supremely Irrational in Responding so Ill to the Designs of God in Regard to us*

Is it not indeed a strange thing that we, who ought to belong wholly to God, show less zeal in executing His will, in the order of our eternal salvation, than men of the world exhibit for miserable temporal interests? Nevertheless, many who call themselves Christians do so in spite of the gospel, which anathematizes riches, honors, and pleasures, and declares that salvation is the one thing necessary. The man of the world is inspired by a passionate desire to procure the false goods of this world for himself; and many who call themselves Christians have only a very moderate desire to be saved; they think of it very little, and even then it is with indifference; they do not make a serious business of it, and, of all their anxieties, it is the least. The man of the world carefully puts aside everything which forms an obstacle to his projects; he watches, he keeps himself on his guard; and yet many who call themselves Christians care little for what exposes their salvation to peril; even when they perceive that there exists an obstacle to their salvation, it is only with difficulty they decide to put it away; they love the occasion which exposes them to it, often they will not leave it; and it is only difficulty that they are persuaded to separate themselves from it. The man of the world does not hesitate to make any sacrifice which will enable him to attain his end; and, not taking into account any probable chances, he always aims at what is most certain, never neglects any means of success, braves fatigue, perils, even death itself; whilst, on the contrary, many who call themselves Christians are pusillanimous and devoid of energy in what has regard to salvation; they aim always at doing the least possible, not examining whether what is asked of them is the best means whereby to save themselves, but whether it is absolutely necessary, if they could not really dispense themselves from it; the smallest difficulties repel them, restraint frightens them; they do not think either of repairing past losses by amassing more virtues and merits, or of taking precautions against dangers in the future, or of sending before them into heaven spiritual riches which will be their happiness throughout eternity; they only aim at not ruining themselves completely, that is to say, not to damn themselves. Oh, if we had but as much zeal to save ourselves as the man of business has to enrich himself, as the soldier has to obtain advancement; if we but did for heaven what the world does to obtain a position, to gain a lawsuit, to succeed in commerce, or to recover lost health, how soon should we become great saints! So true are the words of Our

Lord, that the children of this world are wiser in regard to the trifles which they call their affairs than the children of light in regard to the affair of their salvation. *Resolutions and spiritual nosegay as above.*

EIGHTH MONDAY AFTER PENTECOST

SUMMARY OF TOMORROW'S MEDITATION

e will meditate tomorrow upon the exercise of meditation, as being after our rising, on which we meditated last Saturday, the first act of the day, and we shall see: First, its excellence; Second, the preparation we must make for it. Our resolution shall then be: First, never to fail to make our meditation, and, in order to do so, to make it immediately after our rising, because a meditation which is delayed is often a meditation which is left undone; Second, to prepare ourselves for it by an habitual life of recollection, and especially by the practice of laying down the subject of our meditation the evening before. Our spiritual nosegay shall be the words of David: "Unless Thy law had been my meditation, I had then perhaps perished in my abjection."(Ps. 118:92)

MEDITATION FOR THE MORNING

Let us adore Our Lord Jesus Christ, the perfect adorer of His Father, rendering to Him His homage in prayer and finding His delight in this holy exercise. Let us admire the zeal with which He applies Himself to it. He begins His prayer when beginning to live; He perseveres in it all his life long; He perseveres in it even after His death, upon our altars, without speaking of the continual prayer He makes in heaven. What homage ought we not to render to Him from this point of view!

FIRST POINT

✝ *The Excellence of Meditation*

Prayer is everything, in a word, which is sublime in religion; it is an elevation of our mind and our heart towards heaven (St. John Damascene); it is intimate intercourse with God (St. Gregory Nazianzen); it is the union of the soul with its Supreme Good (St. Ephrem); it is the occupation of the angels in paradise permitted to men upon earth; it is the life of heaven begun here below. By prayer we raise ourselves above all that passes away, and we leave it beneath our feet; by it, understanding that God alone is all, we throw ourselves upon Him, we cast our hearts into His, that we may love and serve only Him and live only for Him. What can be more sublime and at the same time, more necessary? "Unless Thy law had been my meditation" says David, "I had then perhaps perished in my abjection. Thy justifications I will never forget, for by them Thou hast given me life."(Ps. 118:92,93) It is because in fact meditation alone is able to keep up in the soul that lively faith in the great truths of religion, of the importance of salvation, of the sanctity of our mysteries, of the extent and of the details of our duties, without which salvation is impossible; it alone can prevent the routine, the relaxation, the successive cessation of all the conservative practices of piety, and put away the illusions in which we are so apt to indulge in regard to the state of our conscience; it alone can form and preserve in the soul the spirit of humility, of mortification, of meekness, of all the virtues necessary to salvation, and it was this which made St. Bonaventura say: "Without prayer there is no progress in virtue;" and the pious Gerson: "Without the exercise of meditation no one, except it be by means of a miracle, attains to true Christian life." But meditation is not only necessary, it is also infinitely advantageous on account of the virtues of which it is the source. It renders that easy to the soul which without it would be difficult, if not impossible. By means of meditation we taste God, we are filled with love for Him, we learn to have a horror for sin, to hate the world and ourselves, to fly from vices, to practice virtue, to aim at purity of intention in all our actions, to have a reverence for holy things, and charity for our neighbor. Lastly, meditation is everything that is sweetest in religion. Let us ask the holy souls who practice it habitually as it ought to be practiced, and they will tell you that it is a delicious moment for them, that it is a moment of paradise upon earth; let us imitate them and share in their happiness. "Oh, taste and see that the Lord is sweet." (Ps. 33:9) Do we hold meditation in high esteem? Do we look upon it in the bottom of our hearts as the greatest of all good things?

SECOND POINT

✝ *Preparation for Meditation*

In order to become a man of prayer we must: First, be heartily determined to keep our conscience pure and to mortify our passions. He who does not care to mortify himself and to become better cannot hope to succeed in this holy exercise. He who will not detach himself from earth cannot rise to heaven. Second, we must love recollection and break off our life of thoughtlessness, which, consuming itself in vain imagination, in loss of time, in greediness after riches, makes the soul spend itself upon all kinds of objects and grants to nature all that it asks. To be dissipated all day long and to be recollected in prayer are two things which are incompatible. Third, lastly, we must, the evening before, prepare the subject of our meditation, occupy ourselves with it when we are betaking ourselves to rest and in the morning when we rise. Is it thus that we have hitherto prepared ourselves for meditation? *Resolutions and spiritual nosegay as above.*

EIGHTH TUESDAY AFTER PENTECOST

SUMMARY OF TOMORROW'S MEDITATION

e will meditate tomorrow on the method of making our meditations, and we shall see that it consists: First, in penetrating ourselves thoroughly with the subject of our meditation; Second, in examining our conscience with regard to this subject, and by a good act of contrition renouncing the faults of which this examination makes us aware; Third, in asking God for His grace to execute aright the good resolution contained in the act of contrition. We will then make the resolution: First, to follow this exceedingly simple method in our meditations; Second, often to recall to ourselves, during the day, the good sentiments and the resolutions of the meditation. Our spiritual nosegay shall be the words of David: "My eyes are ever towards the Lord." (Ps. 24:15)

MEDITATION FOR THE MORNING

Let us adore Jesus Christ at prayer in the Garden of Olives. He is there on His knees with His face prostrate against the ground (Luke 22:41; Matt. 26:39). How completely this spectacle ought to teach us to abase ourselves before God in prayer through the sentiment of our nothingness in presence of His infinite majesty. Let us thank Our Lord for giving us this example and ask of Him grace to profit by it.

FIRST POINT

✝ *The Importance of Penetrating ourselves thoroughly with the Subject of the Meditation*

Doubtless, O my God, when we present ourselves before Thee in prayer, we ought, before anything else, to be thoroughly penetrated with Thy adorable presence, since nothing is so well calculated to keep us, during the whole time our meditation lasts, in an attitude of attention and reverence. We ought to implore the assistance of Thy Holy Spirit, since we cannot otherwise have even a single good thought. But after that, nothing is more necessary than that we should be thoroughly penetrated with Thy divine teachings in regard to the subject of our meditation and on the reasons for conforming our conduct to it; for these are the two elements of which every subject of meditation is composed. Thy divine teachings, O Lord, which are to be deducted from what Thou hast said, done, or thought upon the subject we are meditating, are they not of all things in the world the most worthy of our serious reflections? What can be more just than to consider them with thanksgiving, admiration, and love for the infinite goodness which wills to instruct us? What more reasonable than that we should afterwards penetrate ourselves with the reasons which should lead us to conform our conduct to them, to assimilate, if I may so say, these divine lessons, not by means of subtle speculations and a course of reasoning more suitable to some subject we are studying than to an exercise of prayer, but by pious affections and holy aspirations? Alas, I acknowledge with sorrow, O my God, that for want of occupying myself with this first portion of meditation, my faith is weakened, my convictions lessened, and I do not feel as strongly the necessity of leading a better life.

SECOND POINT

✝ Examination of Conscience, Followed by an Act of Contrition, the Second Portion of Meditation

After having seen what I ought to be, O Lord, what can be more natural than to examine what I am, in what my sentiments differ from Thy sentiments, my actions from Thy manner of acting, my words from Thy divine language, and whether, living as I do, I could present myself with confidence before Thy heavenly Father, who has said that He will receive into His Paradise none but those who bear a resemblance to Thee (Rom. 8:20). I shall therefore have to examine my faults, to study their source, and to put away from me the occasions of them. After having, by means of this examination, recognized my guilt, ought I not, O Lord, to deplore so sad a past, bitterly to regret having served Thee so ill, be filled with shame in Thy presence, and make resolutions to lead a new life: practical, special resolutions, present resolutions adapted to the present day? Alas! Lord, I confess with sighs that I have failed and that I fail nearly every day in observing these holy rules, and this is the reason why I perform my meditations so ill.

THIRD POINT

✝ To Ask for Grace to Execute our Resolutions, the Third Part of Meditation

I shall make all these considerations and all these resolutions in vain, all will be useless to me, O my God, without the help of Thy grace. Thou hast said, Lord, and I believe it, that man can do nothing without Thy help (John 15:5); but this grace, how shall I obtain it from Thy mercy? Thou hast also said, and I believe it: It will only be by prayer (John 16:24), but it must be a fervent prayer; that is to say , an ardent desire to conform my life to the virtue or the truth upon which I have been meditating; a humble prayer accompanied by confidence; recourse to the merits of Our Lord, to the intercession of the Most Blessed Virgin, to St. Joseph, to the holy angels, to our holy patrons, and the saints which the Church honors today. Alas until now I have not asked this, or I have asked it badly, and hence the want of putting into practice so many resolutions, but henceforth I will pray earnestly, with humility and confidence, and Thou wilt hear me. *Resolutions and spiritual nosegay as above.*

EIGHTH WEDNESDAY AFTER PENTECOST

SUMMARY OF TOMORROW'S MEDITATION

e will meditate tomorrow upon two principal difficulties which are met within meditation: First, distractions; Second, aridities and other trials. We will then make the resolution: First, to lead a more recollected and detached life, which will be a means of drying up the source of many of our distractions; Second, never to be discouraged by the state of powerlessness in which we may find ourselves during our meditation, but to remain quietly humiliated in the presence of God, admiring His goodness which bears with us and loves us in spite of our wretchedness. Our spiritual nosegay shall be the words of David: "In a desert land, and where there is no way, and no wafer, have I come before Thee." (Ps. 62:3)

MEDITATION FOR THE MORNING

Let us adore Our Lord Jesus Christ praying to His Father so perfectly that no distraction turns Him away from it, and, at the same time, often with so much distress that He falls into an agony; but this agony, instead of making Him give up prayer, only excites Him to prolong it all the more (Luke 22:43). Oh, what an admirable example! How happy the soul that is faithful enough to imitate it!

FIRST POINT

✝ *Remedy against Distractions in Meditation*

Be Thou blessed, my God, who, whilst permitting that we should have distractions in meditation, hast in Thy goodness acquainted us with the remedies we may use against this evil before, during, and after meditation. Before meditation, we must prevent distractions by drying up the sources of them, which are: First, curiosity for news, eagerness about the affairs of this world, an ill-regulated attachment to some occupation of other, a too lively affection for creatures, dissipation of the mind and of the senses; Second, the unhappy habit of allowing ourselves to be carried away by the first thought which is pleasing to us; for instance, a wandering of the imagination, which runs after the past, the present, and the future; Third, carelessness, which will not submit to restraint, or prepare, on the preceding evening, the subject of meditation, or think of it at night during moments of wakefulness, or in the morning from the moment of awakening until the time arrives for making the meditation, or penetrate itself, when beginning, with the sense of the holy presence of God and with the desire of making a fervent meditation. Is it not true that we have left open until now all these sources of distraction? Is it astonishing, then, that we should have such distractions? During the meditation: it is, as soon as I shall perceive a distraction, to humble myself and be ashamed at such a want of respect towards God, to have recourse to Thee, O Lord, saying with the apostles: "Lord, teach us to pray." (Luke 11:1); to resume my meditation at the point where the distinction took hold of me, and simply to continue it without trouble or uneasiness. Lastly, after the meditation, to carry away with me a deep humility on account of all my distractions; to apply myself to make amends for a meditation so ill-performed by performing in a better manner the actions which follow it, and making a strong resolution to pass the day in a manner all the more holy in proportion to the faulty manner in which I have made my meditation, and thereby repair my defects in this exercise. Alas! I have done nothing of the kind, O Lord, and Thou knowest it. I am confounded in Thy presence, and will do better in the future.

SECOND POINT

✝ *Remedy for Aridities in Meditation*

How happy I should be, Lord, if I could but imitate David, who, in the midst of abandonments, of obscurities, and of aridities, rendered Thee his homage in prayer with as much fervor as in the season of consolations. (Ps. 62:3) The holy king comprehended that, in the midst of these trials, the Christian soul ought not to retrench aught in its exercises, or be troubled and complain, be sorrowful or discouraged. Make me also understand it, O my God! Enable me to follow in patience and humility the four points of my method of meditation, which are: The study of my subject, the examination of my conscience, contrition, and a prayer for Thy grace to make me execute my good resolutions. If I have no taste for this exercise, it will only be all the more meritorious and fruitful. Thou wilt accept it in expiation of my sins; Thou wilt make of it a ladder whereby to arrive at humility, by convincing me that my evil nature can produce nothing that is good; and thus I shall make better meditations, because I shall come forth from them in a more humble frame of mind. From thence I will raise myself to a greater love of Thy infinite goodness, deigning to love a creature so miserable as I am, for Thy saints teach me that these abandonments are often only an artifice of Thy love to excite my soul to desire Thee with more ardor, to seek Thee with greater zeal, to take hold of Thy grace with more eagerness, and to follow it with more fidelity when it presents itself. (St. Gregory in St. Matt) *Resolutions and spiritual nosegay as above.*

Eighth Thursday after Pentecost

SUMMARY OF TOMORROW'S MEDITATION

e will meditate tomorrow on the value of time and the proper manner of employing it. We will then make the resolution: First, to economize every moment by always employing it usefully; Second, to avoid frivolous reading and conversation, and other ways of wasting time. Our spiritual nosegay shall be the words of the Holy Ghost: "Son, observe the time." (Ecclus. 4:23)

MEDITATION FOR THE MORNING.

Let us adore the infinite goodness of Our Lord, who has bought us and arranged time for us that we may prepare in it for eternity, the sole aim to which all our actions here below ought to be referred. Let us beg of Him to make us sensible of the value of time and to give us grace never to abuse it.

FIRST POINT

✝ *What is the Value of Time*

Time is worth, First, as much as heaven; because heaven is the reward assigned by God Himself to the right employment of time. A single moment well employed was worth to the good thief, spite of all the crimes of his past life, the possession of paradise, and even if by the holiness of our life we are worthy of paradise, one more moment well employed will be worth to us an added degree of glory and of happiness throughout eternity, that is, so to speak, a new heaven in heaven itself. Time is worth, Second, as much as the blood of Jesus Christ; for His blood is the price at which all the moments of our life have been bought; it is, as it were, the money which represents the value of time. If, then, this blood calls itself precious, time ought to be precious to us in the same proportion, that is to say, beyond all speech; for who could express the value of this blood, a single drop of which would have sufficed to redeem a thousand worlds? Time is worth, Third, as much as God Himself; for every moment well employed will be worth the possession of God to us throughout eternity. Fourth, time is of such great value that God gives it only drop by drop, if I may so say, without ever granting two moments at once. Now we can only enjoy one short moment of it, which passes like lightning; and if we fail to take hold of it in its flight, it is lost forever, lost irrecoverably; for time passed never returns, nor another time which might repair it, because of the reason: First, that the other time is already due to God, and that which is due cannot be used to pay other debts; Second, that time, seeing it may be taken from us at any moment, is the most uncertain thing in the world, and that a thing which is so uncertain cannot be assigned as the payment of a debt which is certain. Whence it follows that it is our duty to act, in regard to time, as those do who, not having large revenues, do not expend the smallest portion of them in useless expenses, and derive the greatest possible advantage from those that they have. Is it thus that we have looked upon time?

SECOND POINT
✝ *The Way in which to Use Time Properly*
First We must perform at each moment what God asks of us in regard to that moment. Time being God's and not ours, we have no right to put it to any other use except that which He wills, to give up the smallest particle of it to the like or dislike of the moment, and to take counsel of caprice respecting the employment to be made of it. Second, we must do everything with a view to pleasing God. God recompenses only what is done for Him. The Pharisees might perform as many good works as they chose; Jesus Christ declared that they would not receive any recompense for them, because they did them that they might be esteemed by men, and not from a desire to please God. Oh, what merits are lost in this way! Third, we must do everything in the best possible manner. "In all thy works keep the pre-eminence." (Ecclus. 33:23) To do things negligently and imperfectly when we are proposing to do them for God, is to be wanting in respect to God; for the more eminent the person is for whom we are laboring, the more what we do for him ought to be carefully per formed and perfect in every respect. For whom are you performing that action? St. Ignatius asked, on a certain occasion, one of his brethren who was negligent in his office. I am doing it for God, he replied. So much the worse,

St. Ignatius answered; if you had been doing it for me I would have forgiven you for having done it badly; but as it is for God you are performing it you are inexcusable to put so little zeal into it and to do it so carelessly. *Resolutions and spiritual nosegay as above.*

Eighth Friday after Pentecost

SUMMARY OF TOMORROW'S MEDITATION

e will meditate tomorrow upon the obligation of employing our time rightly and not losing the smallest portion of it. We shall see that this obligation is: First, a divine precept; Second, a natural right. We will then make the resolution; First, to be always busily occupied; Second, to occupy ourselves especially with the work which is in the order of our duties for the actual moment. Our spiritual nosegay shall be the words of God to Adam: "In the sweat of thy face shalt thou eat bread." (Gen. 3:19)

MEDITATION FOR THE MORNING

Let us adore Jesus Christ employing for the glory of His Father and the salvation of men all the time which He passed upon earth not a moment given to pleasure, to personal satisfaction (Rom. 15:3). He did everything from the desire to please God His Father. (John 8:29) Let us thank Him for this great example, and render to Him all our homage.

FIRST POINT

✝ *The Obligation to Employ Time Properly is a Divine Precept*

Even if we were the children of an innocent Adam, a divine precept would oblige us to utilize time by work, since it is written that God placed man in paradise that he might work therein (Gen. 2:15). How much more, then, are we obliged to do so. we who are the children of a guilty Adam, to whom it has been said: "In the sweat of thy face shalt thou eat bread, "a general law which weighs upon the whole of the human race without distinction, upon the rich as well as on the poor, upon the great as well as on the little! And this law was confirmed by Jesus Christ declaring that the useless servant shall be cast into the abyss (Matt. 25:30), that the tree which is sterile shall be cast into the fire (Matt. 3: 10), that, lastly, all will have to render to Him an account of all the talents confided to them; and these talents, what are they if they be not their faculties, which idleness paralyzes, or which it abuses; if it be not time, of which each moment ought to bear fruit before God? "If any man will not work, neither let him eat;" says Jesus Christ by His apostle (2 Thess. 3:10) he is unworthy to live, and occupies a useless place in the order of creation.

SECOND POINT

✝ *The Obligation of Employing Time Well is a Precept of Natural Right*

Natural right forbids us from dishonoring human dignity in our person, to abuse the gifts of God, and to compromise our salvation. Now the loss of time, First, dishonors human dignity in our person; for it is a shame for man to grovel in inaction, to drag along an existence here below which is of no use, and to be nothing more than a useless burden upon earth; Second, it is an abuse of the gifts of God, that is to say, first, of time, which is a gift of His munificence, then of our faculties, which idleness enervates and emasculates, numbs, and ends by stifling; Third, it compromises our salvation, for experience teaches us that idleness is the mother and mistress of all the vices; it engenders them, develops and strengthens them (Ecclus. 33:29); it was the cause of the immorality and the ruin of Sodom: so true is it that there are no faults which it cannot make man commit, no kind of chastisement which it cannot draw down from heaven (Ezech. 16:40). It has ruined the greatest men: Samson, David, Solomon, after having been saints whilst they were laboring, were ruined by idleness (Ad frat. erem. serm. vi. inter Op. St. Aug.). The reason is easy to conceive. As the body is developed by exercise and is strengthened by fatigue, whilst it is rendered effeminate by inaction and loses its vigor in a state of immobility, so in like manner the soul is enervated by idleness, loses its energy, and languishes in a state of inaction. When in this sad condition, the heart is dried up, the imagination wanders, the mind goes astray by occupying itself with useless thoughts. We look upon as a happiness all the means of which we can make use for getting rid of time of which we do not know what to do, and in consequence we take our weary idleness into dangerous society, and indulge in foolish conversations, which are sometimes free and devoid of decency. We use and absorb our faculties in vain curiosity, in frivolous reading, in reveries, and henceforward there is no counting upon virtue. We are accessible to all kinds of temptations, impressionable to all kinds of vices. The demons, who know this well, seize upon these wretched moments, and come in crowds to tempt the soul. There are the demons of pride and self-love, the demons of impurity and sensuality, the demons of cupidity and the love of riches, who all join together in making the assault, and we succumb. It was this which made Cassian say that for one demon who tempts the man that works there are a thousand who besiege an idle man (Cassian, Lit. Book 10,100:19). In presence of these facts, who is there that will not understand the obligation laid upon us of spending time well and never giving up the smallest portion of it to idleness? What reproaches have we not to address to ourselves on this subject! What moments have we not lost in idleness! Let us regret this sorrowful past of ours and let us resolve to make a better use of time in the future. *Resolutions and spiritual nosegay as above.*

EIGHTH SATURDAY AFTER PENTECOST

SUMMARY OF TOMORROW'S MEDITATION

e will consecrate our meditation of tomorrow to the consideration of six ways in which time is lost, in order that we may be upon our guard against the misfortune of subjecting ourselves to so great a loss. Our resolution shall be: First, never to remain idle, and to occupy ourselves always in something that will be of use in regard to our salvation; Second, to sanctify all our actions, even the most ordinary among them, such as our meals, our recreations, our work, and even our sleep by the pure intention of pleasing God. Our spiritual nosegay shall be the advice given in the Holy Scriptures: Do not allow the smallest particle of the time which God has given you to be lost (Ecclus. 14:14).

MEDITATION FOR THE MORNING

Let us adore Jesus Christ as the supreme Judge to whom we must render an account at the judgment day of all the moments of our pilgrimage upon earth. Let us adore Him recommending us by the mouth of the Wise Man not to lose the smallest particle of one sole day; and let us ask of Him to enable us to employ our time so well that all our days may be days full of merit and of good works (Ps. 72:10). Let us therefore beg Him with this object in view to make us understand the six ways in which time is lost, so that we may not fall into any of the snares by which so many souls are lost.

FIRST MANNER IN WHICH TIME IS LOST

We lose time, first, by doing nothing. All the faculties of the soul seem to be numbed; we think of nothing, we do not know what to do with ourselves and with our time; or, if we do think of anything, we occupy ourselves with useless reveries, with vain projects and chimerical plans. If we are not sufficient to ourselves, we spend whole hours from morning to night in idle talk, in games and amusements, in visits which have no object, in walks without any aim, in all the pastimes which idleness can invent, and we utterly waste all our moments (Prov. 18:9). Have we no reproaches to address to ourselves on this head?

SECOND MANNER IN WHICH TIME IS LOST

We lose time, in the second place, when we employ it in doing what is wrong. Such is the sin of those who pass their time in reading novels, theatrical pieces, or other books in which morals are but little respected; in criticizing our neighbor and speaking evil of him, in frequenting society which is dangerous, in going to certain soirées where seduction enters into the soul through all the senses, in meditating projects of vengeance, hatred, or injustice, in listening to the inspirations of Satan, who insinuates bad thoughts and evil desires into the soul. What does our conscience say to us on this head?

THIRD MANNER IN WHICH TIME IS LOST

We also lose time in performing actions which are indifferent in themselves, that is to say, which have nothing reprehensible about them in themselves, or in the manner in which they are performed, but which are done mechanically and without any fixed object, or from some fixed object, but one which is simply human and purely natural; for example, we eat only because we are hungry, or because it is the hour at which we take our meal; we betake ourselves to rest because we want to sleep; to repose or to recreation because we are tired; to conversation because it amuses us; we go to see such or such a rare and remarkable object because it feeds our curiosity. Evidently all this is devoid of merit, because it is all done without a view to God. What a loss and what a misfortune! In order to render one of these acts worthy of heaven nothing is wanting but a direction of intention. What reproaches have we not to address to ourselves here!

FOURTH MANNER IN WHICH TIME IS LOST

We lose time when we perform good actions, but which are not in the order of our duties. It is the fault committed by those who forget that the duties belonging to their position must hold the first place, who, having no rule for their conduct, do everything at a wrong time, nothing at a fixed hour; they often think of what they ought to do, and then nearly always decide upon doing what they ought not to do; they occupy themselves with offering long prayers at church when their duties call them to their homes; they employ themselves in pious exercises or good works when they ought to be occupying themselves with household affairs; they watch when they ought to sleep, sleep when they ought to rise, pray when they ought to work, or work when they ought to pray. Do we not recognize ourselves by these characteristics?

FIFTH MANNER IN WHICH TIME IS LOST

We also lose time in performing good works which are in the order of our duties, and this may happen in two different ways: First, when we are in a state of mortal sin; for in this state all works are dead works, incapable of meriting anything for heaven. All the good works we do may doubtless dispose God to grant us His grace to bring us back to Himself, but they are of no value in regard to salvation; Second, when instead of referring our good works to God, we perform them from vanity, to make ourselves remarked and esteemed; when we act under the influence Of caprice or fancy, when in doing good, for example, giving alms to the poor, we are influenced solely by a purely human, a purely natural pity. Let us here examine ourselves. What merits have we not lost, in this manner, because we act without any reference to God, for our own satisfaction, our self-love, or our vanity, and what treasures should we amass in heaven if at each action we said to God: Lord, it is to please Thee I do this; all for Thy love.

SIXTH MANNER IN WHICH TIME IS LOST

Lastly, we lose time by performing with a right intention the good which is in the order of our duties, when we do not do it at the time, in the place, in the manner, and accompanied by the other circumstances which God demands from us. This is the case with certain souls which spoil the good they do by the bad grace with which they perform it; by the wrong time at which they do it; by the disagreeable words with which they accompany it; or some other unfortunate circumstance which they do not take care to put aside. If in these cases all merit is not lost, the sum total of it is at least greatly diminished. What a vast field for examination! *Resolutions and spiritual nosegay as above.*

NINTH SUNDAY AFTER PENTECOST

THE GOSPEL ACCORDING TO ST. LUKE, 29:41-47

"At that time, when Jesus drew near to Jerusalem, seeing the city, He wept over it, saying: If thou also hadst known, and that in this thy day, the things that are to thy peace: but now they are hidden from thy eyes. For the day shall come upon thee, and thy enemies shall cast a trench about thee, and compass thee round, and straiten thee on every side, and beat thee flat to the ground, and thy children who are in thee; and they shall not leave in thee a stone upon a stone, because thou hast not known the time of thy visitation. "And entering into the temple, He began to cast out them that sold therein and them that bought, saying to them: It is written, My house is the house of prayer, but you have made it a den of thieves. And He was teaching daily in the temple."

SUMMARY OF TOMORROW'S MEDITATION

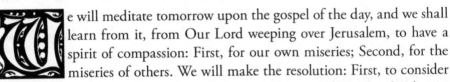e will meditate tomorrow upon the gospel of the day, and we shall learn from it, from Our Lord weeping over Jerusalem, to have a spirit of compassion: First, for our own miseries; Second, for the miseries of others. We will make the resolution: First, to consider our own spiritual miseries without feeling any bitter self-love, or desolation, but with humility and a strong resolution to live a better life; Second, to pity the trials of the Church at least by our prayers, if we cannot do more, the unhappiness of sinners by exercising zeal to bring them back, the misery of the poor by our alms, and the sorrow of the afflicted by the consolations we may be able to give them. Our spiritual nosegay shall be the words of the gospel: "When He drew near the city, He wept over it." (Luke 19:41)

MEDITATION FOR MORNING

Let us adore the Savior of the world shedding tears of compassion over Jerusalem, which He had always so much loved. Let us admire, love, and praise His goodness; He is more touched by the evils hanging over the unfortunate city than by His own interests, and the acclamations of the people who receive Him in triumph do not make Him forget the calamities reserved for its inhabitants. Who would not love so good a God?

FIRST POINT

✝ *On the Spirit of Compassion for our own Miseries*

The Jerusalem over which Our Lord weeps is the type of our soul, in which there is so much to weep over. "Weep for yourselves" (Luke 23:28), said Jesus to the holy women when He was ascending Calvary. We ought to weep, in fact, over our past sins, over our present miseries, over the uncertainty in which the future leaves our salvation, upon the abuse of graces, upon the small progress we make in virtue. God visits us every day by the illuminations with which He enlightens us, by the good movements with which He inspires us, by numerous instructions, by good books, by holy examples, by the blessings, and even by the trials which He sends us; the former to make us feel His goodness, and the latter to make us remember His justice; and it is a thing worthy of tears that we do not appreciate these graces and that we render them useless to us. O my soul, what a subject for compassion! (Luke 19:42) What unhappiness to have so often disregarded the visit of the Lord! (Ibid. 44) Let us weep over ourselves as Jesus Christ wept over Jerusalem, and let us be converted. The design of God in making us see our wretchedness is to render us humble and penitent and to make us lead a better life; and it would be a great evil if we were to derive from such a sight nothing but annoyance, desolation, and discouragement. Let us weep, then, because we are miserable, but let our tears be accompanied by a strong resolution to change our life, and to be filled with humility and confidence in the divine mercy.

SECOND POINT

✝ *On the Spirit of Compassion for the Miseries of Others*

We ought, first, to have compassion for the trials of the Church, who is our mother, our benefactress; she to whom we owe everything, and by whom alone we can be saved. All her evils ought to go to our heart; all her interests ought to be dear to us; it is a duty of filial piety to pray for her, to espouse her cause, and to defend her by all the means in our power. We ought, second, to have compassion for the trials of our country, because Jesus Christ, weeping over Jerusalem, teaches us to love our country, to sigh over her temporal and spiritual misfortunes, and to remedy them, each one of us according to the degree of his power and the sphere of his means, by prayer, by good example, wise counsels, and his support We ought, third, to have compassion on the evil-doing of sinners; instead of being irritated and murmuring against those who do evil, we ought to pity their blindness, pray for their conversion, and zealously use all our endeavors to bring them back; they are the children of God, they are our brethren in Jesus Christ. We ought, fourth, to have compassion on the needs of the poor, succoring them by our alms, and practicing privations so that we may afford them help. We ought, fifth and lastly, to have compassion for the trials of the afflicted, and console them by kind and gentle words, weeping with those who weep, and finding our greatest enjoyment in being able to raise up the sorrowful soul of a brother and to shed a little balm upon his grief. Let us examine whether our compassion extends to these five objects without neglecting any one of them. *Resolutions and spiritual nosegay as above.*

SUMMARY OF TOMORROW'S MEDITATION

We will meditate tomorrow upon the spirit of religion, of humility, and of mortification which ought to be associated with the action of taking our repasts. We will then make the resolution: First, to repeat, with exactitude and piously, the prayers to be said before and after our meals; Second, to partake of all our repasts in a spirit of religion, humility, and mortification. Our spiritual nosegay shall be the words of the Apostle: "Whether you eat or drink, or whatsoever else you do, do all to the glory of God." (1 Cor. 10:31)

MEDITATION FOR THE MORNING

Let us adore Our Lord Jesus Christ taking His repasts during His mortal life. He submitted Himself to eat and to drink like the rest of mankind; but in what a holy manner He did it! How He raised the meanness of the action by the beautiful virtues which He practiced in regard to it! It was the daily object of the veneration of the Blessed Virgin and of St. Joseph; let us admire it with them, and let us render our homage to our adorable Savior taking His repasts in so holy a manner.

FIRST POINT

✝ *The Spirit of Religion which ought to be Associated with our Repasts*

This spirit consists in taking our repasts: first, with a perfect purity of intention, with the sole aim of pleasing God, who wills that we should sustain our bodies in order that we may fulfill the duties of our position; second, with a heart full of love and of gratitude towards the God who gives us our food, who bestows it upon us by the hand of His servants, and treats us better than numerous others who have a table that is inferior to ours, or who are sometimes in need of even what is necessary; third, in a spirit of sacrifice, looking upon the table as an altar on which we ought to offer to God two victims; that is to say, our appetite and the food we take. Is it in these dispositions we take our repasts?

SECOND POINT

✝ *The Spirit of Humility in which we ought to Take our Repasts*

One of the greatest humiliations of mankind here below is the being obliged to eat. He who is called to sit down in heaven at the table of a God, to feed there upon truth and charity to be inebriated with celestial graces, has to abase himself here below to an entirely animal action which is common to him with the beast. He who feeds at the altar on the bread of angels, and even on God Himself, eats and assimilates the flesh of animals. Is it not a strange humiliation? If we consider it only in the natural order, is it not humiliating that man, a being so great, the king of creation, should have to imitate an animal, which browses and ruminates, and, like it, collect together in his body gross food which becomes corrupt and, as it were, a poisonous dung hill? And how humiliating it is for him to take pleasure in this ignominy, and to turn it into an enjoyment; to abuse it, and not to keep himself to what is indispensable; to employ, lastly, in so low an action time which might be so much better employed in many great and noble things for the glory of God, for the good of his neighbor, for the perfecting of his intelligence and of his heart! How much more humiliating still it is for him to be reduced to acknowledge that he is unworthy of this nourishment, base as it is, since, after having sinned, he became unworthy to live, consequently unworthy to taste any food? He receives it from God only by way of a favor, and in addition he is obliged to gain it by work. (2 Thess. 3:10) It was this which made St. Vincent de Paul exclaim: "Miserable man that I am, I have not earned the bread I eat." Do we bring to our repasts this spirit of humility?

THIRD POINT

✝ *The Spirit of Mortification in which we ought to Take our Repasts*

First; this spirit consists in not caring about food and a good table. The saints took their food with sighs, often even steeping their bread in their tears, and only with regret lending themselves to the action of eating, as being a torment and a danger (St. Bernard), because, they said, it was eating which introduced sin into the world; it weakens the spirit, it strengthens the flesh, it engenders the most terrible temptations. Very different from the base souls which attach importance to the quality of their food, they are contented with what is ordinary, without wishing for what is more refined and better prepared, never choosing what is best and leaving the worst to others. If the food is to their taste, they partake of it without any sensual complaisance, blessing God, who feeds them better than they deserve, retrenching something from what is more to their liking, sometimes even taking pleasure in rendering their food insipid and unpleasant to the taste. If the food is not what suits them, they take it nevertheless without complaint, blessing God, who gives them an opportunity of exercising mortification. Second; the spirit of mortification does not limit itself to the interdiction of all refinement in regard to the quality of the food; it also interdicts voracity, which seizes upon what is set before us, the in decent greediness which, dominated by the in temperance of the flesh and the impetuosity of its desires, never thinks that it has eaten enough, and sometimes goes to such excesses that it is not possible afterwards to apply the soul to prayer, to the affairs or other duties of our state. The Christian who has a true spirit of mortification does not listen to the intemperance which the flesh suggests to him; he eats only what is necessary, never satiates his appetite, and eats with the moderation and modesty which characterize a servant of God (St. Bas. Reg.). Have we not many reproaches to address to ourselves on this head? *Resolutions and spiritual nosegay as above.*

Ninth Tuesday after Pentecost

SUMMARY OF TOMORROW'S MEDITATION

We will meditate tomorrow: first, upon the faults to be avoided in conversations; second, upon the virtues to be practiced in them. We will then make the resolution: first, to be on our guard against these faults and to sanctify our conversations by means of the opposite virtues; second, often to remember during our conversations that God is beside us; that He is listening to our words and will make us give an account of them. Our spiritual nosegay shall be the words of the apostle Peter: "Be you in all manner of conversation holy." (1 Pet. 1:15)

MEDITATION FOR THE MORNING

Let us adore Our Lord Jesus Christ conversing in the world, and doing men the favor to hold intercourse with them. (Baruch 3:38) Oh, how holy were His conversations, how far removed were they from all the miserable features which are so often to be met with in ours! (Wis. 8:16) Let us contemplate and bless this adorable pattern.

FIRST POINT

✝ *Faults to be Avoided in Conversation*

The first fault of conversation is dissipation or want of reflection, which is the cause, first, that we lose considerable time in useless speeches; second, that the soul, being subjected to no restraint, becomes unskillful in prayer, meditation, and serious matters (Ecclus. 21:29); third, that we abandon ourselves to immoderate gaiety, to jesting and frivolous talk, to words characterized by scurrility, which are quite unworthy of issuing from the mouth of a Christian, to obstinate and regrettable disputes, to clamor, and vivacious speeches, which are imprudent and to be regretted. "The lips of the unwise" the Holy Scripture says, "will be telling foolish things; but the words of the wise shall be weighed in a balance" (Ibid. 28); do not expect from a man quick to speak either words of wisdom or amendment of life (Prov. 29:20); fourth, we render ourselves disagreeable to our neighbor by always endeavoring to speak, interrupting others, and talking without caring to listen, which is the sign of a fool. (Ecclus. 10:14) The second fault in conversation is the spirit of criticism. We fall upon the absent, we mock at the defects of others, we find something to speak against in every one, above all in those whom we dislike; calumnies, falsehood, deceit, season all that we say, foment divisions, and weaken charity. We exaggerate defects and we diminish virtues, sometimes from vanity, sometimes from wanting to make ourselves esteemed, sometimes from vengeance, anger, and contempt, lowering as much as possible the merit of those whose life, being better regulated than ours, is a reproach to us, and turning into ridicule the good actions of virtuous souls, their maxims and practices of piety. The third fault is anti-Christian discourse, in which we extol the enjoyments of life; we boast of the happiness of those who enrich themselves, who procure for themselves pleasures, and attain to honors and glory; we pity poverty, which the gospel beatifies; we envy riches, which the gospel curses; we make a profession of not suffering humiliation and contradiction, to ministering to our own comforts, of liking to be at our ease, of satisfying our tastes; and the mouth speaking out of the abundance of the heart, we make of the pleasures of the table, of the delights and enjoyments of the world, the ordinary subject of our conversation. Now what can be more anti-Christian, or more opposed to the gospel, than such language as this? Is it not, as it were, an apostasy? Let us here examine ourselves, and see whether our conversations are not often tainted by some of the faults which we have been pointing out.

SECOND POINT

✝ *Virtues to be Practiced in Conversation*

First, charity ought to preside over it; (James 3:1-3) a gentle charity, characterized by a serene expression of face, an affable manner, kind and cordial words; an indulgent charity, which takes in good part and interprets in a favorable manner all that is said; which excuses others, even at its own expense, in so far as prudence permits; which never shows any annoyance at wants of good breeding, rudeness, or infirmities of our neighbor; which accepts with meekness advice, reprimands, mortifications, whatever they may be; an attentive charity, which watches over its words and manners, that it say nothing or do nothing which can give displeasure, but, on the contrary, say and do everything that is amiable in so far as conscience allows; lastly, a communicative charity, which testifies affection for others, joyfully renders them good offices, and interests itself in all that concerns them. Second, humility ought to be associated with charity, the humility through which we look upon ourselves as unworthy to converse with men, after having deserved to converse only with demons, and which, consequently, treats every one with consideration and respect; (Rom. 12:10) listens to others without permitting itself to interrupt them, feels no annoyance at being itself interrupted or not listened to with attention; willingly defers to their opinion in so far as conscience authorizes them to do so, avoids speaking of itself or of what may attract praise and esteem. Third, zeal for good ought to sanctify conversation, by consoling our neighbor in his trials, encouraging him in his annoyances, strengthening him in his weaknesses, raising him up when he is cast down, giving him good advice with discretion, leading him to God and to virtue. (1 Pet. 1:15; Philipp. 1:27) *Resolutions and spiritual nosegay as above.*

Ninth Wednesday after Pentecost

SUMMARY OF TOMORROW'S MEDITATION

e will meditate tomorrow: first, upon the manner in which we ought to conduct ourselves towards the different classes of people with whom we have to converse; second, on what ought to be the most ordinary subject of our conversation. We will then make the resolution: first, to delight to converse with the poor, the simple, and the humble, to console them by good words, rather than with the great, to whom we can be but very rarely of any use; second, always to mingle with our conversation something edifying or useful, and to avoid everything that virtue disavows. Our spiritual nosegay shall be the words of the Holy Ghost: "A man wise in words shall make himself beloved." (Ecclus. 20:13)

MEDITATION FOR THE MORNING

Let us adore Our Lord in His conversation. He converses by preference with the poor, the little, and the simple, and above all with those recommended to Him by His Father (John 17:24), and He holds with them pious conversations calculated to lead them to God; it is thus that He teaches us to converse in a manner worthy of the gospel (Philipp. 1:27). Let us thank Him for the beautiful example which He gives us.

FIRST POINT

✝ *How we ought to Conduct ourselves toward the Different Classes of Persons with whom we have to Converse*

First, whoever may be the persons with whom we have to converse, religion prescribes that we shall always be kind, amiable, and obliging; (Ecclus. 6:5) to treat everyone according to his deserts, his dignity, his character, behaving towards some in a serious manner and in a gayer manner towards others; (Coloss. 4:6) always to avoid affectation in our deportment, pride and austerity, contradiction and dissimulation, so that no one should have to complain of us and that everyone should be edified.(1 Tim. 4:12) Second, if they are persons whom we dislike, we must conceal our repugnance beneath a gracious exterior, and not allow any feeling of annoyance or of austerity to show itself. If, on the contrary, they are persons who are pleasing to us, we must be on our guard against being too free and too frivolous, say nothing which is not according to propriety, and mistrust sensible attachments and too great friendships, which captivate the heart and preoccupy it. We must be friendly towards all, familiar with hardly anyone; and this observation, which is always true, is above all true in regard to persons of different sex. Third, if they are inferiors, poor, simple, or ignorant, charity forbids us to avoid them or to repel them, to grieve them by a proud and disdainful manner, to be melancholy in their presence, and to make use of a pretext for sending them away. It commands us, on the contrary, to welcome them joyfully, to place ourselves within their reach, to speak to them kindly, and to act in such a manner that they shall leave us in a contented frame of mind. Fourth, if they are great personages, humility forbids us to seek their society and to endeavor to insinuate ourselves into their good graces; to use flattery towards them, and to show complaisance, and to utter applauses in regard to what they do or say which conscience reproves. We must, says St. Francis de Sales, treat them as we do fire, and not go too near them; when we are obliged to do so, we must observe the perfect modesty which indicates that we respect them, and a frank liberty which proves that we love them. Fifth, if they are fervent souls, whose conversation tends towards God and virtue, we must seek them out and take pleasure in their society; but if they are persons who are tepid or devoid of religion, it is well to try and gain them over by amenity of language and of manners; and if we do not succeed, and on the contrary, we see that their society is hurtful to us, we must avoid them. Are these the rules which we have followed?

SECOND POINT

✝ *What ought to be the most Ordinary Subject of our Conversations*

Our conversations ought to be first of all edifying; the heart of the wise inspires his lips, says the Holy Ghost.(Prov. 16:23) That is to say, that as the mouth, speaking out of the abundance of the heart, speaks willingly of what it loves, a Christian ought to mingle from time to time in his conversation a few words which are edifying and which have respect to God, salvation, eternity, religion, the Church, the saints, and the imitation of these holy examples. He would not be a Christian who only took pleasure in talk about worldly, vain, and futile things. When our conversations are wanting in this characteristic of edification, they must at least be marked by utility, for it is not worthy of a reasonable man to speak only of trifles and puerilities, about things happening in the town or in the house hold, a thousand things without utility and without an object. Lastly, when our conversations are neither edifying nor useful, they must at least be irreproachable, that is to say, that if sometimes we may have nothing in view but an innocent recreation, we must at least take care that there shall be nothing in what we say that would be disavowed by virtue; that the love of truth shall put aside all deceit in our language, all those falsehoods so familiar to self-love in order to hide a truth which humiliates, to make ourselves esteemed for more than we are worth; to raise ourselves above others, or to lower others beneath ourselves; the love of our neighbor must banish all backbiting or criticism, all raillery in regard to the present or the absent; all tales calculated to sow discord, all the jealousies which cannot bear to hear others praised without trying to lower them; lastly, humility must not be able to find a single word inspired by self-love or vanity to reprehend, meekness must not be wounded by any altercation or dispute, nor the Christian spirit by any worldly maxim contrary to the gospel. Do our conversations bear this character? *Resolutions and spiritual nosegay as above.*

SUMMARY OF TOMORROW'S MEDITATION

e will meditate tomorrow upon the visits which we make in the world, and we will study three principal dangers attending upon them: first, the intentions in regard to them are seldom Christian; second, sins are frequent; third, we are exposed through their means entirely to lose the Christian spirit. We will then form the resolution: first, to make no visits except those which propriety renders necessary; to abridge them as much as possible, and to place our happiness in family life; second, to be on our guard in these in dispensable visits against the dangers to which we are exposed in frequenting the world. Our spiritual nosegay shall be the words of an ancient philosopher: "Every time that I mingled with men, I returned less a man." (Seneca).

MEDITATION FOR THE MORNING

Let us adore Jesus Christ in the visits which He made during His life. He made very few, and He made them in a very holy manner, that He might merit for us the grace of sanctifying ours and of avoiding the dangers to be met with in them. What advantage for us to find in the actions of a God a pattern for our actions and also a grace to enable us to perform them aright! May our hearts be poured forth in praise and thanks at the feet of our divine Savior.

FIRST POINT

✝ *The Intentions of Visits are Rarely Christian*

A Christian intention is that which proposes to itself, as the end of its action, the glory and the good pleasure of God. Now let us question the facts: is it not true that our visits have for the most part an entirely different intention? We make them from purely human and natural views; sometimes that we may amuse ourselves and find in them an agreeable pastime, to keep up intercourse with the world, to satisfy our curiosity, to hear news; sometimes to have it said of us that we are amiable and that our society is agreeable; to make our talents shine, to acquire a reputation or to preserve that which we have already attained, to gain friends who may be of service to us, and obtain positions for us and make our fortunes; sometimes even to maintain dangerous friendships or to satisfy one or other of our passions. Do we not often infuse into our visits intentions like these, which render them culpable or dangerous, or at any rate make us lose time which might be employed for our salvation?

SECOND POINT

✝ *Sins are Frequent in Visits*

First, we often sin therein by words; sometimes they consist in calumnies, or turning into ridicule the defects of our neighbor, a species of gossip in which we pass the whole of society in review, and in which we destroy the reputation of every one; sometimes they are made up of worldly speeches, words in which there is too much license, uttered under the pretext of amusement and of recreation. At other times there is intemperance of language or an interruption of others who are speaking, or there is a morose taciturnity which is disagreeable to others, or a pretentious self-love which endeavors to attract esteem, which pronounces, in regard to everyone and everything, sentences from which there is no appeal, and which will not permit contradiction. It is herein that we realize the words of the Holy Ghost: "In the multitude of words there shall not want sin." (Prov. 10:19) Second, in visiting, we often sin by our actions; we permit ourselves to indulge in too great freedom of manners; we are too jovial and too familiar, especially towards persons of the opposite sex; we permit ourselves, and that is still more serious, a mode of dress and dances which are wanting in modesty, games and amusements in which the spirit of Christian reserve is not observed as it ought to be. Third, we often sin therein by omissions not putting a stop, when we might do so, to all that is said in contravention of the law of charity, modesty, or any other virtue; not taking sufficient care to prevent what may give pain to others; not endeavoring to render our visits pleasant to all, in such a manner that everyone feels the happier and the better for them. Have we not sinned during our visits in one or other of these ways?

THIRD POINT

✝ *We Expose Ourselves in our Visits Entirely to Lose a Christian Spirit*

Visits, says Peter of Blois, make the world revive in even the souls of those in which it was dead (Ep. 8); and, several centuries before his time, a pagan philosopher had said: "Every time that I mingled with men, I returned less a man." (Seneca). How much more reason have we to say, I returned less a Christian! It is because, in fact, it is very rare to frequent the world without running great risk. We lose our time, we imbibe a taste for idleness, a dislike for work and a serious life, for things appertaining to religion and to our salvation; we become imbued with a spirit of effeminacy and relaxation, with all kinds of dissipations and futilities, the love of the world and f amusement; we listen to words and we see things calculated to seduce the heart; we contract dangerous intimacies; we seek to please, above all, persons of the opposite sex, and we too often meet with occasions of sin. And, to add to our misfortunes, the more visits we make, the more we desire to make; they become, as it were, a necessity of life; we multiply and we prolong them, most frequently to the injury of the duties of our position. Is not this our history? *Resolutions and spiritual nosegay as above.*

Ninth Friday after Pentecost

SUMMARY OF TOMORROW'S MEDITATION

e will continue to meditate upon visits, and we will study the rules to be observed before, during, and after our visits. We will then make the resolution: first, to make all our visits in a Christian spirit, with the object of pleasing God, and for God; second, in making them, to watch over our words and our actions, so that we may banish from them anything that may breathe the spirit of the world. We will retain as our spiritual nosegay the words in which Our Savior tells us the object of His visit to this world: "I am come that they may have life, and may have it more abundantly." (John 10:10)

MEDITATION FOR THE MORNING

Let us adore Our Lord in the different visits He made to men; He visited them all in general, through descending from heaven upon earth by the Incarnation; (Luke 1:78) He visited them in particular during His life, as when He visited Zacharias (Luke 19:5); He visits them every day in general and in particular in the Sacrament of the Altar. (Ps. 8:5) Let us love and bless our divine Savior for the great goodness He shows us by this behavior.

FIRST POINT
✝ *Rules to be Observed before our Visits*

We must first of all examine, in the presence of God, whether it is permissible, proper, and useful to make the visit, or whether it is not a dislike to solitude, the love of the world, frivolity, a spirit of dissipation and of curiosity which leads us to make it, rather than a solid reason of duty and propriety. The visit being decided upon after this examination, we must settle the intentions in which it is to be made. These ought to be the same intentions which Jesus Christ would have had if He had been in our place. If those whom we visit are afflicted persons, we must propose to ourselves to honor the suffering Savior in His members, and to imitate Him carrying consolation to all who were in sorrow, for example to Mary and Martha after the death of Lazarus, to the apostles and St. Mary Magdalene after His resurrection. If they are poor persons, we must propose to honor in them Jesus Christ, who was poor, and to treat them with kindness, love, and respect, as being the best friends of the Savior, who embraced their position and chose them to be the foundation of His Church and the apostles of the universe. If they are sinners who have wandered away from God, we must propose to withdraw them from so unhappy a state, and to recall them to a better life, with all the tenderness which a perfect charity inspires. Lastly, whoever they may be whom we visit, we must propose to induce them to esteem Christian truths, a love of the maxims of the gospel, the practice of solid virtues, by frankly condemning the spirit and the maxims of the world, by laboring with zeal to strengthen and perfect in their souls the reign of Jesus Christ, according to the example of the Blessed Virgin, who visited her cousin Elizabeth for the sole purpose of making all who were in her house know and love God. The means for having grace to do all these things in a holy manner is, before we go out, earnestly to ask God for it.(St. Jerome, Ep. 22) Are we faithful to this practice?

SECOND POINT
✝ *Rules to be Observed During our Visits*
Having been received by those whom we are visiting, we ought, first, to salute their angel guardian as being the principal host of the house where we are making a visit; to remember that we are going to converse in his presence, and that we must not allow a word to escape us which would be unworthy of so illustrious an auditor. It would be better still to recall to mind that the Three Persons of the Blessed Trinity are present at our conversation, that they listen to and register all our words in order to ask an account of them at the last day. We ought, second, to pay great attention to our words and our behavior, so that everything in us may not only be irreproachable, but calculated to lead hearts to God, to make them love religion and practice virtue. We ought, third, to terminate our visit as soon as charity and propriety admit, that we may avoid the loss of time. Have we followed these rules?

THIRD POINT
✝ *Rules to be Observed after our Visits*
Having returned home we ought, first, to resume our exercises and occupations with the same zeal as though we had not quitted them, and return to our rule of life with the same exactitude. We ought, second, to purify our interior from all we have heard which has a tendency to disturb the spirit of

piety and of recollection, not lose our time in going over in our memory and representing to our imagination all we have seen or heard, but shut ourselves up in our interior with God, and with perfect freedom of spirit employ ourselves solely with what ought to occupy us. *Resolutions and spiritual nosegay as above.*

Ninth Saturday after Pentecost

SUMMARY OF TOMORROW'S MEDITATION

e will meditate tomorrow upon the last action of the day, which is that of betaking ourselves to rest, and we shall consider: first, the exterior manner of performing this action; second, the interior dispositions with which it must be undertaken. We will then make the resolution: first, to betake ourselves to our repose in a holy manner, by thinking of death, of which sleep is the image, and by means of this thought detaching ourselves from everything which is not God; second, to go to sleep as though in the arms of Jesus Christ, uniting our sleep to His sleep. Our spiritual nosegay shall be the words of the Psalmist: "In peace in the selfsame I will sleep and I will rest." (Ps. 4:9)

MEDITATION FOR THE MORNING

Let us adore Our Lord Jesus Christ lying down as we do, taking rest like us, sleeping like us. "I have slept and have taken My rest," He says by His prophet. (Ps. 3:6) Let us admire and thank our divine Savior, who willed, God though He be, to submit to sleep in order to sanctify it in His person and to merit for us the grace of sanctifying it in ours. (St. Gregory Nazianzen, Oral. 31)

FIRST POINT

✝ *The Exterior Manner of Performing Holily the Action of Betaking Ourselves to Rest*

First, it is a dictate of wisdom that we should take our rest at the hour laid down in our rule, without anticipating it through idleness, effeminacy, or too great a love of rest, as well as without retarding it under the pretext that we neither desire nor are in need of sleep, and that we want to pray, or to read, or to do something else. Second, modesty requires that we should undress our selves decently; that we should lie down in the same manner, remembering that we are in the presence of God and of our guardian angel. Third, religion demands on its side that we should never lie down without having first offered our evening prayer and made our examination of conscience, followed by an act of contrition; that we should take holy water and sprinkle it over our bed to keep away the devil during the night; that, having laid ourselves down, our last action should be the sign of the cross; our last words, Jesus, Mary, Joseph; and that we should then abandon ourselves into the arms of Jesus, that we may sleep upon His bosom and take in Him our repose (Ps. 4:9). Have we observed these rules?

SECOND POINT

✝ *The Interior Dispositions for Performing Holily the Action of Taking our Repose*

First, when undressing, we must have a lively desire to despoil ourselves of ourselves and of all our attachments (Coloss. 3:9), despising ourselves as sinners unworthy to have any clothing after having lost that of innocence. Second, on lying down we must: first, honor Our Lord, who performed the same action, and render homage to the mystery of His death and of His sepulchre; second, we must look upon our bed as our sepulchre, our sheets as our shroud, and upon sleep as the image of death, and be inspired, in consequence, with the sentiments we should desire to have at our last sigh; to accept death with the state of decay which will follow upon it; and we should desire that the world should separate itself from us as we separate ourselves from a corpse, and forget us even as the dead are forgotten. Third, having laid ourselves down, we must offer our repose to God in honor of the repose of Jesus Christ whilst He was on earth, and still more in honor of the eternal repose which the heavenly Father takes in Himself, in His Son, in the Most Blessed Virgin, and in all the saints; then we must enter into the abandonment which Our Lord made of His soul to His Father, and say, when going to sleep, what He said when He was dying: "Father, into Thy hands I commend My spirit" (Luke 23:46), after which we must endeavor to go to sleep with some good thought in our hearts, so that we may also have good thoughts when we awake and that even our sleep may be a prayer in the presence of God (St. Jerome, Ep. 22). Are we faithful to these practices? *Resolutions and spiritual nosegay as above.*

Tenth Sunday after Pentecost

THE GOSPEL ACCORDING TO ST. LUKE, 18:9-14

"At that time, Jesus spoke this parable to some who trusted in themselves as just and despised others: Two men went up into the temple to pray; the one a Pharisee, and the other a publican. The Pharisee standing, prayed thus with himself: O God, I give Thee thanks that I am not as the rest of men, extortioners, unjust, adulterers, as also is this publican. I fast twice in the week; I give tithes of all that I possess. And the publican, standing afar off, would not so much as lift up his eyes towards heaven, but struck his breast, saying: O God, be merciful to me a sinner. I say to you, this man went down to his house justified rather than the other: because every one that exalteth himself shall be humbled and he that humbleth himself shall be exalted."

SUMMARY OF TOMORROW'S MEDITATION

fter having gone through all the actions which belong to a Christian life, we will meditate henceforth upon the virtues which constitute this life. We will begin with humility, of which the gospel of the day makes so magnificent an eulogium, and which may be called the first of the virtues, because it is the foundation of them all. We shall see in our meditation: first, what must be understood by humility; second, how reasonable, thus understood, is humility. We will then make the resolution: first, to make humility our virtue of predilection and to ask it earnestly of God; second, not to allow a single day to pass without performing some interior or exterior act of humility. Our spiritual nosegay shall be the words of the Holy Ghost: "Humble thyself in all things and thou shalt find grace before God." (Ecclus. 3:10)

MEDITATION FOR THE MORNING

Let us adore the Son of God descending from heaven to earth to teach us humility by means of His heavenly doctrine, and still more by His example, since the whole of His life, from Bethlehem to Calvary, was nothing but a continual lesson of humility. Let us confess that as His eternal majesty was continually humiliated, it would be intolerable behavior on our part to be puffed up with pride and vanity. Let us render all our homage to this humbled God.

FIRST POINT

✝ *What we must Understand by Humility*

Humility consists in despising ourselves, because we see that we are supremely contemptible, and to feel it to be only right that others should despise us, because it is right that what is contemptible should be despised. It does not consist, therefore, either in humble words which are contrary to our thoughts, or in a modest exterior hiding a soul which esteems itself and endeavors to obtain the esteem of others. Humility is the frankness of an upright soul which desires only that which it knows to be true, which wills and loves what is true, even when what is true humiliates and confounds it. It says to itself: I have nothing in myself which belongs to me; my mind, God has made it and can withdraw it from me at any moment; a slight derangement of the brain is sufficient to make the greatest intellect lose all its genius, and the wisest all his knowledge, and even his reason. I have no virtue in myself; if there be any in me, it is the doing of grace, and the slightest temptation can overthrow it. Even my body does not belong to me; God has made it such as it is, He has lent it to me, and the slightest accident can change its form or its beauty. To this nothingness of the whole of my being I have added sin, which has rendered me worthy of the eternal contempt of the whole of hell. And as the sum-total of all my miseries, I am incapable of all good, even of one single thought or word, which might be of use for my salvation; capable of all kinds of evil, since there is not, says St. Augustine, any sin committed by a man of which another man would not be capable if the grace of God did not hold him back. Now in such conditions as these I can neither esteem myself nor desire to be esteemed, without being guilty of injustice and falsehood; I ought to despise myself, to love contempt, obscurity, and humiliation, through love of truth, which cries to me from out of the bottom of my conscience that such is the portion of nothingness and of sin. I ought, consequently, to put away from me all thoughts imbued with pride, self-love, ambition, pretension, and susceptibility. I ought to be content to be nothing, and to be looked upon as nothing. Is it thus that I have hitherto understood humility?

SECOND POINT

✝ *Humility Rightly Understood is Eminently Reasonable*

For what is more reasonable than to keep to what is true? And is there not disloyalty in lying to ourselves, in not allowing ourselves to be looked upon as what we are, because it is displeasing to us, as if it could be changed on account of our not confessing it? God, the Author of all good, has sown the good grain in the field of our soul; we, who alone are authors of all that is evil, have sown in it tares; is it seemly for us to glorify ourselves and say: This harvest is my work? What more reasonable, also, when we know the root of an evil, than to tear out the root? Now, the bad passions which are in us pride, ambition, vanity, the love of riches, and other attachments which make us commit so many sins, which render us so unhappy because of the deceptions they inflict upon us, have all of them the common root, which is self-esteem together with the desire to be esteemed; and this root humility destroys. Lastly, what more reasonable than to lean upon an immovable pillar, rather than upon a reed which bends? Now, this is what the humble man does. Being aware of his weakness, he does not lean upon himself, and he does not expose himself to temptation; he counts only upon God, who has promised him His help, and he confides in Him alone, becoming thereby strong with the strength of God Himself, so that he is able to say with the Apostle: "I can do all things in Him who strengthened me." (Philipp. 4:13) "When I am weak, then am I powerful." (2 Cor. 12:10) The proud man dare not undertake anything; and, if he undertake it, he is troubled and annoyed in executing it; the least difficulty discourages him: his self-love fears humiliation and failure. The humble man, on the contrary, after having taken counsel of prudence, goes forward with his eyes fixed upon God, in whom he places all his confidence (Ps. 17:30). He goes forward leaning on the pillar, which is God, not upon the reed of human misery, and is thereby capable of great things. Let us ask of God this treasure of humility, which is the foundation of wisdom, reason, and good sense. *Resolutions and spiritual nosegay as above.*

Tenth Monday after Pentecost

SUMMARY OF TOMORROW'S MEDITATION

e will thoroughly examine, during the whole of this week's meditations, into the truth which we were only able to touch lightly upon this morning: namely, that humility is eminently reasonable; and we shall meditate tomorrow upon a first proof of it, which is that we are nothing, and we will consider, in a second point, the sweetness and consolation which a faithful soul feels in this truth. We will then make the resolution: first, often to recall to ourselves our origin, which is nothingness, so that we may combat the imaginations with which our pride entertains us; second, no longer to deceive the world by endeavoring to appear something, and desiring that others should think of us, esteem and praise us. Our spiritual nosegay shall be the words of the pious Alvarez: "O nothingness! O nothingness! How thou dost displease God when thou dost inflate thy self! O nothingness! What is there in common between thee and praise?"

MEDITATION FOR THE MORNING

Let us adore Our Lord declaring that, notwithstanding His divine perfections, He was, as man, nothing (Ps. 38:6); calling Himself often Son of man that is to say, Son of nothingness. Consequently, during the whole of His life He treats Himself as man, who is nothing. In the bottom of His soul,

He continually makes to God, His Father, the confession that He is nothing, and is content that God should be all. Let us admire these dispositions of His heart, and let us rejoice at the honor He thereby renders to the supreme majesty of God.

FIRST POINT

✝ *Of Ourselves we are Nothing*

All our being is from God. We are only His stewards and administrators; He alone is the proprietor. What were we in the eternity which preceded our birth? We were less than a worm of the earth, less, than an atom in the air: we were nothing. Even now we should be nothing if God, through His wholly gratuitous goodness, had not chosen us from amongst millions of possible beings, without any merit on our part had not drawn us out of the abyss of nothingness. At this very moment we should fall into our first state if God were to withdraw His powerful hand, which holds us suspended, as it were, above the abyss. Oh, what nothingness are we then! "All that is good in me, O my God, all that is good in me, is a present of Thy mercy," says St. Augustine (Ps. 58). How unsuitable is it, then, for a man to esteem himself to be something, no matter how small, and to take pleasure in what he is! It is a falsehood, since it is the truth that of ourselves we are nothing; it is a sacrilegious larceny, because it is appropriating to ourselves that which belongs essentially to God; it is the greatest pride, since it is the raising ourselves presumptuously above what we are. God has said: I alone am Being; I contain in Myself all Being, and I possess it in fullness. (Ex. 3:14) If God is what is, every creature is necessarily that which is not. Yes, my God, "all nations are before Thee as if they had no being at all." (Is. 40:17) With still greater reason I, who am so small a thing in the midst of all the nations, am nothing in Thy sight; and Thy apostle had good reason to say: "If any man think himself to be something, whereas he is nothing, he deceiveth himself." (Gal. 6:3) Let us remain for a time in a state of abasement at the feet of Our Lord to receive the impression of those words, I am nothing; to make it penetrate into the centre of our nothingness, and to affirm ourselves in the deep feeling that we are nothing.

SECOND POINT

✝ *The Sweetness and Consolation which the Feeling of its Nothingness Infuses into the Faithful Soul*

There is in this a truth which the world does not suspect, and which it is even incapable of understanding, but the soul which loves God delights to annihilate itself in His presence; first, because it knows that to make itself little in the sight of God is the means for being loved; that to empty ourselves of self is the means for being filled with God (St. Augustine); and that if God sees nothing in us but what comes from Him, He will love all that there is in us, consequently He will love us; second, because the recognition of our nothingness is the glorification of God. "My daughter," Jesus once said to one of His faithful servants, "I am He who is, and thou art she who is not." Sweet words for a soul that loves! If it would be something, it would renounce it, in order that God alone might be all in all, (1 Cor. 15:23) and to be able to say to Him with a delicious feeling, "Thou art alone, O my God, and outside Thee is nothing." (Job 14:4) It is an ineffable consolation for it to look at itself in the midst of the nothingness in which God has placed it, without in this state to be able to have any other support or any other hope than the omnipotence and entirely merciful goodness of its amiable Father. O God! O my all! The more I feel I am nothing, the more I feel Thou art all, and this thought is my happiness. *Resolutions and spiritual nosegay as above.*

TENTH TUESDAY AFTER PENTECOST

SUMMARY OF TOMORROW'S MEDITATION

e will meditate tomorrow upon a second reason for keeping ourselves humble, which is that we have nothing; that is to say: first, that we have nothing good in us at which we can glorify ourselves; second, the good which is foreign to us is lent to us, to serve for the glory of God and not for ours. After these reflections, we will make the resolution: first, to make an exact division between what belongs to God in us and what belongs to ourselves; there will then remain nothing but what is evil as our portion, consequently, what humiliates us; second, when it seems to us that others esteem us or that we are tempted to take pleasure in ourselves, immediately to make the right division between what is God's and what belongs to us. "Take what is thine and go thy way." (Matt. 20:14) These words shall serve as our spiritual nosegay.

MEDITATION FOR THE MORNING

Let us adore Jesus Christ possessing in Himself all the treasures of grace, all the riches of the wisdom and of the knowledge of God; and in the midst of all these riches confessing Himself, in the presence of His Father, to be poor and needy (Lam. 3:1; Ps. 39:18), because He would not consider as His own any of the gifts of God. His doctrine is not His own, His words do not belong to Him. (John 7:16; 14:28) Oh, what a beautiful example He sets before us, teaching us thereby not to be vain because of anything that is in us, and to look upon ourselves always as having nothing in respect to which we can glorify ourselves. Let us thank our divine Master for so useful a lesson, and beg of Him to establish His spirit of annihilation firmly in our hearts.

FIRST POINT

✝ *We have not in us Anything Good in Respect to which we can Glorify Ourselves*

In point of fact, nothingness, which is our nature, excludes all possession; nothingness is the greatest of "all kinds of poverty, the lowest of all kinds of miseries. If in this state we were sufficiently devoid of sense to glorify ourselves for anything, we should fall beneath the double anathema pronounced by God against the poor proud man and of Jesus Christ against the man in the Apocalypse who believed himself to be rich when he was in the greatest poverty. It is very true that in order that we should appear in this world in the rank of creatures, God created for us a body and a soul, and all that we have, not excepting a single hair; but in creating these things He did not intend thereby to abdicate His property in them. All in the order of nature and of grace belongs to Him, and is His. He has only lent it to us, with the charge to turn it to profit, and at the judgment day to render to Him an exact account of it. Now, things being thus, is it not an extravagance on our part to glorify ourselves for what we have? "What hast thou that thou hast not received?" the Apostle asks, "and if hast received, why dost thou glory as if thou hadst not received it?" (1 Cor. 4:7) It is only a fool who wills to be admired because of his dress which has only been lent to him, which everyone knows does not belong to him, and of which he will be deprived at the moment when he least expects it.

SECOND POINT

✝ *The Good which is in us has been Lent us only to Serve for the Glory of God, and not in any Way for our own*

God declares to us that glory belongs to Him alone; it is His exclusive property, and He will not give it up to others. (Is. 48:2) To make use of His good things for the glorification of the creature, is to act in a manner entirely contrary to His designs. It is to abuse His gifts and turn them against Himself. It is behaving with the greatest insolence to employ His gifts in stealing away His glory from Him. Let us think deeply on this kind of outrage which we commit against God every time that we make use of His gifts for our own glory by esteeming ourselves or endeavoring to obtain the esteem of creatures. Let us beg of Him today and every day of our life to give us the grace never to esteem ourselves because of anything there is in us, and never to seek anything except the greater glory of God. *Resolutions and spiritual nosegay as above.*

Tenth Wednesday after Pentecost

SUMMARY OF TOMORROW'S MEDITATION

e will meditate tomorrow upon a third reason for being very humble, which is that we can do nothing; that is to say: first, that we can do nothing of ourselves; second, that even with the ordinary help of God, we are still weakness itself. We will thence derive the resolution: first, to mistrust ourselves and to put away from us occasions of sin; second, to confide in God and not allow ourselves to be discouraged by our weaknesses. Our spiritual nosegay shall be the words of the Apostle: "When I am weak then am I powerful." (2 Cor. 12:10) "I can do all in Him who strengthened me." (Philipp. 4:13)

MEDITATION FOR THE MORNING

Let us adore Jesus Christ, the only one in this world who is powerful, (Jud. 11:6) annihilating His power so entirely that in the days of His infancy He shows Himself to us under the semblance of the most complete powerlessness; that in a more advanced age he affirms that He can do nothing of Himself; (John 5:30) and that, after His death, He remains in the Sacrament of the Eucharist in a state in which, judging from appearances, He can neither see nor hear, neither speak nor move, that He may teach us to honor God by the humble confession of our powerlessness when He does not give us His aid. Let us thank Him for this lesson which He gives us, and let us render to Him our accustomed homage.

FIRST POINT

✝ *We can do Nothing of Ourselves*

It is Jesus Christ Himself who affirms it: "Without Me you can do nothing." (John 15:5) It is reason itself which tells us so, since of ourselves we are nothing, and can do nothing. We are so miserable that, if God did not sustain us, did not move us, did not concur with us, and did not make Himself at every moment the principle of our action, our powerlessness would be as complete as that of a corpse; (Rom. 11:36) without Him we cannot perform the least action, (Is. 26:12) nor say the shortest word,(1 Cor. 12:3) nor have the least thought, (2 Cor. 3:5) nor conceive the slightest inclination, the least desire which is of any worth in regard to heaven,(Philipp. 2:13) nor make the very least movement. (Acts 17:28) We cannot even attribute to ourselves cooperation with grace, because this cooperation is of itself a grace, nor have the knowledge of the truth that we can do nothing, because this knowledge is one of the greatest graces which God can bestow upon us. Lastly, we are so incapable of all good that it was necessary God should buy for us, at the price of His blood, even the least thought of doing good, even the smallest value of the least prayer, even the least movement of the heart which has salvation for its object. Now, at the sight of such total powerlessness, what ought we to do, if not on the one side to pray and humble ourselves like the poor man who asks for an alms, and, on the other side, thank, bless, and admire God for the continual assistance which we receive from His goodness? Do we do both the one and the other?

SECOND POINT

✝ *Even with the Ordinary Succor Given us by God, we are still Weakness Itself*

Is it not true that, despite of the graces which we receive from God, we often fall, and our life is full of deplorable weaknesses? We are like the paralytic, who cannot move except by means of a helping hand; and, again, even when this hand presents itself, we often will not allow ourselves to be led by it. The smallest temptations are too much for the strength which God offers to us; (Osee 7:9) an imagination, a thought, a bad example, a word of criticism makes us fall; the feeblest passion drags us along with it; the slightest difficulty arrests us. O God, how weak we are We can, by means of prayer, obtain a more powerful grace which would enable us to obtain the victory over our weaknesses; But alas! It is one of our greatest miseries that we pray so little and pray so ill! What must we do then, except be ashamed, in the presence of God, at the sight of our powerlessness, mistrust ourselves, believe ourselves to be incapable of all good through our own strength, capable of all evil if grace did not stop us; watch over our senses, our mind, and our heart, fly from occasions, and then confide in God, who alone is our strength; expect everything from Him, nothing but from Him, and beg Him with our whole soul to have pity on our misery. Let others count upon human means, "but we will call upon the name of the Lord our God." (Ps. 19:8) *Resolutions and spiritual nosegay as above.*

TENTH THURSDAY AFTER PENTECOST

SUMMARY OF TOMORROW'S MEDITATION

e will meditate tomorrow upon the fourth reason for being very humble, which is that we are worth nothing, and that: first, because we are made up of nothing but miseries and subjects for humiliation; second, because what remains in us beyond these miseries is worth nothing. We will then make the resolution: first, to reject from the very first moment all idea of esteeming ourselves because of the graces God bestows upon us; second, to feel that when but little esteem is shown us it is because there is reason in it, and when we are praised a mistake has been made. Our spiritual nosegay shall be the words of the subject of our meditation: "We are worth nothing."

MEDITATION FOR THE MORNING

Let us adore Jesus Christ not being able to endure that it should be said of Him that He is good. (Mark 10:18) All that is in Him, down to the slightest thought, the least action, is of infinite value, and yet He wills to be treated throughout His whole life as though He were worth nothing. He wills to be despised in His words, in His works, in all that He is, as though it were all worth nothing. He wills to suffer the blackest calumnies, the most unworthy treatment, both in His mortal and His Eucharistic life. Let us adore, admire, thank, and imitate Him.

FIRST POINT

✝ *We are Made up of Nothing but Miseries and Subjects of Humiliation*

What is there, in fact, in us which is worth anything, or because of which we can esteem and glorify ourselves? Is it our body? God took it, as regards its beginning, out of the earth. In respect to its actual existence, it is a vessel of uncleanliness, a sink of corruption, hidden beneath a more or less agreeable coat of varnish. As to its future destiny, it will be the food of worms, a mass of decomposition, which men will hasten to bury beneath the ground, that they may not be poisoned by it. Is it our intellectual faculties in which we can glory? Alas! As regards our understanding, how limited it is, what darkness and obscurity there is in it; in our judgments, what temerity and precipitation, what errors and uncertainties; in our imagination, what extravagances, what ridiculous and absurd images; in our knowledge, what defects and ignorance!

The more we know, the more clearly we see that we know nothing; and the knowledge of the philosopher who is sufficiently instructed to be able to measure the field of science, reveals to him his profound ignorance with respect to a thousand more objects than there are stars in the heavens or grains of dust on the earth. Is it the qualities of our heart respecting which we may glorify ourselves? Alas! All the vices exist there as seeds, and there is not a single vice committed by a man of which another man would not be capable if God did not hold him back. All the passions have their root therein; it is like an infected pit, whence exhale a thousand malignant vapors of vanity and pride, of sensuality and impurity, of impatience and a disordered will, of the love of pleasure and of riches. Is it our good actions and our virtues of which we have a high opinion? Alas! Where is the good work in which something evil is not mingled sometimes self-love and vain complaisance, sometimes negligence and tepidity? Is there in us a single virtue such as that possessed by the saints? Have we their humility, their mortification? And what is our whole life except inconstancy in our resolutions, weakness in our temptations, indiscretion in our words, susceptibility in our self-love, distractions and coldness in our prayers? Is it, lastly, the graces which we have received of which we may be vain? But it is that, on the contrary, which ought to put me most to shame. So many graces ought to have made of me a great saint, and I am still miserable and a sinner, still as imperfect, as negligent, as tepid as ever in the service of God. Lord, the abyss of my miseries cries out towards Thee, the depth of my nothingness raises its hands towards Thy mercy. (Hab. 3:10)

SECOND POINT

✝ All which Remains in us, beyond our Miseries, is also Worth Nothing

Everything is worth only according to what it is, and according to what it has or what it can do. Now, it is a truth which has been made clear by our preceding meditations, that we are nothing, that we have nothing, that we can do nothing; therefore we are worth nothing. Moreover, on account of the way in which we have abused our being and the gifts of God, we have deserved to be deprived of all being and to return to nothingness. We have become like the salt which, having lost its savor, is fit only to be thrown into the dirt, and to be trodden down under the feet of the contempt of men. Let us be ashamed, then, that, being worth nothing, we have nevertheless esteemed ourselves so greatly; let us ask God to pardon us for the past, and beg of Him grace to be content, for the future, that we should be despised and looked upon as worth nothing. *Resolutions and spiritual nosegay as above.*

SUMMARY OF TOMORROW'S MEDITATION

 e will meditate tomorrow upon a fifth reason for being very humble, which is that we are sinners: first, we have sinned; second, we are capable of sinning again. We will thence deduce the resolution: first, to elevate ourselves, by means of these considerations, to praise, admire, and love the goodness of God, who is willing to love such miserable creatures as we are: second, to confound ourselves and be humiliated by every temptation to pride which may present itself to us, because it ill becomes so miserable a being to have any esteem for itself. Our spiritual nosegay shall be the words of the holy King David: "My sin is always before me." (Ps. 1:5)

MEDITATION FOR THE MORNING

Let us adore Jesus Christ on the cross teaching us by all His ignominies and all His sufferings how constantly humble he ought to be who has had the unhappiness of sinning one single time. Our divine Savior bore only the shadow and appearance of sin, for which He made Himself security and the victim; it is enough to cover Him with confusion, (Ps. 68:8) and to make Him in His own sight as it were an object of anathema and of malediction. (Gal. 3:13) O heavenly Father, what then ought we to think of ourselves? If nothing more than the appearance only of sin rendered Thine own Son infamous and abominable in His own eyes, what ought we to feel, who in reality have sinned, have sinned so often, and are capable of sinning again?

FIRST POINT

✝ *We ought to be very Humble because we have Sinned*

If we had only committed one single sin during the whole of our life, it would be enough to keep us forever in the lowest degree of humiliation. It would be better never to have been created than to make use of our creation in order to offend God. By sinning we abase ourselves beneath everything which is most miserable, even below the clay of the earth, which is superior to us in that it has the honor of never having offended God. What is a man who has committed but one single venial sin? He is a being who has a bad heart, who has offended his benefactor and his father, who has wounded Him sometimes by actions, sometimes by words. Is there not matter herein to make us ashamed and humiliated? But above all, what is a man who has committed a mortal sin? He is an exile from heaven, a creature condemned to eternal punishment, a rebel against his God, a traitor who has been faithless to his oaths, a deicide who has crucified Jesus Christ in his heart and trodden underfoot the blood of the Testament. O opprobrium! O ignominy! And what is it then if he has committed this great offence many times, if he has multiplied it like the hairs of his head? No, we shall never be able to conceive the contempt which such a man as this deserves. Do not let it be said that all this has been pardoned. First, no one can be sure that it has been. (Eccles.9:21) We know quite well that we have deserved hell; we do not know, we shall never know in this life, whether we do not still deserve it. What matter for humiliation! But even if we had had the revelation of our pardon made to us, we should even then be only as a creature who has escaped hell, like a brand torn from the burning, a criminal released from perpetual servitude, who had deserved to be always trodden under foot by demons, to be the object of their insults and of their deadliest contempt. Now when we have deserved to be thus treated, is it reasonable to be proud and haughty, not to be able to bear a slight humiliation? Ought we not, on the contrary, to keep ourselves always in a state of the most profound humility and to be covered with confusion?

SECOND POINT

✝ *We ought to be very Humble because we are still Capable of Sinning*

We are so wicked that we might say to God every morning like St. Philip Neri, and with far greater reason than he: "Lord, do not trust to me; for if Thou dost not take care, I shall betray Thee." O profound wretchedness! we cannot answer for ourselves for one single moment. (1 Cor. 10:12) There is not a moment in our life in which we might not commit a mortal sin, and not a mortal sin after which we might not die and be punished everlastingly. For that nothing more is needed than a proud thought, as is shown in the case of the rebel angels; a word of calumny, an impurity, according to St. Paul, a desire, a look, according to what Jesus Christ says; and who is there who has not cause to fear certain delicate occasions, certain unhappy moments, in which the heart is so weak and so forsaken that it hardly recognizes itself? Who has not cause to fear that pride is only made captive and not annihilated, that sensuality only slumbers and is not really extinguished? Alas! So many others have fallen who were worth more than we. And what is there that could reassure us? Is it a certain kind of good that we have done? But even if, like the apostles, we had left all to follow Christ, if like them we had evangelized nations, and worked miracles, we have only to look into hell and we shall see that Judas did all that. Might it be graces received?

But the angels received more than we have; they were free from all kinds of passion and they did not persevere. Might it be a life exempt from great faults? But in order to be damned it is not necessary to have committed great sins, it is enough not to have done the good we ought to have done, to have been a faithless servant, not to have put our talents to account. After that, who could have any pride, who would not despise himself down to the very lowest degree? *Resolutions and spiritual nosegay as above.*

Tenth Saturday after Pentecost

SUMMARY OF TOMORROW'S MEDITATION

e will meditate tomorrow upon a sixth reason for being very humble, which is nothing more than our own pride, and we shall see what a subject of humiliation it is for us: first, to esteem ourselves so highly; second, to desire to be highly esteemed when we really merit nothing but an entirely contrary opinion. We will then make the resolution: first, often to address to God this aspiration: "Lord, have pity on me, for I am a proud man;" second, never to say or do anything from a motive of self-love. Our spiritual nose gay shall be the words of the Psalmist: "It is good for me that Thou hast humbled me." (Ps. 118:71)

MEDITATION FOR THE MORNING

Let us adore Jesus Christ so deeply hidden in the Sacrament of the Altar in order to teach us to despise ourselves and not to wish to make a parade of ourselves; let us say to Him with Isaias: "Verily, Thou art a hidden God." (Is. 45:15) Let us admire Him in this state, and ask of Him a share in the grace of His hidden life.

FIRST POINT

✝ *We ought to be very Humble at our having so High an Opinion of Ourselves*

What a state of confusion we are in when we lie so boldly to our conscience, when the least want of vigilance, of combats, and of prayers puts us constantly in the wrong! We do not know ourselves, and like him who fancies himself to be rich because he neglects looking into the embarrassed condition of his affairs, and imagines himself to be safe because he shuts his eyes to the danger, in health because he is not conscious of his malady, we fancy ourselves to be perfect because we do not perceive our defects. Everyone knows our weak point; we alone are not aware of it, whether it is that, seeing it too near at hand, the eye confounds itself with the object, or whether, looking far beyond ourselves, we escape from our own ken; whether it is, lastly, the excessive love we bear ourselves which prevents us from seeing ourselves such as we are. Even when, knowing ourselves better, we allow that what is good in us comes from God, we nevertheless enjoy it and we contemplate ourselves in our own merit, like a vain woman looking at herself in her mirror; we are pleased that we rather than another should be the person on whom heavenly gifts flow down; and without saying so to ourselves we appropriate to ourselves the most beautiful of these gifts. We recount to ourselves our acts of humility, of patience, of disinterestedness; we make use of them as of so many aids for enabling us to con fide in ourselves and for rendering us a good testimony of our own righteousness. Lastly, we have a high opinion of ourselves because of our imagining that we have conquered self-esteem. After having raised ourselves above vulgar sentiments, we fall back upon ourselves, and we take pleasure in receiving from our own hands the incense we refuse from the hand of another, and to feed within ourselves upon a certain hidden and interior vainglory, which is all the more exquisite in that, putting everyone else under ourselves, we suffice for ourselves and have no need of any extraneous aid. What a heap of misery! What a subject for confusion! Here indeed is the poor proud man, whom the Lord detests. (Ecclus. 25:3,4)

SECOND POINT

✝ *We ought to be very Humble at Wishing to be so Highly Esteemed, when we Deserve it so Little*

Although our conscience tells us that we do not deserve esteem and praise, we desire to be esteemed and praised, and we seek to be in every kind of way. In our conversations we wish to be praised and approved, to say something which will make others esteem us; the least eulogium, the least mark of esteem goes to our heart and awakes in it a secret complaisance; whilst, on the other hand, nothing more than the mere semblance of contempt, and the slightest want of consideration, is sufficient to overwhelm and irritate us. We are so tenacious of praise, that there is no man, however obscure he may be, whose praise is not agreeable to us and which does not excite in our heart a vain complaisance. We wish to be preferred to others, and we are averse to their superiority to such a degree that we can hardly bear to hear any one praised without attempting to depreciate the praise by criticism of one kind or another. How calculated to put us to shame are such dispositions existing in a soul so miserable as ours! What! To be obliged to confess to our conscience that we deserve nothing but contempt, and yet to wish, at no matter what price, to be honored, praised, and esteemed! Is it not an unworthy pretension, shameful and very capable of covering us with confusion? *Resolutions and spiritual nosegay as above.*

ELEVENTH SUNDAY AFTER PENTECOST

THE GOSPEL ACCORDING TO ST. MARK, 5:31-37.

"At that time, Jesus going out of the coasts of Tyre, came by Sidon to the sea of Galilee, through the midst of the coasts of Decapolis. And they bring to Him one deaf and dumb, and they besought Him that He would lay His hand upon him. And taking him from the multitude apart, He put His fingers into his ears, and spitting, He touched his tongue, and looking up to heaven He groaned, and said to him: Ephpheta, which is: Be thou opened. And immediately his ears were opened, and the string of his tongue was loosed and he spoke right. And He charged them that they should tell no man, but the more He charged them, so much the more a great deal did they publish it; and so much the more did they wonder, saying: He hath done all things well; He hath made both the deaf to hear and the dumb to speak."

SUMMARY OF TOMORROW'S MEDITATION

We will tomorrow interrupt our meditations upon humility that we may meditate upon the gospel of the day. This gospel presents to us two remarkable facts: first, a miraculous cure worked by Jesus Christ; second, a beautiful eulogium on the Savior pronounced by the witnesses of the miracle. From the meditation on these two facts we will deduce the resolution: first, every day to lend a docile ear to grace, and to watch over our tongue carefully that we may not sin in our words; second, to apply ourselves to performing our ordinary actions in a perfect manner. Our spiritual nosegay shall be the words which the people, according to what is told us in the gospel, said: "He hath done all things well." (Mark 7:37)

MEDITATION FOR THE MORNING

Let us adore Jesus Christ making the journey from the confines of Tyre to Sidon, and from Sidon to the lake of Galilee. Oh, how holy was this journey!

The good pleasure of His Father was the principle of it; (John 8:29) charity was its motive: He was going to cure a deaf-mute; and a divine modesty was its rule. O God, grant me grace to make all my journeys in this manner, and to be edified by everything which takes place in Thine.

FIRST POINT

✝ *The Miraculous Cure Operated by Jesus Christ*

Hardly had Jesus Christ reached the end of His journey, before a deaf-mute was brought before Him and He was entreated to heal him. O charity of the Savior! He cures him immediately by touching his tongue and his ears, whilst at the same time uttering a deep sigh and looking up towards heaven. (Mark 7:34) How much more worthy of our sighs and tears are the spiritual deaf-mutes with which the earth is covered; the deaf who keep the ears of their heart closed to the inspirations of grace, to the remorse of the conscience, to the word of God, to holy books, to good examples; the mutes who do not pray or who pray ill, who are silent in society when the glory of God requires that they should speak, at times to impose silence upon the blaspheming tongue which attacks religion, wounds charity, outrages modesty, at times to mix some words tending to edification in wholly worldly conversation. Alas! am I not of the number of these deaf-mutes? O Jesus, say to my ears in my meditations, in my readings, or when I listen to Thy holy word, Ephpheta, that is to say, Be opened, and then, speak Lord, Thy servant will listen. (1 Kings 3:9) Open the ears of my heart, as Thou didst open those of the woman of Philippi, who was evangelized by St. Paul. (Acts 16:4) Unloose my tongue, as Thou didst unloose the tongue of the mute in our gospel, that it may speak of Thy glory, that it may exalt and bless Thee, that it may expose to Thee my miseries, and call down upon me Thy mercies; that it may speak to my neighbor of all that may edify him and lead him to Thee. But above all, Lord, govern my tongue, the origin of the greater portion of my faults, that it may abstain from all sharp words, from all calumny and vanity, from all that is calculated to give pain to others, to wound modesty or religion, to scandalize or to tend to evil, and that it may serve, on the contrary, to edify others, to exhort them to all that is good, to console the afflicted. (1 Cor. 4:3)

SECOND POINT

✝ *The Beautiful Eulogium Pronounced on Jesus by the Witnesses of the Miracle*

"He hath done all things well." (Mark 7:37) exclaimed the witnesses of the cure on which we have been meditating. Admirable words, and the most beautiful eulogium which can be made upon Jesus Christ; it is an eulogium on God Himself and His adorable Providence. We ought to respect these words in the midst of the revolutions of this world and the events which we cannot understand. We are troubled and scandalized at seeing empires which crumble, families which perish, the crime and impiety which everywhere prevail, religion and right which are oppressed. At such a spectacle we ought to say: Providence presides over all; it has its hidden designs, we do not understand; but without understanding them, we ought to respect them, to love them, to bless them, to proclaim that they are the doing of infinite wisdom, power, and holiness; all that God does is well, we ought always to repeat to ourselves. We ought to apply these words to ourselves, not in the sense that we do all things well like God, but in order to recall to ourselves in each one of our acts that the whole of our holiness consists in doing all things well; that the perfection of our ordinary actions is what God demands of us, and that to seek virtue elsewhere would be a deplorable illusion. *Resolutions and spiritual nosegay as above.*

Eleventh Monday after Pentecost

SUMMARY OF TOMORROW'S MEDITATION

 e will meditate tomorrow upon a seventh reason for being humble, which is often to ask ourselves, What am I in comparison with the saints? And in order to understand this reason we will consider: first, that to appreciate ourselves at our real value we must take, as points of comparison, the virtues of the saints; second, that this comparison is deeply humiliating for us. We will then make the resolution: First, often to ask ourselves, How would a saint perform this prayer, his action; how would he employ this present day? Second, to humble ourselves every day, saying, Oh, how far am I from being what the saints were! Our spiritual nosegay shall be the words of David: "I will make myself meaner than I have done, and I will be little in my own eyes." (2 Kings 6:22)

MEDITATION FOR THE MORNING

Let us adore and bless God, the Father of Our Lord Jesus Christ, who from all eternity has chosen us and called us to be saints. (Eph. 1:3,4) Let us thank Him for so beautiful and glorious a vocation, and let us ask of Him grace to fulfill it rightly.

FIRST POINT

✝ *In Order to Appreciate Ourselves at our Real Value, we must Take for Points of Comparison the Virtues of the Saints*

Baseness inspires us sometimes to make perfidious comparisons. It leads us to compare our life with the life of great sinners or of worldly persons who are only half Christians, and it tempts us to say, "I am not like this person or that; my life is not in the least degree scandalous; there are no great immoralities or notable disorders in it which are worthy of reproof." At other times, by means of a still more dangerous piece of deceit, it makes us compare ourselves with certain pious and devout souls in which a malignant spirit finds some defects of character to be reprehended, certain susceptibilities springing from self-love or other imperfections from which we flatter ourselves that we are exempt. In consequence we imagine ourselves to be better than these pious souls, and we take pleasure in ourselves. What deplorable reasoning! What matters to us, who desire to save ourselves, the conduct of those who do not care about compromising or risking their salvation? If we are free from the defects which characterize certain pious persons, have we the virtues which compensate them? Do we think that we shall be justified when we appear before the tribunal of the sovereign Judge, because we shall be able to say to Him: I do not commit the faults of such a one; I have not the defects of such or such a person? If we aspire after paradise, we ought to know that paradise is reserved for the saints, only for the saints; and that whoever is not holy will not be able to enter therein. If, then, we desire to be saved, let us compare ourselves with the saints, and correct, in accordance with these beautiful examples of holiness, the too high opinion we entertain of ourselves. Is this what we do?

SECOND POINT

✝ *The Comparison between our Life and that of the Saints Is deeply Humiliating for us*

Where indeed are to be found in us the virtues and the sentiments of the saints? Where is the humility of a St. Dominic, who delighted in contempt as being the most delicious thing in the world; who, when he was about to enter the gates of a town, fell on his knees, and with tears in his eyes besought Heaven not to make thunder and lightning fall upon the walls which were about to receive so great a sinner? Where is the lively faith of a St. Gregory, which transported mountains? Where is the spirit of prayer of a St. Antony, who, finding the long nights of winter too short, complained that the sun by its light distracted him in his holy intercourse with God? Where is the spirit of mortification of a St. Catherine of Siena, who wept over the necessity of granting some small solace to her body? Where is the passion of St. Teresa for the cross, that saint who could not bear to live without suffering? Where is the love of St. Vincent Ferrer for Jesus crucified, the love which made him melt into tears on hearing three sentences read of the Passion? If such are the virtues of the saints, where are ours? Let us make the comparison before God, who will judge us. St. Antony, after conversing one day with St. Paul the hermit, came back with his eyes cast on the ground, sobs in his heart, and confusion on his face, proclaiming that he did not deserve to be called a religious, and that he must change his life. What ought we then to do after contemplating so many saints so extraordinarily raised by grace and so deeply abased by humility? Let the sight at any rate make us recognize our poverty, humble and confound us, and make us begin a better life (Prayers of the Offertory). *Resolutions and spiritual nosegay as above.*

ELEVENTH TUESDAY AFTER PENTECOST

SUMMARY OF TOMORROW'S MEDITATION

 e will meditate tomorrow upon an eighth reason for being humble; it is that self-esteem and the passionate desire to be esteemed, two vices which are precisely the opposite of humility, are supremely odious to God. After these two considerations we will make the resolution: first, often to humble ourselves before God on account of this depth of misery which exists in us; second, never to say things tending to make us esteemed, or to utter what is to our disadvantage in order to make others imagine that at any rate we are very humble. Our spiritual nosegay shall be the words of St. Paul: "No flesh should glory in His Sight." (1 Cor. 1:29)

MEDITATION FOR THE MORNING

Let us adore Our Lord Jesus Christ abasing Himself in the presence of God His Father to the level of the lowest amongst men, (Is. 53:3) even to the level of a worm of the earth. (Ps. 21:7) It is thus that He teaches us not to esteem ourselves, and not to desire the esteem of others.

FIRST POINT

✝ *How Odious a Thing is Self-esteem in the Sight of God*

God hates self-esteem to such a degree that, seeing in His temple the publican laden with iniquities, but who is covered with confusion and humbles himself, and the Pharisee, who is an exact observer of the law, but who indulges in self-esteem and takes pleasure in his righteousness, He pardons the first and condemns the second. It is to tell us that the self-righteous is farther from the kingdom of heaven than the sinner who humbles himself. Elsewhere He pronounces an anathema on the man who delights in his own wisdom; (Is. 5:21) He curses him who confides in man, (Jer. 17: 5) that is to say, in himself, because he himself is only a man; and He declares by His saints that whoever is displeased with himself is pleasing to God, and that whoever is pleased with himself is displeasing to God. (St. Bernard) This truth shines forth throughout the whole of the Scriptures. The king of Assyria held himself in high esteem because he had been the instrument of divine justice against Jerusalem. Thou dost take pride in thyself, said the Lord to him by His prophet. My hand shall crush thee and thy great army, that all ages may learn that I hate the ax which glorifies itself at the expense of him who hews with it, and the rod which raises itself against him who carries it. (Is. 10:15) And it is remarkable that God has such a hatred of self-esteem as to have chosen for the performance of the greatest of His works the most incapable of men, so that human pride might never be able to attribute to itself the glory of them. (1 Cor. 1:29) In order to convey His people out of Egypt, He made choice of Moses, who, during forty years, had known nothing beyond the desert and his flock; in order to overthrow the innumerable army of Madian, He made use of only three hundred men; to throw Goliath to the ground, He chose only a shepherd and his sling; to deliver Bethulia, besieged by one hundred and forty thousand men, He made use of one simple woman; to convert the pagan world, He took twelve fishermen, who were unlearned, cowardly, and timid. O Lord, who, after having contemplated such examples, would dare to open his heart to self-esteem?

SECOND POINT

✝ *How Odious to God is the Passionate Desire to be Esteemed*

Esteem and glory are things which belong exclusively to God, (1 Tim. 1:17) and the poor and miserable creature who dares to pretend to them incurs His hatred, like the thief who attempts to steal the property of another. God created all things for His glory. (Deut 26:19) He created man's intelligence that it might praise Him, the heart of man that it might love Him, the world to proclaim His providence, the skies to declare His glory. To wish, then, to attract to ourselves esteem and praise is to profane vessels destined to contain nothing but the glory of God; it is to pervert the order and the plan of His providence; it is to frustrate the end which He proposed to Himself in giving a being to intelligent creatures. This is why God resolved to abase every thing which exalts itself;(Baruch 5:7) and this is why Jesus Christ said: "Woe to you when men shall bless you", if you take pleasure in what they say, and "blessed shall you be when men shall hate you." (Luke 6:26,22) "Take heed," He continues, "that you do not your justice before men, to be seen by them." (Matt. 6:1) When you give alms, try to ignore it yourself, and let God alone know it. When you fast or perform good works, take care that men do not perceive it, even if you were obliged a strange precaution, the singularity of which shows us how much we ought to fear the esteem of men even should it be necessary, in order to hide the thing from them, to "anoint your head and wash your face". (Matt. 6:17) Could God tell us more plainly how He reproves those who prefer human glory to the glory of God? (1 John 12:43) *Resolutions and spiritual nosegay as above.*

ᴇʟᴇᴠᴇɴᴛʜ ᴡᴇᴅɴᴇꜱᴅᴀʏ ᴀꜰᴛᴇʀ ᴘᴇɴᴛᴇᴄᴏꜱᴛ

SUMMARY OF TOMORROW'S MEDITATION

e will meditate tomorrow on a ninth reason for being humble; it is the love which God has for humble souls. First, we will establish the fact of this love. Second, we will study the marvelous effects of it. We will then make the resolution: First, not to make excuses when we are reproved and when nothing obliges us to justify ourselves. Second, willingly to consent to be thought an awkward person, having no intelligence, or judgment, or memory. Our spiritual nosegay shall be the words of the Psalmist: God looks down complaisantly upon the humble. (Ps. 112:5,6)

MEDITATION FOR THE MORNING

Let us adore the complaisance which the Holy Trinity takes in the humiliations of the Incarnate Word. His Divine Son humbles Himself in the crib, and God shows how pleasing this humiliation is to Him by sending His angels to announce His birth to the shepherds, and by the heavenly star which led the kings to adore Him. He humbles Himself on the borders of the Jordan by receiving baptism from John, confounded with sinners; and the adorable Trinity declares from the height of heaven that it finds in Him its complaisance. He humbles Himself upon the cross, and it reveals His greatness by the sun which is darkened, the earth which trembles, the rocks which are rent, the dead who rise. Let us thank God for the great lessons enclosed in these prodigies.

FIRST POINT

✝ *The Love of God for Humble Souls*

"To whom shall I have respect," says the Lord in Isaias, " but to him that is poor and little, and of a contrite spirit, and that trembles at My words?" (Is. 66:2) Who is he that glorifies Thee, and consequently pleases Thee, O Lord, says Baruch, if it be not he who humbles himself for the evil he has done, and blushes for it, and dare not even raise his head or his eyes? (Bar. 2:18) God always looks with complaisance upon the humble heart: "A contrite and humble heart, O God, Thou wilt not despise!" (Ps. 1:19) "In a contrite heart and humble spirit, O Lord" says Daniel, "let us be accepted." (Dan. 3:39) My kingdom, says Jesus Christ, is for those who are humble like little children: "Amen I say to you, unless you become as little children, you shall not enter the kingdom of heaven." (Matt, 18:3) And St. Peter teaches us that God gives to the humble His grace and His love; (1 Pet. 5:5) St. Paul assures us that He draws near to them and consoles them, (2 Cor. 7:6) that His predilection is for souls which are nothing in their own eyes, and that it is those whom He chooses for His great works. (1 Cor. 1:27,28) The reason of this great love of God for the humble is that He loves the truth, (Ps. 1:8) and that the humble soul has the true feeling of what it really is, of its poverty and its misery; whilst the soul which is under the empire of self-love has a false idea of its own merit; it exists in an atmosphere of false hood, esteeming itself and desiring to be esteemed. The soul which loves truth even when it humbles it is so pleasing to God that He places in it all His delights; He pours forth His whole heart and all His love into it. Who then would not desire to be very humble, since it is a means for gaining the heart of God and for being loved by Him?

SECOND POINT

✝ *The Marvelous Effects of the Love of God for Humble Souls*

The author of the Imitation thus recounts the tenderness of the divine love for the humble soul. When God, he says, sees it in trouble He consoles it; (2 Imit. 2:2) when He finds it sunk in the feeling of its own nothingness He draws near to it (Ibid.) and gives it a great abundance of graces (Ibid.); and in proportion as it humbles itself He raises it to glory (Ibid.); He reveals to it His secrets, and draws it sweetly to Himself (Ibid.). The lower it descends into the abyss of its miseries, the more God raises it in grace here below and in glory in heaven. (Luke 1:52) When it has something to ask of Him, its prayer is always well received. (Ecclus. 35:21) Even when it does not know how to speak to God and feels itself incapable of praying, humility supplies all that is wanting and stands in place of it. God beholds it and sees that it is filled with low and humble sentiments in presence of His greatness and His infinite holiness; He sees that it is ashamed and confounded at its own coldness and its insensibilities, its distractions, and its aridities, and He is content; He looks upon its prayer as being perfect. (Jud. 9:1) The publican cannot say anything else save the humble words: "God, be merciful to me, a sinner," (Luke 18:13) and these words are worth everything to him: they are worth his justification. If the humble soul be assailed by a thousand temptations, and afflicted by falls, and if, instead of giving way to being vexed by self-love, it humbles itself peacefully and asks forgiveness like the publican, it issues victoriously from its temptations and corrects itself of its backslidings. Lastly, the humble soul is an elect deposit of grace and predilection, because in its fidelity it leaves to God all the glory and attributes none of it to itself. Mary was chosen from among all other creatures to be the mother of God only because she was the most humble (Luke 1:48), and St. Teresa was elevated to such lofty contemplations only on account of her humility. "When I was," she says, "confounded in the presence of God to such an extent as to present myself at the foot of His throne like a little worm crawling in the dust, it was then that He seized me and united me to Himself." What a lesson for us! What an encouragement to be very humble in the presence of God! *Resolutions and spiritual nosegay as above.*

ELEVENTH THURSDAY AFTER PENTECOST

SUMMARY OF TOMORROW'S MEDITATION

e will meditate tomorrow upon a tenth reason for being very humble; it is the special affection which the saints have had for humility. We will make this clear in the first point, and we shall see in the second point how we ought to endeavor to render ourselves like to the saints. We will then make the resolution: first, to recall to ourselves in temptations to self-love how humble the saints were, and to be ashamed and confounded by the comparison; second, often to ask of God grace to imitate the saints in their generous contempt for all vanity and for all self-love. Our spiritual nosegay shall be the words of St. Augustine: "Why canst thou not do what these have done."

MEDITATION FOR THE MORNING

Let us adore Our Lord Jesus Christ laboring from the first moment of His incarnation down to His latest sigh to teach us humility by His example, and continuing after His death to teach it to us by the great examples set up by

His saints, whom He rendered participators in His life of humility upon earth before rendering them participators of His glory in heaven. Let us thank Him for the care He takes to instruct us and for the desire He has to make us very humble.

FIRST POINT

✝ *On the Special Affection which the Saints had for Humility*

Even before Jesus Christ came David had said: I have chosen contempt for my portion (Ps. 83:2; 2 Kings 6:22). St. John Baptist had said: Every day I desire to become less in the opinion of men, that the Messias may be more honored. I desire to efface myself that He may appear (John 3:30). It is He who is the master; as for me I am but as a sound which is lost in the air, and of which nothing remains a moment after (John 1:23). I am not worthy to untie the strings of His sandals (Luke 3:16). Mary places herself in the lowest rank of creatures. She calls herself a poor servant (Luke 1: 38), and far from attributing to herself the honor of her divine maternity, she says that the great things which had been done in her were entirely the act of the divine mercy (Luke 1:54), and on that account she devoted herself with all the more love to the obscurity of a poor dwelling. Jesus Christ appears, and passes through life in humiliation; and His apostles, filled with His spirit, esteem it a great cause of joy to have be deemed worthy of humiliation. (Acts 5:41) St. Paul finds his happiness in opprobrium (2 Cor. 12:10; Gal. 1:10), and calls himself the chief of sinners (1 Tim. 1:15). After the apostles come twelve millions of martyrs, who joyfully lose their reputation upon earth, believing that they are only beginning to be disciples of Jesus Christ from the moment in which they begin to be humiliated (St. Ignatius, Martyr). To the martyrs succeed the hermits, who go and hide from the eyes of men their merits and their virtues. Then come the saints of all conditions and of both sexes, who strive to do good in secret, blush to be surprised in a good work, are afraid of esteem as they would be of a dangerous rock, of praise as though it were a scourge, are calm in the midst of calumny and contempt, and esteem themselves to be worthy only of confusion. St. Ignatius looked upon himself as an ulcer, whence infected matter was forever flowing; St. Vincent Ferrer as a hideous corpse, horrible to the sight, unsupportable to all who approach it. St. Francis Xavier is in his own eyes nothing but an abominable sinner, who stands in the greatest need of being recommended to God, because of the infinite multitude of his sins; St. Francis Regis considers himself worthy to be trod under foot by everyone; and when perverse men strike and outrage him, he exclaims that they are doing him a great favor, and that he deserves to be treated in a much worse manner.

And who has not heard St. Vincent de Paul utter from the bottom of his heart that touching prayer: "O God! I am not a man, but a poor worm crawling over the earth, not knowing whether it is going and only trying to hide itself in Thee, O Jesus, who art all my desire. I am a poor blind man, who cannot advance a single step in virtue unless Thou boldest out the hand of Thy mercy to lead me." O humility of the saints, how you confound my self-love and my vanity!

SECOND POINT

✝ *How we ought to Endeavor to Resemble the Saints in the Practice of Humility*

If the saints, so eminent as they are in merit and in virtue, reached heaven only by humiliating themselves and wishing to be humiliated, what likelihood is there that I shall arrive there by an entirely opposite road? Jesus Christ has placed in the firmament of His Church these admirable examples of humility that we may see how the soul is saved. When the saints, who had so many merits, nevertheless despised themselves so greatly, and made of contempt their delight, how inexcusable are we, with so many defects as we have, to esteem ourselves and to desire to be esteemed I The saints, considering all the graces which they had received, all that these graces, put largely to profit, had produced in them of what was most perfect in holiness, said in the bottom of their hearts: "If such or such a sinner had received as many graces as I have done, I believe that he would have better profited by them; whilst I, if I had been in his place, with passions as violent as his, in an atmosphere as dangerous, and an ignorance as great, I believe that I should have behaved worse than he has done. "Whence they came to the deeply felt conclusion: "I am therefore the greatest of sinners, I deserve nothing but contempt and confusion." (St. Peter Damian) Why should not I myself come to the same conclusion? Is it reasonable of me to esteem myself and to desire to be esteemed? Oh, how humble I ought to be! *Resolutions and spiritual nosegay as above.*

Eleventh Friday after Pentecost

SUMMARY OF TOMORROW'S MEDITATION

e will meditate tomorrow upon an eleventh reason for being very humble; it is that humility is the foundation and the guardian of all virtue. We will thence deduce the resolution: first, to watch over ourselves carefully in order to shut the door of our heart to all kinds of self-love, and constantly to maintain an attitude of humility; second, to oppose to the temptations of self-love these acts of humility, or others similar to them: My God, take pity on me, for I am proud; To Thee be glory, to me shame and confusion. Our spiritual nosegay shall be the words of St. Bernard, which will also be the subject of our meditation: "Humility is the foundation and guardian of the virtues."

MEDITATION FOR THE MORNING

Let us adore Our Lord, who, beholding the great love which His Father entertained for humility, came and humbled Himself in this lower world, making Himself therein a man like us, hiding His divine nature, veiling all His perfections, and subjecting Himself to all our infirmities. Let us offer our homage to Our Savior thus humiliated in order to give glory to God, and to us an example of which our pride was sorely in need.

FIRST POINT

✝ *Humility is the Foundation of all Virtue*

If you asked me, says St. Augustine, What is the most fundamental thing in religion? I should answer: It is humility. What is the second? What is the third? I should still reply: It is humility. Humility is the first condition for doing all things well for praying, for communicating, for having intercourse with our neighbor, for conquering temptations, for triumphing over our passions. Self-love can produce nothing but sin, or the false virtues, void of all merit, of the pagan philosophers, because it is only a miserable egotism which acts for itself alone, and which God cannot consequently recompense; it is a vicious inclination, which makes us live and act without having faith or grace, and solely from natural motives. Humility, on the contrary, the true seat of grace, the seed of glory, the characteristic of the elect, makes us live a supernatural life, and all the virtues repose upon it, as upon their foundation, First. Faith. The humble soul easily believes, because it mistrusts its own intelligence, because it finds its happiness, on the one hand, in abasing the presumption of its thoughts before the infinite knowledge of God; and on the other side, in enlarging its short-sightedness by everything that the divine light wills to reveal to it. Second. Hope. The soul which is devoid of humility counts upon itself and never thinks of confiding in God. The humble soul, on the contrary, is happy to hope, because, not confiding in itself, it is glad to be able to throw itself upon God, who never forsakes those who trust in Him. Third. Charity. The humble soul loves God with all its heart, because the more miserable it sees itself to be, the more rejoiced it is to behold that the divine mercy is greater still than all its miseries; the smaller it sees itself to be, the more inclined it is to love the eternal greatness which abased itself to such profound littleness; the more unworthy it feels itself to be loved by so holy a God, the more it loves Him and attaches itself to Him. The humble soul is not less disposed to be charitable towards its neighbor to the extent of suffering everything from him without making him suffer aught, because it believes him to be much above itself. Fourth. Conformity to the will of God, which is the sum total of all virtue. The humble soul is resigned and courageous beneath the weight of all trials, because it says to itself: I have deserved far worse for my sins; what is all that I suffer compared to hell, where I deserve to burn eternally? So true it is that humility is the foundation of all virtue. Have we hitherto rightly understood it?

SECOND POINT

✝ *Humility is the Guardian of all the Virtues*

Humility is to virtue and to merit what the source is to the brook, the root to the tree, the foundation to the building. In vain we may have practiced many virtues and acquired merits; if humility does not protect and cover them, if self-love or a complaisant glance cast upon ourselves intervenes, all merit disappears, our virtues become vices, our acts fruits of death, worthy of reprobation. In the same way that the brook separated from the fountainhead ceases to flow, that separated from its root the tree does not bear either blossom or fruit, that separated from its foundation the building falls down, so, separated from humility, all virtue vanishes, all merit departs. Self-love feeds upon it, and nothing is left for heaven. Is not this very sad? We have labored much, we have performed actions very holy in themselves, we had wherewith to obtain a beautiful place in paradise, and behold, it is all reduced to dust which is carried away by the wind: the breath of vanity has dissipated it all. Whence we ought to conclude that the more good works we perform, the more deeply humble ought we to be, lest pride and vanity, greedy of feasting upon praise, take from us the whole merit of what we have done. O humility, guardian of all virtue and of all merit, how worthy art thou of all our esteem and of all our efforts! *Resolutions and spiritual nosegay as above.*

SUMMARY OF TOMORROW'S MEDITATION

e will meditate tomorrow upon a twelfth reason for being very humble, which is that: first, humility is the mother of charity; second, that it is the beauty of it. We will thence deduce the resolution: first, to treat everyone with consideration and kindness, and to find happiness in the delicate attentions, the amiable kindnesses which charity inspires and which humility executes; second, to suffer all things whatsoever from every one and not to make any one suffer. Our spiritual nosegay shall be the words of St. Paul: "With honor preventing one another." (Rom. 12:10)

MEDITATION FOR THE MORNING

Let us adore Our Lord Jesus Christ bringing into the world the virtue of humility, of which even the very name was unknown before He came, and thereby preparing the way for charity, of which He was about to establish the reign here below. Let us thank Him for this double blessing, and let us conceive a great desire thoroughly to profit by it.

FIRST POINT

✝ *Humility is the Mother of Charity*

It is only the humble soul which always shows towards its neighbor those delicate attentions, that esteem and respect, and that kindness of behavior which constitute true charity, First: Charity, says St. Paul, is patient; (1 Cor. 13:4) it suffers everything from others, without making any one suffer. Now humility perfectly understands how to do so, but not pride, which is essentially impatient, and incapable of suffering contradiction, contempt, and a want of consideration. (Prov. 13:10) Second: Charity is neither jealous, envious, nor ambitious; far from envying the happiness of others or being annoyed at their success, it wishes it for them as much as it would for itself; it has so little ambition that there is nothing, however vile and low it may be, which it does not embrace with all its heart from love towards its neighbor. Now humility does all these things in simplicity, and pride will not hear of it. Third: Charity, continues St. Paul, is not puffed up, does not know what it is to command arrogantly, to reprove with bitterness, to speak harshly, still less to treat any one whatever with contempt. Now humility excels in all these holy things, whilst pride acts in an entirely opposite manner. Fourth: Charity is disinterested, and humility is also. As it does not esteem itself and esteems others as being better than itself, it places the interests of others always before its own. Pride thinks and acts in a quite opposite manner. Fifth: Charity does not allow itself to be irritated; it is never embittered against or annoyed with any one, no matter what cause for displeasure it may receive. Humility is capable of this moderation, but not pride. Sixth: Charity does not think of the evil that has been done it, or which its enemies wish to do it; and far from considering it as an injury or calling down vengeance upon it, it dissimulates it, excuses and forgives it. Now we may expect all these dispositions from humility, but not from pride, Seventh: Lastly, charity, far from rejoicing over the faults of its neighbor, places all its happiness in seeing him advance in the paths of justice and in seeing himself surpassed by others in virtue. (1 Cor. 13:6) Now it is thus that humility thinks and reasons. Pride, on the contrary, impatient of all superiority or preference of others over itself, cannot hear any one praised without trying to lessen what is said by an expression of censure. Let us examine by means of these seven characteristics whether a sincere humility has produced in us true charity.

SECOND POINT
✝ *Humility is the Charm of Charity*
Nothing is more amiable than the society of the man who is really humble. As he esteems himself to be the last of all, he is full of consideration and attention towards every one. Convinced that no one owes him anything and that he owes everything to others, he treats every one with honor and respect; he suffers contradiction, want of consideration, even contempt and reproaches, as things which are due to him; he seems not to perceive any want of attention, any criticizing words, or any ridicule; and he meets them with nothing but amiable manners, gracious words, and all the good offices which he can render. In him there is never any sign of haughtiness; he never shows by his tone in speaking any attachment to his own ideas and his own will; on the contrary, everything in him is modest, simple, and amiable. He is never offended, and does not know anything about the susceptibilities of self-love. Now who is there who does not understand how full of pleasantness must be the society of such a man? It is the fruit of humility. *Resolutions and spiritual nosegay as above.*

Twelfth Sunday after Pentecost

THE GOSPEL ACCORDING TO ST. LUKE, 10:23-37.

"At that time Jesus said to His disciples: Blessed are the eyes that see the things which you see. For I say to you, that many prophets and kings have desired to see the things that you see, and have not seen them; and to hear the things that you hear, and have not heard them. And behold a certain lawyer stood up, tempting Him, and saying: Master, what must I do to possess eternal life? But He said to him: What is written in the law? how readest thou? He answering said: Thou shalt love the Lord thy God with thy whole heart, and with thy whole soul, and with all thy strength, and with all thy mind; and thy neighbor as thyself. And He said to him: Thou hast answered right: this do, and thou shalt live. But he, willing to justify himself, said to Jesus: And who is my neighbor? Jesus answering said: A certain man went down from Jerusalem to Jericho, and fell among robbers, who also stripped him, and having wounded him, went away, leaving him half dead. And it chanced that a certain priest went down the same way, and seeing him passed by. In like manner also a Levite. when he was near the place and saw him, passed by. But a certain Samaritan, being on his journey, came near him; and seeing Him was moved with compassion. And going up to him, bound up his wounds, pouring in oil and wine: and setting him upon his own beast, brought him to an inn, and took care of him. And the next day he took out two pence, and gave to the host, and said: Take care of him: and whatsoever thou shalt spend over and above, I, at my return, will repay thee. Which of these three, in thy opinion, was neighbor to him that fell among the robbers? But he said: He that showed mercy to him. And Jesus said to him: Go, and do thou in like manner."

SUMMARY OF TOMORROW'S MEDITATION

ccording to our usual custom, we will tomorrow interrupt our meditations upon humility that we may meditate upon the gospel of the day. We shall there admire, in the person of the good Samaritan, two beautiful characteristics of Christian generosity: first, his noble sentiments towards an enemy who despised him; second, his still more noble conduct. We will thence deduce the resolution: first, to render to our neighbor all the good offices which we may have an opportunity of doing, whatever it may cost us; Second, to treat with special kindness all of whom we may have cause to complain, and always to render good for evil. We will retain as our spiritual nosegay the words of St. John: "Let us not love in word nor in tongue, but in deed and in truth." (1 John 3:18)

MEDITATION FOR THE MORNING

Let us adore Our Lord offering us in the parable of the good Samaritan; (Luke 10:23) a touching example of Christian generosity, of that beautiful virtue, the virtue which is the quality of great souls, which is not only charity, but charity accompanied by sacrifice, and which shone forth in the whole of Our Savior' s life. Presented in the person of a priest or a Levite, it would produce but little impression, because such persons, when doing good, would only be fulfilling a duty of their position; but presented in the person of a stranger passing along the road, it is invested with a more striking character. Let us receive this divine lesson with sentiments of respect, gratitude, and love.

FIRST POINT

✝ *The Noble Sentiments Entertained by the Samaritan towards an Enemy who Despises him*

The Jews despised and hated the Samaritans as a nation who had deserted their belief and their worship, who had separated themselves from the people of God and adored a golden calf. They would not hold any intercourse with them, and would have imagined themselves to have been soiled if they had eaten and drunk at their table, or admitted them to their own. Nevertheless and how admirable it is the Samaritan of our gospel loves even those who hate him and who despise him. He meets on his road with a Jew whom he has never seen, whom he does not in the least know; but he sees in him a man, a man who suffers, who is unhappy, who is forsaken. It is sufficient to touch his heart. He is traveling, and wishes to reach the end of his journey quickly; but in presence of such misfortune he forgets his own interests; interruptions count as nothing. Others have passed along the road and have not honored the wounded man by a single glance; but such bad examples as these do not influence him; he stops, draws near, and tries to console the sick heart, to solace the wounded body. It is thus that Christian generosity acts. It does not see any reason for hatred or diminished love in a diversity of opinions or beliefs, in the hatred which ill-disposed hearts bear towards the wretched, in the contempt they show them, in the character of an unknown person or a stranger, in their own interests being compromised, or in the example of the rich man who has no bowels of compassion. Very different from those narrow minds who will not be charitable except on condition that others will think like them, it does not esteem itself to be the only one who thinks aright, or if it be certain that it is in possession of the truth, it only pities those who have not the same happiness, and endeavors by dint of charity to bring them back to what is true. It pities those who dishonor through hatred and contempt their noble character of Christian, and deems itself happy to be able to render them good for evil, a gentle word for a hard one, a testimony of affection or of esteem for a hateful or contemptible act. No one in its eyes is unknown or a stranger; it sees in all men, made after the image of God, children of God, members of Jesus Christ, heirs of the kingdom of heaven; and on account of these titles they are all dear and honorable; to render them service, no sacrifice is too great, no interruption inconvenient, no bad example sufficient to make them deviate from the line of charity. Let us here examine ourselves and see whether we find in ourselves these characteristics of Christian generosity.

SECOND POINT

✝ *The Noble Conduct of the Samaritan towards an Enemy who Despises him*

It will be in vain that we shall imagine we are accomplishing the precept of charity, if we do not pass from sentiments to acts. Works are the language of the heart; it is by its fruits and not by its leaves that we judge of the goodness of a tree. Therefore the Samaritan had hardly looked at the poor traveler who had been robbed, who was ill. and covered with wounds, and who had no one to succor him, before he descends from his horse, goes up to him, washes his wounds with the wine he had brought with him for his journey, soothes them with a little of the oil he had about him, and then, putting him upon his horse, takes him to the nearest inn. There he gives a sum of money to the mistress of the inn, recommending her to take great care of him, and promising to pay her on his return all that the wounded man might have cost her. What a beautiful example of disinterestedness and of generosity! He does not spare anything, he sets no bounds to his alms. Let us then admire such noble conduct! The good Samaritan shows his love not merely in words, but in works and in truth. This is the true characteristic of charity. (1 John 3:18) He gives all that he has the wine, the oil, and the money with which he had supplied himself. He does not love who does not dispense his possessions or his money when his neighbor is in need of them. In addition to his possessions and his money, the good Samaritan gives himself. What a touching spectacle it is to see him on his knees before the poor wounded man, himself dressing his wounds, purifying the flesh with wine, correcting the acidity of the wine with the soothing nature of the oil, then binding up all the wounds! How beautiful it is next to see him taking his dear patient in his arms, placing him as gently as possible upon his horse, conveying him to the nearest inn, laying him on his bed, as a mother would her child, and, after giving his orders and his money in order that he might be treated in a proper manner, promising to return as soon as possible and pay all that his patient might have cost. It is thus that true charity devotes itself; it is not afraid of trouble, and it is a pleasure to it to sacrifice body and soul for the welfare of its neighbor. *Resolutions and spiritual nosegay as above.*

TWELFTH MONDAY AFTER PENTECOST

SUMMARY OF TOMORROW'S MEDITATION

e will meditate tomorrow on a thirteenth reason for being very humble; it is that therein consists the secret of our happiness even in the present life, and in order to understand it we shall see: first, how unhappy is the man who is devoid of humility; second, how happy is the truly humble man. We will then make the resolution: first, always to have a great deal of consideration for everyone, even for our inferiors; second, not to require any consideration to be shown to ourselves, and to receive with great gratitude, as a thing which is not due to us, the kindness bestowed upon us. Our spiritual nosegay shall be the words of Our Lord: "Learn of Me, because I am meek and humble of heart, and you shall find rest to your souls." (Matt. 11:29)

MEDITATION FOR THE MORNING

Let us adore the ineffable goodness of Jesus Christ, who has enabled us to find happiness here below in the accomplishment of His will, and, above all, in the practice of humility. Let us thank Him for all His goodness and render to Him all our homage.

FIRST POINT

✝ *How Unhappy is the Man who is Devoid of Humility*

If the man who is not humble considers himself, he beholds his wretchedness with nothing but sorrow and annoyance; he is sad and somber in his temper on account of it. and his melancholy makes him a burden to others and to himself. If, after looking at his own person, he casts his eyes on his neighbor, the advantages which others possess excite his jealousy. A preference which is not granted to him, a slight reproach, or even a charitable piece of advice, saddens him and fills his soul with vexation. A check in a project wherein he hoped for success; a word of censure or of ridicule; a look, a gesture, forgetfulness of certain small attentions which he believed were his due, is enough to discourage and cast him down. In the smallest sign of contempt he finds the source of a great grievance, as is seen in the favorite of Assuerus, who shed tears of despair because the esteem of one single man in the empire was not accorded to him. It is a susceptibility which is annoyed, which is uneasy and offended at everything. There is no need for him to seek a cause out of himself; his own temperament is sufficient to render him unhappy. The suspicions he conceives, the rash judgments he forms, the imaginations which have no foundation, are enough to render him gloomy and discontented. (Prov. 11:2) Let us here examine our past lives, and we shall see that the greater portion of our troubles comes from hence. Who could give expression to the sadness and melancholy which our imagination has excited in us with regard to the unfavorable opinion which we fancy has been entertained of us? What trouble and uneasiness have been inflicted on our minds on account of a small humiliation which we have received, a reproof addressed to us, or the thought that we have not been respected as much as we ought to have been!

SECOND POINT

✝ *How Happy the really Humble Man is even Here Below*

Our Lord has promised peace and happiness to humble souls. "Learn of Me," He says, "Because I am meek and humble of heart, and you shall find rest to your souls," (Matt. 11:29) and He keeps His word to all who strive to be really humble. The humble man is always content and tranquil; he receives trials with meekness, believing that he deserves them; he sees the privileges possessed by others without feeling any vexation, esteeming that the last place is good enough for him. Words which touch his reputation do not affect him: if he is spoken well of, he pities the men who are deceived about him; and if he is spoken evil of, he is content that others should think of him as he thinks of himself. Being thus freed from the anxieties which human judgments cause others to feel, he is immovable like a rock in the midst of the waves of opinion which ebb and flow around him: he does not trouble himself any more about them than about the wind which blows, and goes on occupying himself in well-doing, and the What will they say? He treads under foot and does not give it a thought. To do well and let what will be said, is his motto, not from a sentiment of proud contempt which raises itself above what is said by man, but from a sentiment of true humility. "I am nothing," he says; nothingness is not offended at anything, nothingness does not pretend to anything, nothingness is not troubled at anything, nothingness does not attach itself to anything; "And filled with these humble sentiments, he enjoys God alone in all things.

God only suffices him, and he is happy. God alone is all in all to him, and he cannot conceive that it is possible to desire anything else when we possess Him. *Resolutions and spiritual nosegay as above.*

TWELFTH TUESDAY AFTER PENTECOST

SUMMARY OF TOMORROW'S MEDITATION

e will meditate tomorrow upon a fourteenth reason for being very humble; it is because humility is: first, the remedy for all our miseries; second, the key of all graces. We will then form the resolution: first, to make our miseries serve daily to increase our growth in humility, by humbling ourselves profoundly before God; second, to carry into our prayers a deep sentiment of our littleness and of our unworthiness to speak to God. Our spiritual nosegay shall be the words of the Imitation: "The most useful of all knowledge is to know how to despise ourselves." (1 Imit. 2:4)

MEDITATION FOR THE MORNING

Let us adore Our Lord covered with the appearance of sin and the form of a slave abased down to nothingness. (Philipp. 2:7) Let us render our homage to our divine Savior in this state. The more He abases Himself for us, the more respect and love we owe Him.

FIRST POINT

✠ *Humility is the Remedy for all our Miseries*

We have all of us passions to conquer, and we do not know how to reach the end of them; temptations to overcome, and we do not know how to get rid of them; prayers and spiritual exercises to perform, and often our minds are so distracted, our hearts so arid and disgusted, that we do not know how to acquit ourselves of them. Now humility, the true universal remedy, cures all these weaknesses. It attacks all our passions at once, weakens them, casts them down almost without a combat, and reduces them by taking from them their principal food, which is self-love. Under the inspiration of humility, the soul, ashamed of itself, sees the passions which exist in it under the form of so many hideous lepers, the sight of which excites horror; it is filled with profound abasement and cries out towards Thee, O Lord, from the bottom of the abyss (Ps. 124:1): "Have pity on my great misery, O my God. How canst Thou endure me? How canst Thou love me who am so poor and so mean? Oh, I am worth nothing. How miserable I am, how I deserve the contempt of all creatures, and still more Thine, O Lord." And in this humble state no passion can stand its ground. Our temptations also have no power of resistance. The tempted soul turns towards God and is confounded. "Lord," it says with St. Teresa, "behold what my evil nature is capable of producing. I know well that plant of my garden. Thanks, Lord, for having shown me what I am, a corrupted nature, an abyss of miseries; all kinds of vices have their seeds in my heart. How ill then would it become me to indulge in self-love, to look upon myself as being anything and to desire that others should esteem me! How ill it becomes me to count upon myself and to expose myself to occasions of sin! I will fly from them, Lord, and with Thy help I will triumph over my enemies." But it is above all in states of powerlessness to pray, in aridness and distractions, that humility is the supreme remedy. Then the soul is confounded in the presence of God; ashamed of its insolence, which forgets the respect due to so lofty a majesty; ashamed of its misery, which does not even know how to ask God for the spiritual alms of which it has need; then it quietly resumes its prayer where it left it off and continues it in a spirit of humility. If aridness or distractions return, the soul recommences its exercise of humility, without being troubled and without vexation; and thus it performs all its prayers, the best assuredly which it can perform, for the best prayer is that from which we issue forth the most humble. Oh, what an excellent remedy then is humility for all our miseries!

SECOND POINT

✝ Humility is the Key of all Graces

The Holy Spirit says so: "God gives His grace to the humble." (James 5:6) The reason is: first, because all graces are attached to prayer, and because the prayer of the humble soul is always granted. (Ecclus. 35:21) The publican cannot say anything more than a few humble words, and those words obtain for him his justification; whilst the prayer of the soul which esteems itself and is pleased with itself is always rejected by God. Second, as the waters of heaven cast themselves down from the mountains into the valleys, so the waters of grace do not stay upon the souls which lift themselves up in their own esteem like mountains, or which do not descend by humility below the common level, but they concentrate and collect together in the souls which abase themselves in their own eyes. A humble soul is a large vessel into which God sheds His graces in proportion to its depth. Such is always the way in which God proceeds;

the more humble a soul is, the higher He raises it in grace. "Let us humble
our souls before Him and humbly wait for His consolation." (Jud. 8:16,20)
Resolutions and spiritual nosegay as above.

Twelfth Wednesday after Pentecost

SUMMARY OF TOMORROW'S MEDITATION

e will meditate tomorrow upon a fifteenth reason for being humble;
it is that not to be humble is to run after the vainest thing there
is in the world, which is the esteem of men; and in order that
we may be deeply imbued with this thought, we shall see how
vain this esteem is: first, in its principles; second, in its effects. We will thence
deduce the resolution: first, to have God alone in sight in all our actions, and
to put away from us with supreme contempt any thought of vanity which may
mingle with our intentions; second, not to attach any importance to the praises
or testimonies of esteem which may be addressed to us. Our spiritual nosegay
shall be the words of the Psalmist: "The Lord knoweth the thoughts of men,
that they are vain." (Ps. 93:11)

MEDITATION FOR THE MORNING

Let us adore Our Lord Jesus Christ recommending us never in our actions
to aim at gaining the esteem of men, but to think only of pleasing God. (Matt.
6:1) Let us thank Him for so useful a lesson, and beg of Him to enable us
thoroughly to understand all the vanity of the esteem of men.

FIRST POINT
✝ *How Vain in its Principles is the Esteem of Men*

When we are praised, or when marks of esteem are bestowed upon us,
self-love is very ready to tell us that it is a homage rendered to our merit, a debt
which is paid to us; but in reality nothing is more false. Sometimes on the part
of our flatterers it means nothing more than mere civility, the fear of wounding
our susceptibility, which they know to be very great, the desire of pleasing us,
the knowledge they have that we like to be praised, and they laugh behind
our backs at the weakness which they caress to our face; some times it is an
encouragement bestowed upon our weakness, a help given to our cowardice,
which without such aid would fall to the ground. At other times it is the charity
which thinks no evil and sees nothing but good in all things, which, honoring
Jesus Christ in us, treats us with consideration, speaks to us with respect, loves

us with cordiality. Often, also, it is a prejudice in our favor, a blind friendship formed by flesh and blood or by social relations. Then, the mind regulating its movements in accordance with the attachments of the heart, all that we do, all that we say, seems worthy of praise, and nothing but virtue and spiritual riches are seen where God often beholds nothing but poverty and misery, and great talents where truth sees nothing but what is very ordinary. Oftener still, if indeed it be not always, it "is ignorance and falsehood. We are praised and esteemed because we are judged in accordance with deceitful appearances, because our characters are not known. Oh, how rare would the language of flattery be upon earth if the eyes of men could but see what in reality the persons are of whom they speak. Ignorance in those who praise us may, indeed, excuse the language of which they make use, but we who know the truth respecting ourselves, is it reason able in us to take pleasure in it? If we were to go and say to a poor man reduced to the last degree of indigence, covered with rags and ulcers, we admire you, great prince; you are immensely rich, no one is your equal in beauty and in grace, nothing could be more magnificent than your attire," and if we found that the poor man took pleasure in such language, we should say he had lost his senses; and yet this is exactly our own history. We are poor in every respect, we are nothing, we have nothing, we can do nothing, and yet we take pleasure in hearing others say that we are rich in merits and virtues, and, however false may be the praises which are given us, we are delighted to listen to them, caring very little about what we really are in the sight of God, but only about what we are in appearance and in the opinion of men. What folly, what simplicity is ours! Ah, these praises and these marks of esteem ought rather to be considered by us as they were by the saints, an insult inflicted upon our extreme poverty. "Receive praises as though they were mockeries and insults," said St. Francis Xavier. " Those who flatter me, scourge me," said another saint; and truly, if we did but know ourselves, we could not be of any other opinion.

SECOND POINT
✝ *How Vain the Esteem of Men is in its Effects*

Let me be praised or blamed; let me be esteemed or despised; let me be forgotten or let me be unknown, what does it signify? The judgment of man raises me on high today: what have I gained? Am I less miserable on account of it? No, doubtless, only I have added to my miseries one more piece of ridicule, that of taking pleasure in esteem which I do not deserve. I have added to my ills one more malady, the swelling up of my pride, which has swollen me without making me any greater. Tomorrow, effacing the picture which it had painted, the judgment of men makes me out to be small and contemptible, unworthy of attracting towards me a single glance. What have I lost thereby? Nothing at all but a useless amusement, a little noise highly dangerous to my self-love and my vanity. Alas! I have no need that others should speak to me of the good that is in me, I speak only too much of it to myself. The opinion of men is therefore nothing more than wind and smoke; it gives us nothing, and it takes away from us nothing; and all that can be said of us, whether it be good or whether it be evil, does not make us either better or worse. Therefore, to desire to be esteemed by men is a thing so vain that we cannot help being ashamed of it; there is no one who would not blush at being suspected that he desired praise. We like the good we do to be known, but we do it in such a way as to make others think that it is in spite of ourselves it has become known. We seem as though we suffered violence in listening to praise; we reject it, but it is in such a manner as to incline others to imagine that we merit still greater praise. How strange it is! The esteem of men is so vain that we are ashamed of it, and yet it so sweetly flatters our heart. Ah, it is because we are created to be praised and esteemed by God throughout eternity; but that will be realized only in so far as we shall disabuse ourselves of the passion of being esteemed by men upon earth. *Resolutions and spiritual nosegay as above.*

Twelfth Thursday after Pentecost

SUMMARY OF TOMORROW'S MEDITATION

e will meditate tomorrow upon a sixteenth reason for being very humble; it is that we have within us a seed of self-love, which as a mortal poison: first, corrupts the gifts of God; second, engenders all the vices. We will then make the resolution: first, to watch with special care over all the movements of our heart, that we may keep alive the spirit of humility within it; second, gladly to seize upon all opportunities for humbling ourselves. Our spiritual nosegay shall be the words of the Imitation: "Do not imagine you have made the least progress as long as you do not esteem yourself to be the lowest of all creatures." (2 Imit. 2:2)

MEDITATION FOR THE MORNING

Let us adore the dispositions of the heart of Jesus abased with the feeling of His littleness and of His nothingness in presence of the lofty majesty of

His Father. (Ps. 38:6). Let us bless Him in this state, wherein He teaches us to despoil ourselves of the vain esteem of ourselves, which is so harmful to our souls and so dangerous for our salvation.

FIRST POINT
✝ *Self-love Corrupts the Gifts of God in us*
God has given us a body, the masterpiece of all the visible creation; a mind which feeds upon intelligence and truth, capable of attaining all distances, the height of the heavens as well as the depths of the abyss, which embraces the in finite and cannot content itself with anything less. Now, self-love perverts these so excellent gifts to the extent of converting them into a misfortune, or at any rate into a danger in regard to our salvation. He who esteems his body and takes pleasure in it makes of it an idol of insane vanity, as hurtful to his soul as it is unworthy of his great and eternal destinies. He who holds his talents in esteem attracts to himself the chastisement of the proud, presumes upon his own intelligence, and allows himself to be blinded. Oh, how many will be lost for having adored their own minds and who have had too high an opinion of its conceptions! Why have they not fewer talents and more humility? He who esteems the qualities of his heart and glorifies himself for them puts into it a worm which eats them and spoils them at their root. God has indeed given us the grace of prayer, by which we may obtain all things; but if self-love mingles with our prayer it will be accursed and condemned by God, like the prayer of the Pharisee, who, whilst he was thanking God, spoilt his thanksgiving by the vain complaisance he took in himself. God, to the grace of prayer, has, of course, added the grace of good works and the acts of different virtues, but if self-love is mingled with these good works, the whole merit of them will be lost. He who has a high esteem of his own virtue puts it to death; he who has a high opinion of his own piety kills it; he who takes pleasure in the good works he does spoils his harvest, throws down his edifice, destroys his work. What self-examinations may we not make on this point! How many merits have we not lost!

SECOND POINT
✝ *Self-love Engenders all the Vices*
"O esteem of men" said St. Francis Xavier, "what evil you have done, what evil you do, what evil you will do!" Hence comes ambition, with its intrigues and its baseness; we desire to be spoken of, to be raised up beyond what we really are, no matter at what cost, and for the satisfaction of our pride we are ready to over throw society and to make bloody wars. Hence the desire

for riches, with its iniquitous proceedings for making a fortune, in order that others may speak of us and that we may attract observation. Hence luxury in our clothing and our furniture, because the common herd looks at and admires such magnificence. Hence the vanity which feeds upon the vapor of praise, which cannot bear to receive a counsel, a reproach, even an inadvertence, and is angry if it suspects that it is not appreciated according to its own estimate, as though it were a monarch that attempts were being made to dethrone. Hence human respect with all its baseness and weakness. What will be aid, what will be thought of me, if I do or do not do such or such a thing? And rather than submit to a word of reproval, duty is sacrificed, (Prov. 24:25; Gal. 1:10) evil done from complaisance towards theirs, and we affect to be worse than we really are. (St. Augustine, Conf. lib. 2 100:9) Hence impatience and ill-temper, which cannot bear either contradiction or reverses. We will not allow that we deserve the least blame, that we deserve to be punished by God and forsaken by men. Hence the calumnies which conscience reproves, the freedom of speech in which we indulge. What will be said if I do not talk in the same way as others? Hence lies and equivocations or reticences, whether employed to justify ourselves when we are guilty or to give others a good opinion of us. Hence such hatred, or at any rate coldness, towards those whom we fancy do not esteem us; hence the kind of adoration for those who appear to have a high opinion of us, the complaints with regard to such as do not render to us the honor we believe to be our due; hence the envy we feel with respect to the merits of others; lastly, the preoccupations of the mind and of the heart, which render all prayer and all virtue impossible. O God! how true it is that self-love engenders all the vices! What a great misfortune it is to be always receiving the incense of praise, what great happiness to be at least sometimes misconceived! *Resolutions and spiritual nosegay as above.*

Twelfth Friday after Pentecost

SUMMARY OF TOMORROW'S MEDITATION

e will meditate tomorrow upon a seventeenth reason for being very humble; it is: first, that self-love is a wall of separation between God and us, second, that self-love is incompatible with virtue. We will then make the resolution: first, to prefer always that which causes us to be hidden rather than that which places us in evidence, that which humbles us rather than that which raises us; second, to avoid as much as possible opportunities for showing ourselves off and attracting observation.

Our spiritual nosegay shall be the words of the Apostle: "Let us not be made desirous of vain glory." (Gal. 5:26)

MEDITATION FOR THE MORNING

Let us adore Our Lord Jesus Christ suffering throughout the whole of His apostolic life all the blame cast upon Him. Some indeed said, "He is a prophet; He is the Christ," but others added, "No, He is not, He is a deceiver, He is a man who loves pleasure, wine, and good eating; He is a Samaritan, a heretic, an impious man, an enemy of the temple and of the holy nation. If He delivers the possessed, it is in the name of Beelzebub. He is Himself possessed. Can any good thing come out of Nazareth? Of a truth this man cometh not from God, for He does not observe the Sabbath." And in the midst of all these speeches Jesus is silent. He accepts the humiliation and offers it to His Father in expiation of the susceptibilities of our self-love. Let us admire, thank, imitate Him.

FIRST POINT

✝ *Self-love is a Wall of Separation between God and Ourselves*

First, it is a fact confirmed by experience that inasmuch as humiliations borne in a Christian manner bring God near to us and unite us with Him, so the complaisance which the heart feels in esteem and praise, the vexation which contempt and blame inflict upon it, removes God from us and separates us from Him. The reason is, that the esteem in which we take pleasure develops in us pride, which God detests; while contempt rightly borne develops in us humility, which God cherishes. Second, self-love distracts us from God. It suffices that the soul, which at first proposed to itself God alone and desired nothing but His good pleasure, begins to think that it is looked at, that it is praised and admired; at that moment it is turned away from God, stopped in its progress, and inclined to act only from vainglory. All kinds of praise or marks of esteem, unless they are disavowed by a frank humility, dissipate, preoccupy, and seduce the heart, dazzle it and charm it. It is a kind of enchantment which pursues us in our prayers, our acts, and our intentions, separates us from God and makes us forget heaven. It is what made an author say, "I mistrust a virtue exposed to too great a number of spectators; the least look cast upon it may "inflict a mortal wound;" and it is this which has made so many saints love a hidden life. Have we hitherto considered this danger and do we distrust it?

SECOND POINT

✝ *Self-love is not Compatible with any Kind of Virtue*

What virtue, in fact, could harmonize with self-love? Could it be faith? But faith desires that we should look upon our own minds as ignorant and not able to comprehend anything in the supernatural order, which cannot without temerity examine into subjects beyond its own level, which consequently ought, with the simplicity of a child, without discussion or examination, to accept what is told to it by Holy Church. Now he who is not humble cannot submit to anything of the kind; hence doubts and temptations against faith. Could it be charity? But he who looks upon himself as being superior to others imagines that pre-eminence is always due to him, that the best share of everything belongs to him, that every one should bow down to his decisions and yield to his will; now, all that is incompatible with charity. Could it be wisdom and prudence? But he who is inebriated with a good opinion of himself throws himself rashly into all kinds of difficulties and dangers, prefers his own ideas to the advice of wise men, makes of himself a master of all subjects and speaks like a doctor. Could it be knowledge of ourselves? But the good opinion of our own merit, like a prism placed before our eyes, changes the color of objects, and hinders us from seeing ourselves as we really are. We have faults which shock every one, and we alone do not even suspect them. We will not even allow ourselves to be warned about them; the most moderate kind of advice embitters and revolts us. Could it be, lastly, the love of God? But divine love is comprehended only by the soul that despises itself. It belongs only to the soul that is conscious of its own baseness and profound misery to appreciate as it ought how good, merciful, and wondrously loving God is, to lower His greatness to our littleness, His holiness to our misery, His goodness to our ingratitude. Then only, then alone, it exclaims with St. Francis Assisi, and with its heart set on fire with love: "Who art Thou and who am I, my God?" or with St. Augustine: "O God, the abyss of my misery reveals to me the abyss of Thy mercy. Oh, how well Thou dost deserve my love in return for the love Thou dost bear to a creature as miserable as I am!" Let us sigh in the presence of God at the obstacle which self-love has hitherto placed in the way of our progress in all the virtues. *Resolutions and spiritual nosegay as above.*

SUMMARY OF TOMORROW'S MEDITATION

 e will meditate tomorrow upon an eighteenth reason for being very humble; it is that in our self-love we have the shame of carrying about with us a treacherous thief who: first, takes away our merits; and, second, takes them often away without our being conscious of it. We will then make the resolution: first, in all our actions to direct our intention towards God alone, often saying to Him before and during our actions: All to please Thee, O my God; second, carefully to put away from us all other aims which might vitiate our intention. Our spiritual nosegay shall be the words of Jeremias: "See, O Lord, and consider, for I am become vile." (Lam. 1:11)

MEDITATION FOR THE MORNING

Let us adore God as the last end as well as the first principle of the whole of our being. In His presence we are but nothingness and sin, and we have no right to do anything, to say anything, or to think anything which has any other end save Him alone. To Him essentially belong all honor, all glory, and everything related to us. Let us abase ourselves in presence of His adorable majesty, and be filled with humble sentiments regarding ourselves.

FIRST POINT

✝ *Self-love Takes from us the Merit of our Good Works*

We ought to keep ourselves on our guard against self-love as we should be on our guard against a thief who was trying to rob us of all that we have which is most precious. What, in fact, have we that is more precious here below than our good works, which are, as it were, the money with which heaven is bought, and with which we may obtain at any moment of our existence an increase of glory and of happiness for all eternity? Neither riches nor treasures are worth a possession so great. The humble man preserves this possession in all its integrity, and adds to it the new merit of humility, which infinitely elevates His actions; but self-love squanders the whole of this treasure. It will have done us no good to have labored much, to have given ourselves an infinity of trouble and anxiety; if self-love intervenes, not only will there remain nothing of what might have enriched us, but we shall even be poorer than we were at first. That which might so greatly have profited us will turn against us, and we shall have nothing to expect from God excepting the punishment of the proud. What a loss, what a misfortune, not to be humble! This is why Our Lord repeated so often in His Sermon on the Mount: "Take care not to do your good works before men, that you may be seen of them, otherwise you will receive no reward from your Father who is in heaven. When you give alms try to ignore it yourself, by avoiding to take pleasure in your good works, and let your left hand be ignorant of what your right does. Then your heavenly Father, who seeth in secret, will recompense you for it. When you pray, do not let it be in the sight of the world, but delight to pray in secret, and your heavenly Father, who seeth in secret, will reward you. (Matt. 6:1, et seq.) Oh, how good then it is to be humble, to close our eyes to all human judgments, and to think only of the good pleasure of God alone! What strange compensations does not self-love offer us! If we had given all our goods to the poor, spent our lives in good works, delivered up our bodies to the flames, all would have no merit in the eyes of God, if self-love has intervened as the determining motive. Let us here examine ourselves in the presence of God. How many have not been the actions of our life from which self-love has taken away all the merit! What riches lost for heaven, and in their place, perhaps, reasons for condemnation at the tribunal of God!

SECOND POINT

✝ Self-love often Takes from us the Merit of our Works when we are not Aware of it

As what is familiar and long continued ends by being no longer observed, so self-love, which hardly ever leaves us, escapes our observation and hides itself from our eyes. It is the pulsations of the heart, which are not remarked be cause they are habitual, or it is because it hides itself under an appearance of virtue. We fancy we are laboring for God, and we are laboring only for ourselves. The good is seen on the surface, and at the bottom it is self-love which, unknown to us, has put all in motion. We began the action with an upright intention; then motives springing from self-love intervened and took possession of the heart because they were more in harmony with its natural egotism. Hence so many illusions which enter into piety and good works; hence the impatience and vivacity which we imagine to be the ardor of zeal; hence the discouragements when self-love is not paid on the spot by the hoped-for success. Let us examine ourselves upon so important and practical a subject. *Resolutions and spiritual nosegay as above.*

THE GOSPEL ACCORDING TO ST. LUKE, 17:1-19.

"At that time, as Jesus was going to Jerusalem, He passed through the midst of Samaria and Galilee. And as He entered into a certain town, there met Him ten men that were lepers, who stood afar off, and lifted up their voice, saying: Jesus, Master, have mercy on us. Whom, when He saw, He said: Go, show yourselves to the priests. And it came to pass, as they went they were cleansed. And one of them, when he saw that he was made clean, went back, with a loud voice glorifying God: and he fell on his face before His feet, giving thanks: and this was a Samaritan. And Jesus answering said: Were not ten made clean? And where are the nine? There is no one found to return and give glory to God, but this stranger. And He said to him: Arise, go thy way; for thy faith hath made thee whole."

SUMMARY OF TOMORROW'S MEDIATION

e will tomorrow interrupt the course of our meditations upon humility, that we may meditate upon the virtue of gratitude recommended to us by the gospel of the day. We will consider this virtue: first, as a precept of the natural law; second, as the soul of society and of the family. We will then make the resolution: first, to show ourselves, in all circumstances, grateful to those who oblige us, even if they should be our inferiors, and for the smallest services rendered to us; second, to do all the good we can to our fellows, without counting upon their gratitude. Our spiritual nosegay shall be the words of the Apostle: "Owe no man anything, but to love one another." (Rom. 8:8)

MEDITATION FOR THE MORNING

Let us adore Our Lord Jesus Christ complaining in the gospel that out of the ten lepers whom He had cured one only had come to thank Him; "And where are the nine?" Let us bless Him for this lesson, and ask of Him grace to profit by it.

FIRST POINT

✝ *Gratitude is a Precept of the Natural Law*

If the natural law obliges us to love our fellows even when they have offended us and have done us evil, what do we not owe towards those who have done us a service or shown a tender interest in us? Love demands love; he who receives is under obligation, and the benefit granted calls for a return of gratitude. He who does not pay his debts is unjust; but he who does not pay the debt of gratitude is worse still he is vile. It is a soul without delicacy and honor, which does not understand that every good heart ought to be grateful, and that the sweetest of enjoyments is to declare the benefit which has been received, and to give back as much in return. It is a soul which is base and lowered beneath the level of savages, who show themselves to be grateful for a service; it sinks below the level of even the animals, of which many show themselves to be grateful to their masters and benefactors, even exposing themselves to death in order to defend them. It is, finally, an ungrateful soul, and that is saying everything, for ingratitude, the most odious of vices, is a hideous product of pride and malignity, founded upon the idea that he who gives seeming to be greater than he who receives, pride, being jealous of domination, cannot bear to make this avowal of inferiority. Hence it is that the proud is ashamed to confess that he has received a benefit; he hides it as much as he can; he is annoyed when it is recalled to him. Hence it is that nothing is so quickly forgotten as a benefit, and that the number of the ungrateful is infinite. In order to dispense themselves from gratitude, they try to imagine interested motives on the part of their benefactor; they search out in him for faults to be censured, wrongs to be reprehended; and if they can render him the slightest service, they make use of it in order to free themselves from the debt of gratitude. "I have rendered all back to him," they say. Evil words are these! The good man never forgets the benefit he has received even when he has rendered one as good in return, or even when he has had the happiness to do still more. Have we nothing to reproach ourselves with on this head? Let us examine our conscience.

SECOND POINT

✝ *Gratitude is the Soul of Society and of the Family*

The world subsists only by means of an interchange of good offices. God, in order to link us together by the sweet ties of charity, has willed that we should all of us have need the one of the other: superiors have need of the service of inferiors; inferiors of the assistance and protection of their superiors; equals of the aid of their fellows. Let us traverse all the conditions, all the ranks of the social ladder; all ages from infancy to maturity, from maturity to old age; we shall see that nothing can go on in this world without a mutual interchange of services. Now these interchanges which are so necessary to society are caused by gratitude, which provokes them, which develops them, which renders them sweet and amiable, which is, in a word, the soul of them, whilst ingratitude is annoyed by them and often disgusted. Gratitude brings near to us the hard of which we have need, ingratitude puts it away; gratitude desires to fly to our aid, in gratitude is ready to forsake us; gratitude binds social links closer together, ingratitude loosens and dissolves them. And this is still more true in regard to family life. Which are good families, if they be not those where children and parents, husbands and wives, masters and servants, are always endeavoring to give pleasure to one another? And where shall we meet with these delicate attentions excepting where they are the fruit of gratitude? Which are bad families, if they be not those where children are ungrateful, servants devoid of gratitude, where masters consider themselves to be dispensed from all gratitude towards their inferiors, under the pretext that they pay them, as though affection and devotion could be repaid by money? *Resolutions and spiritual nosegay as above.*

ThIRTEENTh MONDAY AFTER PENTECOST

SUMMARY OF TOMORROW'S MEDITATION

e will consider tomorrow in our meditation: first, that if, in accordance with what we meditated upon this morning, we owe gratitude to men for their benefits, we owe much more to God; second, how we ought to acquit ourselves of this gratitude. We will then make the resolution: first, to make acts of gratitude towards God at the sight of the heavens, the beauties of nature, and still more at the sight of churches and of crosses; lastly, for every good thought with which the goodness of God inspires us; second, to be faithful in making our thanksgiving after holy communion, after our meals, and in the evening. Our spiritual nosegay shall be the song of the Church: "Let us give thanks to the Lord our God."

MEDITATION FOR THE MORNING

Let us give thanks to God, teaching us the duty of gratitude towards Him, first by His Apostle: "In all things give thanks," St. Paul says, "for this is the will of God." (1 Thess. 5:18) "Give thanks always for all things;" (Eph. 5:20) then by His Church, which every day at the holy sacrifice proclaims it loudly: "Let us give thanks to the Lord our God; it is truly meet and just, right and salutary, that we should always, and in all places, give thanks to Thee, O holy Lord." Let us bless Him for this lesson, and with this object in view render to Him all our homage.

FIRST POINT

✝ *The Duty of Gratitude towards God*

We owe thanksgivings to God: first, on account of our existence, which is a gift of His love; He has chosen us from out of millions of possible creatures to give us a being; second, for our preservation, which is, as it were, a second creation, belonging to every moment, and which consequently calls for, on our part, a continual hymn of thanksgiving; third, for all the evils of the soul and the body which He spares us from in preference to numbers of others who are attacked by them; fourth, for all the sins which we have not committed, thanks to His preventing grace; fifth, for all spiritual and corporeal benefits, whether they are those which are common to all or those which are conferred specially upon us; sixth, for all the beings which surround us and which have been created for us, animals and plants, air, water, fire, the heavens and the earth; seventh, for the care His providence takes of us at every moment, directing the course of the world, disposing the seasons, sending His rain upon the earth, regulating all events with so much attention that it presides over even the fall of one of the hairs of our head, with so much assiduity that even during our sleep it watches by our bedside. And where shall we find words to express what we owe Him for the numerous benefits which belong to a superior order? A God incarnating Himself in the bosom of a virgin; a God born in a crib; a God living by labor and toil; a God scourged, crowned with thorns, crucified between two thieves; a God covered with ignominy; a dying God; a God surviving Himself in the Eucharist and remaining there hidden, forsaken, so often offended by irreverences, profanations, and sacrileges; a God pursuing us with His graces, offering us His sacraments, instructing us by His Church, which He always maintains as a faithful depository of His doctrine! O my God! My God! How can I ever thank and bless Thee sufficiently? "Let us, therefore, love God, because God first hath loved us." (1 John 4:19) We should be all the more inexcusable not to be grateful for so many marvels, seeing that our interests render it a duty that we should be so. The more grateful we are towards God, the more new graces will we attract towards us. Like the waters of rivers which return to the sea and afterwards come back transformed into clouds, dews, and rain, which reproduce the same rivers, so the waters of grace, carried back by gratitude to God, who is their principle, will return to us in rains of divine grace; whilst ingratitude stops the course of graces, dries up like a burning wind the source of piety, the dew of mercy, and places an obstacle in the way of all the designs of God with regard to us. (St. Bernard, in

Cant. Serm. 51) Oh, what a wrong we have hitherto inflicted upon ourselves by reason of the little gratitude we have shown for all the benefits which we have received!

SECOND POINT

✝ *The Manner in which to Pay our Debts of Gratitude to God*

The Church teaches us this, when she says in the preface of the holy sacrifice that we must thank God always and everywhere. First, we must thank Him always. As in our existence there is not a single moment which is not a benefit bestowed by God, there is therefore not one in which our gratitude ought not to ascend to God. Every moment at our waking, as well as every evening when we lie down, we should say, "Thanks, my God!" Every time that the clock strikes, when considering how many persons here below are tried by troubles which we are spared, how many have died during the past hour, we must exclaim, "Thanks, my God!" Lastly, our life ought to be an uninterrupted thanksgiving towards God, our benefactor. Second, we must thank God everywhere, that is to say, in the home, where He places us and provides for all our wants; in our travels, wherein Refurnishes us with means for going from one place to another; in the town, where He brings together all that is necessary to supply the necessaries and the comforts of life; in the country, where He makes the earth bring forth its harvests and the fruits which make us live; at table, where He gives us suitable food; at recreation, wherein He arranges our amusements and pleasures; everywhere, in a word, since everything is full of benefits. *Resolutions and spiritual nosegay as above.*

Thirteenth Tuesday after Pentecost

SUMMARY OF TOMORROW'S MEDITATION

 e will meditate tomorrow upon a nineteenth reason for being very humble; it is that self-love is a deceiver which: first, hides from us what we are; second, hides from us what our neighbor is. We will then make the resolution: first, to be on our guard against the deceptions of self-love, and no longer to look upon them as being realities; second, never to say or do anything which shall be to the advantage of self-love. Our spiritual nose gay shall be the maxim of the Imitation: "He who knows himself well is vile in his own eyes, and takes no pleasure in the praises of men." (1 Imit. 2:1)

MEDITATION FOR THE MORNING

Let us adore Our Lord Jesus Christ taking, as His share, when He was on earth, an obscure and hidden life, to teach us not to listen to the inspirations of self-love, which push us on to make an appearance in the eyes of others. In vain His relatives say to Him: "Manifest Thyself to the world." (John 7:4) He does not listen to these counsels of flesh and blood, which seek the glory of men rather than the glory of God. (John 12:43) Let us thank Him for this example and ask of Him grace to profit by it.

FIRST POINT

✝ *Self-love Hides from us what we are*

It is remarkable to see how self-love deceives us. All the reasons for rendering us contemptible are not sufficient to make us humble, whilst the least advantage which we imagine we possess fills us with vanity. How is that? First, it is because we are determined at all costs to have a good opinion of ourselves; we shut our eyes to our miseries, in order that we may see only our good side. We look at ourselves from this point of view with complaisance, we entertain ourselves with it, we entertain others with it; speaking only of ourselves, approving only what we ourselves do, forgetting nothing which is calculated to make others praise us and taking all the praises we receive as being incontestable truths, all the consideration of which we are the object as debts which are paid for us. Second, we appropriate to ourselves the small amount of good which God has placed within us, saying: This is your good, your virtue, your merit Then we increase and exaggerate it; he who is poor in virtue and in talents looks upon himself as being rich both in the one and the other; he who has only mediocre talents believes that he has remark able talents; and he who has only the appearance of virtue imagines himself to be solidly virtuous. Willingly we constitute ourselves to be innovators, critics, and censors, because we believe ourselves to be more clever than others. Not content with appropriating and exaggerating what is good in us, we dissimulate what is evil to such a point that that which strikes all eyes escapes us, and is for us as the words of a closed and sealed book; or if we cannot hide it, we lessen it, or we clothe it in seductive colors which almost cause it to be loved; we excuse it by human frailty; lastly, we cover it with the good we do, in order to make it forgotten. In this way we reach the point at which we do not know ourselves, and the mind, being duped by the heart, deceives us. Such or such a man believes himself to be humble, patient, detached, and when an opportunity arrives he shows himself to be proud, impatient, filled with attachments. Another man trusts in his virtue, and the most serious kinds of falls are a consequence of the ignorance in which he lives.

SECOND POINT

✝ *Self-love Hides from us what our Neighbor is*

By means of tactics which are opposed to those which have to do with ourselves, self-love increases the evil to be found in others and hides the good which exists. He who does not see the beam in his own eye discerns the smallest straw in the eye of his neighbor, and observes the least defects in others. A manner of speaking or acting, now too simple and now too artificial; the tone, the air, the behavior, nothing escapes him, and, flattering himself to be exempt from the faults which he censures, he arrogates to himself a superiority over them and delights in it. Hence the inclination to criticism and raillery; hence the readiness to believe what is evil, the slowness to believe what is good, the suspicions which are caused by the slightest indications of a defect, and the difficulty of believing in a virtue supported by the strongest proofs. It gives us pain to listen to eulogiums upon others, and we take a malignant pleasure in lowering those who are raised. It is only with difficulty we see their merit; we try not to see it and we lessen it as much as we can. All praise is met by criticism; beside the merits which cannot be denied a defect is placed. It is thus that self-love hides from us what our neighbor is. Let us observe this injustice, that we may preserve ourselves from it. *Resolutions and spiritual nosegay as above.*

Thirteenth Wednesday after Pentecost

SUMMARY OF TOMORROW'S MEDITATION

e will meditate tomorrow upon a twentieth reason for being very humble, which is that self-love is: first, a never-ceasing danger; second, often a more serious danger than we suspect it to be. We will then make the resolution: first, never to seek after praise and esteem; second, never to make any endeavor to hide what is humiliating to us. Our spiritual nosegay shall be the counsel of the Holy Spirit: "Humble thy heart." (Ecclus. 2:2)

MEDITATION FOR THE MORNING

Let us adore the Holy Ghost giving us this counsel: Humble your heart and serve God in all humility and patience. (Ecclus. 2:2,4) He could not give us more useful advice, for self-love every moment exposes us to danger, often of a more serious kind of danger than we dream of. Let us thank the Holy Spirit for a counsel so precious.

FIRST POINT

✝ *Self-love is a Never ceasing Danger*

Self-love is constantly at work around us, occupied in seducing us, as well in little matters as in great, in solitude as well as in the world, in private as well as in public. Always and everywhere it is at the door of our heart, with its arrow in its hand ready to pierce us. We labor with our minds or with our hands; it is there to tell us that we are doing well, and to congratulate us; to persuade us that we do better than others; that we are more clever, more intelligent; or if we do not succeed, to fill us with vexation; to put us into a bad temper, and to make us dream of something or other in which we believe we are superior to our rivals. If, instead of working, we do nothing, self-love is still there, making our imagination wander back to the past to praise us for what we have done; to the future, to dream about what we will do, what we shall become, and to compliment us upon it; upon persons of our acquaintance, to penetrate into their hearts that we may see what they think of us; or to assist at conversations where we suspect that they are speaking of us. If we converse it invites us to prove that we are intelligent, to speak of ourselves and of what we are doing, to hide what humbles us, only to let the good side of us be seen, to put in relief whatever lowers others, even if we should be obliged to lie in order the better to succeed. Hence the taste for a spirit of raillery and criticism, because it makes us enjoy the superiority which a person who turns another into ridicule seems to have over the one who is ridiculed, his wit if the arrow be shot with delicacy in a diplomatic manner, and, lastly, the fault which is criticized, and from which we imagine ourselves to be free. If we give up ourselves to the practice of good works and of virtues, self-love is still there to compliment us, to intimate that we are worth more, that we have more merit, that we do more good than many others. Lastly, if we are endeavoring to acquire sincere humility, it is still there to assure us that we are really very humble, that we know ourselves; it even feeds itself on our belief that we are contemptible. What can we do with so determined an enemy, of whom it has been said that it is the first thing which lives in us and the last which dies? We must remember that no one has more self-love than he who imagines he has none; we must mistrust ourselves and our heart ceaselessly; we must often cry out to God, "Lord have pity on me, for I am proud."

SECOND POINT

✝ *Self-love is a more Serious Danger than we Imagine it to be*

Be afraid of self-love, says St. Bernard; it is an arrow which pierces but slightly the mind and the heart, but it does not make a slight wound; it inflicts death upon him who is not on his guard (St. Bernard, on Ps. 40). We easily forgive ourselves the vain complaisance of self-love in regard to ourselves, and we neglect it as a matter of no consequence in regard to our salvation. Such feelings as these are so sweet! We smile at them and we love them. Doubtless a fugitive thought of self-love is not a mortal sin; but to allow self-love to take to itself the merit of our works, is that nothing? To occasion the subtraction of graces which put to profit would have been the means of procuring for us many others, and without which perhaps we should not be saved, as it happened to St. Teresa when God showed her the place she would have occupied in hell if she had not rejected a movement of self-love is that nothing? But after having repressed this first feeling of self-love, a second will come, then a third, and thus our self-love will go on always growing, and heaping up in us a mass of pride which will in the end close to us the kingdom of heaven; moreover, the habit of being pleased with ourselves will prevent us from seeing what are the virtues we do not possess, the faults we have to correct, and we shall thus arrive at the hour of death without being prepared for it; lastly, self-love, when it is not suppressed, will lead us to the commission of all kinds of vices, to presumption, to ambition, to the vain pretensions suggested by susceptibility, to luxury and to the desire for riches, to a dissipated, worldly, effeminate, and sensual life; lastly, to our eternal ruin. Self-love doubtless tells us that we shall not fall into these excesses; but a blind man is never better seduced than when the precipice on the edge of which he is about to put his foot is hidden from him. Hermits, after eighty years of penitence, have been known to ruin themselves through self-love. It is written that "pride goeth before destruction, and the spirit is lifted up before a fall". (Prov. 16:18) Let us be afraid of making the sad experience of it. *Resolutions and spiritual nosegay as above.*

Thirteenth Thursday after Pentecost

SUMMARY OF TOMORROW'S MEDITATION

 e will meditate tomorrow upon a twenty-first reason for being very humble; it is: first, that self-love is a folly: second, that self-love makes us lose our senses in regard to our conduct. We will then make the resolution: first, to put away from us, at the very moment that we perceive it, all complaisance about ourselves and all desire to be esteemed; second, never to say anything which shall be to our own advantage, and cheerfully to accept all the humiliations we may meet with. Our spiritual nosegay shall be the words of Scripture: "Where humility is, there also is wisdom." (Prov. 11:2)

MEDITATION FOR THE MORNING

Let us adore Jesus Christ hiding Himself in the Eucharist with all His divine grandeurs, in order to teach us to have the good sense not to make ourselves slaves to the opinion of others, or worshippers of reputation, and to content ourselves with the esteem of God alone, who will not allow to pass without recompense anything we do for Him in secret. (Matt. 4:4,6,18) Let us render to Him our homage of admiration, of praise, and of love for so precious a lesson.

FIRST POINT

✝ *Self-love is a Folly*

Where is the man who does not sometimes surprise himself indulging real follies of self-love in his mind and his imagination? Where is the man who would not blush if all the world should know the chimerical projects, the ridiculous reveries, the absurd suppositions, which self-love puts into his head a true phantasmagoria which would make any one laugh who knew of it? Who, when rendering justice to himself, has not cried out: What a fool I am to indulge in such thoughts! Sad folly of humanity, indeed, which inspired St. Vincent de Paul to utter these humble words: "I am the most ridiculous and the most foolish of men." Have we not more reason than this holy priest had to apply these words to ourselves? Have we not indulged in the folly of believing ourselves to be capable of all kinds of positions, always wishing to raise ourselves higher and higher, without ever saying: It is enough; the folly of desiring to be preferred to every one else, looking upon ourselves as being more clever, more intelligent and able to do better than they; the folly of always clinging to our own ideas, without taking counsel of others who are wiser than we are; the folly of desiring to be esteemed by everyone, never being able to bear a want of consideration, a criticism, a reproof, and not yet being able to understand that it is not possible to please everyone, that society is so formed that everyone studies the weak side of his neighbor that he may cast against it the arrows of his satire; that even when there is nothing wrong to be reprehended, intentions are interpreted, reservations supposed, in such a manner that no one ever has been or ever will be safe from criticism? Do we not indulge in the folly of preoccupying ourselves to excess with human judgment, with the opinion of our fellows, that miserable quality in which there is nothing constant save its inconstancy, nothing established except its caprice, which so often exalts the contemptible man and depreciates him who is the most honorable? Do we not aim at reputation, which is a thing so idle, which serves here below only to fill us with pride if it is our portion, to trouble us and render us unhappy if it be against us, and which will be of no service to us in the future life unless the esteem of God accompany it? For what will it serve us to have been praised upon earth if we are tormented there where we shall be? (St. Augustine.) Do we not, lastly, indulge in the folly of begging right and left for the esteem of men, even that of persons for whom we have not the least respect, to feed upon and delightedly enjoy the smallest mark of consideration we receive from them, a word, a procedure, a look, a nothing, provided we can conclude from them that we are thought well of, and that when opportunity arises such persons will speak of us to our advantage? Peter de Blois justly compares those men who are ambitious of reputation, who spend the whole of their existence in the pursuit of a thing so vain, to the spider, which exhausts and spends itself to catch nothing more than a fly in its web. Let us be confounded in the presence of God at these follies of self-love, the principle of the insanity of unfortunate beings who have lost their reason, and who, nearly all of them, imagine themselves to be kings or great nobles; and let us feel that it is supreme wisdom to content ourselves with the esteem of God alone: the only solid esteem, the only esteem which is of use in regard both to time and eternity, the only esteem we are sure of having when we will.

SECOND POINT

✝ *Self-love often Robs us of Good Sense in our Conduct*

The man whom self-love dominates says to himself as the men of Babel did: "Let us make our name famous." (Gen. 11:4) At these words he loses his senses, he casts himself blindly into rash enterprises, without mistrusting his own intelligence, without taking counsel; he comes in contact with obstacles and they bruise him. Even when he feels he has deceived himself, he will not allow it, and making it a false point of honor not to go back, he goes deeper into the bad undertaking in which he is engaged, without any fear of compromising his fortune and that of the simple souls who had trusted in him, and his honor, and sometimes even the honor of religion, so true are the maxims of the Holy Ghost: "Where pride is, there also shall be reproach." (Prov. 11:2) "Hast thou seen a man wise in conceit? There shall be more hope of a fool than of him." (Ibid. 26:12) and those other words: "Where humility is, there also is wisdom."

(Ibid, 11: 2) It is the same thing as saying that humility is the counselor of good sense, that the humble man is full of good sense, that he reflects before acting, that he mistrusts himself; he takes counsel, he does not undertake more than he can do, he keeps from adventurous enterprises and has nothing to do with what he is not sure of. Let us examine if it be thus that we act. *Resolutions and spiritual nosegay as above.*

Thirteenth Friday after Pentecost

SUMMARY OF TOMORROW'S MEDITATION

 fter meditating upon so many reasons for being very humble, we will now meditate on the means of becoming so, and we will consider: first, that the first means is to have it strongly at heart to acquire humility; second, that it is a labor of the whole of our life. Our resolution shall be: first, often to ask God for this virtue as being the most necessary thing in the world; second, cheerfully to accept all opportunities of humbling our selves. Our spiritual nosegay shall be the words of the Holy Ghost: "Humble thy spirit very much." (Ecclus. 7:19)

MEDITATION FOR THE MORNING

Let us adore God, finding in humility such great attractions, such powerful charms, that He delights to look upon the humble; (Ps. 12:6; 137:6) and that having to choose a mother. He gives the preference to her whom considers to be the most humble, (Luke 1:18) to which St. Bernard adds: "Mary, by her humility, conceived the Word of God incarnate." O Lord, couldst Thou better teach me to understand how this virtue ought to be dear to me above all others, and how greatly and constantly I ought to have it at heart to acquire it?

FIRST POINT

✝ *We ought to have it Greatly at Heart to become Humble*

To become humble is a difficult enterprise, which often requires more strength of soul and more true courage than are necessary to expose our life upon a battlefield. All that wounds our self-love touches us so to the quick, that it is only great energy of character and of will that can triumph over it. To become humble is an affair of supreme importance of which we must think far more highly than of fortune or of health, than of reputation and of all earthly possessions, since eternity depends upon it. We must therefore take greatly to heart holy humility, desire it ardently even as we desire what we most esteem, earnestly ask it of God, and often meditate upon the inestimable value of it. We must read by preference books which speak of it, and delight in everything that leads us to and confirms us in it; for example, simplicity in our clothing and in everything of which we make use, modesty in our manners and language, charity, which, far from blushing at it, takes pleasure in the society of the poor and the insignificant; which, far from imagining itself to be lowered by rendering to its neighbor the most humble services, is glad to seize upon all opportunities of doing so. Lastly, we must imitate the man of business, who has it greatly at heart to make a fortune, and who consequently pursues his aim night and day, looks out narrowly for everything that may lead to it, and never loses an opportunity of enriching himself; every evening he goes over his accounts, balances his losses and his gains, and takes precautions either not to incur the same losses the next day or to add fresh profits to preceding ones. Thus ought we to act in regard to humility, which is the great fortune to be amassed by the Christian, his riches and his treasure; every day we must take for our text the acquisition of this virtue, refer to it all our spiritual exercises, meditations, communions, visits to the Blessed Sacrament, and every evening we must examine our conscience on this subject, that we may see at what point we have arrived, what is our progress, and what have been our falls. Is this our practice?

SECOND POINT

✝ *The Acquisition of Humility is a Labor of the Whole of our Life*

Humility being, on the one hand, the most essential of virtues in regard to salvation, and, on the other, the one which we are most in danger of losing (since self-love, which seeks to deprive us of it, is a danger which meets us at every moment, which follows us into retreat as well as into exterior relations, which mingles with our thoughts and imaginations, as well as with our words and our actions), it becomes evident that a constant uninterrupted vigilance is necessary with respect to it. If we neglect ourselves one single day, immediately self-love will either come and whisper to us about our merits, our talents, our virtues, and that in language which will sound so sweetly in our hearts that we shall allow ourselves to be seduced, or else men, seconding therein the perfidious intentions of self-love, will come and applaud us, often even against their own conscience and from pure flattery, and we shall be simple enough to accept their false praise as being so many truths, and we shall take pleasure in it, without thinking of the judgment of God, the only equitable judge of persons and of things. The labor is therefore one which endures throughout our whole life. If even we had applied ourselves during sixty or eighty years to acquire humility, we should have to go on applying ourselves to it still as we did the very first day, in order to persevere until our last sigh and die in humility. One moment of pride before death would be enough to damn us eternally, and no one can answer for himself in regard to so delicate a point. There is therefore no other means of salvation but to take constantly to heart, and with great firmness and constancy, to become humble. Let us beg of God to penetrate us with this truth! *Resolutions and spiritual nosegay as above.*

Thirteenth Saturday after Pentecost

SUMMARY OF TOMORROW'S MEDITATION

e will meditate tomorrow upon another means for becoming humble, which is: first, to exercise ourselves in the practice of humility; second, to apply this practice to all the details of life. We will then make the resolution: first, to be very humble in all our prayers; second, to maintain in all our relations with our neighbors manners and a language conformable with humility. Our spiritual nosegay shall be the words of the sage: "Pride is hateful before God and men." (Ecclus. 10:7)

MEDITATION FOR THE MORNING

Let us adore Jesus Christ in His crib; humiliated in His infancy; humiliated in His mature age; humiliated in His death; humiliated in the Eucharist. Let us render to Him our homage of adoration, of praise, and of love in these different states, and let us beg of Him to communicate to us the grace of them.

FIRST POINT

✝ *Humiliation, or the Practice of Humility, is the Best Means of Rendering us Humble*

There is an essential difference between humiliation and humility. Humiliation is an external fact which does not depend upon ourselves, and to which we are often subjected without desiring it. Humility is an internal fact, a disposition of the soul, which, believing itself to be contemptible, accepts humiliation as being a thing which it deserves; it is what we may call humility in practice, and what we believe to be the best means for becoming humble. In point of fact, neither the arts nor the sciences are learnt except by practice; the man who limited himself to understand the theory of medicine, of architecture, or of painting without proceeding to the practice of them would never become either a good doctor, or a good architect, or a good painter. With still stronger reason, he who does not exercise himself by means of humiliation in the practice of humility will never be humble. There is in humiliation something which makes nature afraid, and this fear, like all other kinds of fear, is only cured by affronting that which causes affright, and by proving in this way to ourselves that there was no reason to have been so troubled. At the beginning we hesitate; by degrees as we advance we become bolder; and we end not only by overcoming, but by loving humiliation, like St. John of the Cross, who desired no other recompense for all his apostolic labors except the contempt of man: "Lord Jesus, to be despised for Thy sake, that is the sole recompense I desire for all that I have done for Thee" he said to Our Lord, who had appeared to him. It is because humiliation is the direct path which leads to humility, (St. Bernard, Ep. 87) in the same way as patience leads to peace, study to knowledge. Whoever desires to be really humble ought to walk in the way of humiliation. In the same manner as an exterior act of pride produces or develops the interior sentiment, so an exterior act of humility, or, what is the same thing, a humiliation well received, increases in us the spirit of humility, because practice acts more strongly upon the will than thought or desire, because an object which is present touches us more than an object which is absent, and because experience teaches better than theory. Therefore Jesus Christ was not content with merely precepts of humility and with having a deep feeling of it in His heart; the whole of His life was a series of humiliations. And why, following His example, should we not accept them? There is nothing bad in contempt except what there is in our refusing to suffer it. Nothing is so contemptible as the horror we feel of contempt. A true humility accepts willingly a great or a small humiliation. He who cannot suffer the slightest mark of contempt has not the slightest humility, and we shall never make progress in virtue excepting in so far as we shall be content to be abject and counted as nothing in the opinion of others. Let us measure the degree of our virtue by this principle.

SECOND POINT

✝ *In what the Practice of Humility Consists*

Humility may be practiced: first, in our relations with God, by behaving in His presence like a poor man who has nothing; like a sick man who is ashamed of his infirmities; like a worm, crawling in the dust at the foot of His throne, saying to Him with a feeling of deep abasement, O Lord, I am nothing and Thou art all; I can do nothing and Thou canst do everything; I am filled with horror and shame of myself, so profound is my wretchedness, whilst Thou dost ravish heaven with Thine infinite amiability! Oh, how agreeable to God is a soul which is in this state, and how many graces does it not attract towards itself! Second, we can practice humility in our relations with our neighbor, always taking for ourselves the least share and the lowest place, treating every one with great consideration and respect, willingly seeing all held in greater esteem than ourselves, and rejoicing to be looked upon as possessing neither wisdom nor knowledge; so that we may, at the expense of our own self-love, honor the humiliations of the Incarnate Word, receiving with a good grace advice, reproaches, even contempt, without trying to justify ourselves; never speaking of ourselves; suffering contradiction meekly and without impatience; loving to occupy ourselves with the lowly and the simple, and preferring their society to that of the great and the rich. It is by such behavior as this that the saints established and perfected themselves in humility, and it is in following their example that we shall succeed in doing so ourselves. Third. Humility may be practiced in ourselves, by cheerfully suffering such of our natural defects as humiliate us; by often keeping present to ourselves of how little worth we are, how little intelligence and judgment we possess, how insignificant is our virtue compared with that of the saints; and by turning away promptly from anything that self-love attempts to say to us about our merits and our graces; lastly, and above all, by counting as nothing the opinion of men, and placing ourselves in our own opinion below everyone else, below even the greatest sinners and infidels, who, if they had received as many graces as we have, would perhaps have been much better than we are; below even the devils, who committed only one single sin of pride, whilst we have committed so many. Let us here examine our conscience. Are these practices of humility familiar to us? *Resolutions and spiritual nosegay as above.*

Fourteenth Sunday after Pentecost

THE GOSPEL ACCORDING TO ST. MATTHEW, 6:24-33.

"At that time Jesus said to His disciples: No man can serve two masters; for either he will hate the one and love the other, or he will sustain the one and despise the other. You cannot serve God and Mammon. Therefore I say to you, be not solicitous for your life, what you shall eat, nor for your body, what you shall put on. Is not the life more than the meat, and the body more than the raiment? Behold the birds of the air; for they neither sow, nor do they reap, nor gather into barns, and your heavenly Father feedeth them. Are not you of much more value than they? And which of you, by taking thought, can add to his stature one cubit? And for raiment, why are you solicitous? Consider the lilies of the field how they grow; they labor not, neither do they spin, but I say to you, that not even Solomon in all his glory was arrayed as one of these. And if the grass of the field, which is today, and tomorrow is cast into the oven, God doth so clothe: how much more you, O ye of little faith! Be not solicitous, therefore, saying, What shall we eat, or what shall we drink, or wherewith shall we be clothed? For after all these things do the heathens seek. For your Father knoweth that you have need of all these things. Seek ye, therefore, first the kingdom of God and His justice; and all these things shall be added unto you."

SUMMARY OF TOMORROW'S MEDITATION

e will consecrate our meditation tomorrow to the sentence which occurs in the gospel of the day: "Seek ye, therefore, first the kingdom of God and His justice;" that is to say, let your salvation be your principal affair. And to excite ourselves rightly to fulfill the command of Our Savior, we shall consider: First, the supreme importance of salvation; Second, the means whereby we may save ourselves. We will thence deduce the resolution: First, always to keep our conscience in order, and never to remain twenty-four hours in a state which would compromise our salvation; Second, to refer the employment of every moment to our salvation, proposing to ourselves as an end to please God in all things. Our spiritual nosegay shall be the words of the gospel: "Seek ye, therefore, first the kingdom of God and His justice." (Matt. 6:33)

MEDITATION FOR THE MORNING

Let us adore Jesus Christ teaching us in the gospel not to allow ourselves to be so taken up with the affairs of this world as to neglect our salvation. Let your first solicitude, He says to us, be your salvation, and holiness, which is the sole means of obtaining it. Let us thank Him for such useful and necessary advice.

FIRST POINT

✝ *The Supreme Importance of Salvation*
In order to fill ourselves with a lively faith in this truth, let us first question the saints the men who studied the best during their lives, and who have learnt it by experience since their death. As long as they lived upon earth they believed that they never could do enough in regard to so serious a matter, and they were always afraid of never doing enough; the whole of their life was continually occupied in pursuing it day and night, and in constantly advancing this great

affair. Abraham forsakes his country, his possessions, his family; Moses prefers the sufferings and the poverty of the people of God to all the pleasures and all the treasures of Egypt. Under the Old and the New Law hermits bury themselves in deserts, hide themselves in caverns, become extenuated by fastings and watchings; martyrs allow themselves to be devoured by flames, torn by wild beasts, deluged in blood; multitudes of others lead a life of purity, of prayer, and devotion in the midst of the world; and now that they are in heaven, far from believing that they have done too much, if they could feel any regret it would be not to have done a thousand times more for an affair in which success gives so much happiness, and in which an unhappy issue is so terrible. And I, my God! What have I done for my salvation in comparison with Thy saints? Are there in heaven saints who have been saved by living as I live, by praying as I pray, without mortifying themselves any more, without being more humble, more recollected, more generous in serving Thee? Let us consult the lost themselves on this question. Upon earth salvation was the least of their cares, but now, oh, how differently they think! How bitterly they regret and will regret always to have esteemed anything more than they did salvation! Let us ask these unhappy ones, in the midst of the flames which devour them, whether the sacrifices demanded by salvation are excessive, compared with hell; let us ask them what they would do if God were to put again in their hands the great affair so unhappily conducted the first time. With what ardor they would labor at it! How they would tread all obstacles under foot! How well they would pray! How holily they would live! If, after having consulted those who know by experience the importance of salvation, we consult God, He will reply that it is for our salvation He created everything; the universe, with its laws and its miracles, and the mysteries of the crib, of Calvary, of the altar, of the Church, and the sacraments; and that the greatness of the means reveals the supreme importance of the end. If afterwards we consult ourselves, our reason will tell us that salvation ought to be the great business with which we ought to be occupied at every moment, because, of all kinds of matters, it is the only personal one, the only necessary, the only urgent one. Let us meditate upon these three things. It is the sole personal affair. It is a matter which concerns me more than my fortune, my honor, my life; it has to do with my destiny during eternity, and this destiny depends so much upon myself that God, all powerful though He be, cannot save me without my co-operation. His the sole thing necessary. I can do without all the rest, but to do without heaven and to have hell in exchange is not possible. If I had to cut off my arm, tear out my eye, allow the whole world to perish, I would prefer all that, rather than lose my soul. Lastly, it is the sole thing that is urgent. No one can answer for tomorrow; the more we put it off, the more difficult it is to break off habits, and the more diminished do graces become. I ought never to live for twenty-four hours in a state in which I should not desire to die. Is it thus that we understand salvation?

SECOND POINT
✝ *The Means of Acquiring Salvation*
The first means is to say to myself before each action that I am going to perform, each decision that I am about to make, of what use is it in regard to my salvation? Is it a thing which will be in opposition to the interests of my salvation, or only dangerous, or even only useless in regard to my salvation? If it be so, I ought to interdict it to myself; my salvation is my all; I ought not to amuse myself with anything which does not tend towards it, still less stop at what may expose it to risk, less still to what may compromise it. On the other hand, is it what will be advantageous for my salvation? Then I ought lovingly to embrace it, without examining whether it is a matter of precept or of counsel. The man of business always aims at the greatest gains, at the most efficacious and surest means of enriching himself. Why should I do less in regard to my salvation? The second means is to begin from this very day ardently to pursue this great affair, and in order the better to succeed, to embrace everything which I know to be most perfect. There is no room here to say, later on, when I am free from such or such a care, I will live in a better manner; the affair of salvation is a very urgent affair, which is compromised by any kind of delay. There is no saying, I am not obliged to aim at perfection. To aim at perfection is a strict precept, and heaven is made only for the perfect, or the saints. (Matt. 5:48) The third means is to detach our hearts from everything that will not be of any use in regard to our salvation. Since salvation is all in all for us, why should we tie ourselves to anything else? Any attachment we may have which will be a tie, which will bind us and expose us to risk our salvation? Let us here examine our conscience; are we faithful to these three means of salvation? *Resolutions and spiritual nosegay as above.*

SUMMARY OF TOMORROW'S MEDITATION

esuming our meditations upon humility, we will meditate tomorrow upon a new means for becoming humble, which St. Paul teaches us when he says: "You are dead, and your life is hid with Christ in God," (Coloss. 3:3) and we shall see that this hidden life: first, cuts down the root of the greater number of temptations against humility; second, renders humility easier. Our resolution shall be: first, never to say or do anything with a view to the esteem of creatures; second, to love modest and quiet positions, which will leave us less in sight and will make us to be less spoken of. Our spiritual nosegay shall be the words of the Apostle to the faithful of his day: "You are dead, and your life is hid with Christ in God" (Ibid.).

MEDITATION FOR THE MORNING

Let us pour forth our hearts in admiration, love, and praise of the hidden life of Jesus Christ. The God of glory hides Himself under the veil of mortal nature; He hides Himself in the womb of a virgin, and His virginal conception itself remains hidden beneath the veil of marriage. When He appears upon the earth, the whole universe ignores Him; He grows up, and allows His divine knowledge to be ignored by all the people, until they say of Him: Where did He learn what He knows, seeing that He has never studied? During thirty years He is hidden in the dwelling at Nazareth; during the three years of His mission He allows it to be said of Him: He is a deceiver, a lover of good cheer, a Samaritan; that is to say, a heretic, an impious man, possessed by the devil; and at the time of His passion He allows it to be said of Him: He is the least of men, a worm, a thief, an assassin; Barabbas is preferable to Him. Let us render our homage to Jesus Christ thus hidden to teach us to love a hidden life, as an element of Christian humility.

FIRST POINT

✝ *A Hidden Life in God with Jesus Christ Strikes at the Root of the Majority of Temptations against Humility*

The first temptation against humility is to esteem ourselves and to desire to be esteemed. It is difficult not to yield to this temptation when we feel ourselves to be honored, esteemed, and praised by everyone. The odor of the incense burned in our honor turns our head, intoxicates us, and we finish by becoming proud beings. The hidden life, on the contrary, keeps away from us the honors, praises, and applauses which possess so great a power of seduction, and of which St. Francis de Sales said: "I cannot think of them without trembling; I have not a soul strong enough to resist them." It leaves man in the presence of God and of himself: in presence of God, who sees what we really are; and when beneath the eyes of such a judge, we are not tempted to esteem ourselves or to desire to be esteemed; and when in presence of ourselves, alone with our conscience, we see ourselves such as we are, we feel the falsity of all human opinions, we easily recognize that we are worth nothing and that we are not worthy of any esteem. The second temptation lies in what the world says to us, urging us to come out of our obscurity and to place ourselves in evidence: You are not made, it tells us, for this obscurity in which your life passes in so sad a manner, for this nullity to which you are reduced; you were born for something quite different, for a position equal, at any rate, to the one held by this person or that, who is certainly not worth more than you are. Why, then, bury yourself alive and conceal yourself? Be silent, deceiving world, he answers who has learnt to enjoy a hidden life; be silent; if I were to listen to you, you would make of me a man who indulges in pride here below and who would be lost here-after. Oh, how much more I delight to hide myself here below that I may appear one day in glory! In my modest life you cannot seduce me either by your words or your example. There I enjoy God alone, with His infinite amiabilities. (Ps. 30:21) I will speak to Him and He will listen to me, a holy intercourse which will be for me as a beginning of Paradise. (Job 31:27) A third temptation lies in the speeches made to us by the devil. It is all very well for you to speak as you do, the enemy of our salvation objects in his turn, but all the same it is a good thing to force men to esteem and praise you, to occupy a position in which you will be looked up to, to exhibit in it all the riches of your nature and of your mind, to conquer envy or to condemn it to silence. It is still better, answers the man who leads a hidden life, to live ignored in God with Jesus Christ. It is much more safe, for if I sought to please men I should no longer be a Christian; (Gal. 1:10) it is much more agreeable, for I am much more tranquil and quiet in it; it is much more noble, for I am able to raise myself therein above public opinion instead of being the slave of it; it is much more honorable in regard to God, for it is saying to Him that He only suffices us.

SECOND POINT

✝ *A Hidden Life in God with Jesus Christ Renders Humility Easy*

When we are hidden in God we only count that as real and worthy of attention which God knows of us and thinks of us: God, who not only sees what is exterior in actions, but who penetrates to the bottom of the heart; and by these means the soul is able to free itself fully from human opinion. As we are hidden with God in Jesus Christ, the soul remains in the society of His holy example, of His adorable maxims, of His humble heart; and in such society as this, in presence of the King of the humble, the friend of the humble, who could be otherwise than humble? A day will come, the soul which understands this mystery says to itself, in which Jesus will appear in His glory, and then I shall appear with Him. But until then I ought to remain hidden with Him, as He was in His crib, as He was in His tomb. Therefore, no more praise, no more glory for me here below. I do not desire it. I desire to appear only with Him when He shall appear in glory; and meanwhile I will live hidden in God, in the bosom of eternal light. I will see it, I will admire it, I will delight in it, and enchanted with so beautiful and sweet a spectacle, I will no longer have any eyes for the vanities, the false honor and glory of the world. *Resolutions and spiritual nosegay as above.*

Fourteenth Tuesday after Pentecost

SUMMARY OF TOMORROW'S MEDITATION

e will meditate tomorrow upon a last means for becoming very humble; it is a life of trial; and we shall see: first, how useful this life is for making us humble; second, how useful in its turn is humility to enable us to bear in a Christian manner the trials of life. We will then make the resolution: First, to receive all crosses and all trials as warnings that God gives us to humble ourselves beneath His hand; Second, to receive them consequently with perfect resignation. Our spiritual nosegay shall be the words of St. Peter: "Be you humbled, therefore, beneath the mighty hand of God." (I. Pet. 5:6)

MEDITATION FOR THE MORNING

Let us adore Jesus Christ in His holy passion, admirable in His humility and His patience. The state of suffering to which He is reduced, His face covered with blood and spittle, His head crowned with thorns, His body torn, His feet and His hands pierced, the mockery of all the people. His death between two thieves as being the most guilty of the three, cover Him with confusion; on the other hand, the humble sentiments which He has of Himself, laden as He is with all the sins of the world, like the scapegoat destined to, die for the whole people, make Him feel these severe trials to be light; and render His patience invincible. It is thus that in Him patience and humility seem to give one another the hand and to sustain each other. Let us thank Him for this great example and ask of Him grace to imitate it.

FIRST POINT

✝ *How Useful a Life of Trial is to Make us Learn Humility*

The life of man, says the Holy Ghost, is a life of constant trial; for the same reason it is a life of constant humility. There are trials of suffering and of infirmities; therein is a lesson of humility, teaching us that we are always in a state of continual dependence upon God, who is the supreme Master of health and sickness, and that when we are well we ought not to be proud, as though health were our own doing; and because, in addition, having sinned, we deserve always to suffer as a penance for our faults. There are trials arising from want of success in our enterprises; therein is a lesson of humility, which tells us that we have not much intelligence, ability, or prudence; that we ought to be modest and not prefer ourselves to others. There are trials arising from reverses of fortune which oblige us to descend from the position we had occupied; therein is a lesson of humility which preserves us from the pride engendered by higher positions. Prosperity swells the heart and leads to contempt of our inferiors; reverses bring us down, destroy our pretensions, and dispose us to entertain humble sentiments in regard to ourselves. There are trials arising from humiliations; others speak or think ill of us, and do not render us the justice which is our due. We are treated without consideration, and are despised; therein is a lesson of humility, which recalls to us that, being nothingness and sin, we deserve nothing but contempt; that we are always treated too well, and that present humiliations are a grace for which we can never be thankful enough towards God, since it is the only path by which we can arrive at the attainment of humility. (St. Bernard) There are trials arising from temptations, which incline us to evil and against which we must constantly maintain a painful combat; therein is a lesson of humility which recalls to us that our nature is evil and cannot of itself produce anything but sin; (Council of Orange) that we ought to mistrust ourselves, avoid occasions which expose us to sin, keep ourselves continually abased in the sentiment of our profound wretchedness. (Nahum 3:14) Finally, we should never finish if we at tempted to describe all the trials of this present life; but all of them have one characteristic in common, which consists in the fact that, by making us feel our misery and our weakness, they lead us to have recourse to God, as to our sole source of strength, our sole support, (Ps. 119:1) and to imitate the dove of the deluge, which, not finding any resting place upon the earth, returned to take refuge in the ark. God is the true ark wherein the afflicted heart finds its consolation, the weak heart its strength, the tempted heart its defense. Let us examine whether we have made use of our trials to become more humble, more detached from ourselves, and more united to God.

SECOND POINT
✟ *How Useful Humility is to Enable us to Bear all Kinds of Trials in a Christian Manner*

A proud man can bear nothing; he is angry with and revolts against the cross; he will not understand that he deserves to suffer and that he needs to do so; and God, who holds pride in horror, leaves him a prey to his impatience and his bad temper. A man who is humble accepts, on the contrary, the cross with a good grace; he feels that, being a sinner, it is only right that he should suffer, and that he ought to accomplish in his own flesh what is wanting in the sufferings of Jesus Christ, and to unite the members with their head in the participation of trials, even as they will be united in the participation of glory; that, lastly, whatever he may suffer, he deserves to suffer still more. On His side, God, touched by this humble frame of mind, assists him, supports him, protects him under the weight of the cross, and renders it sweet and even delightful to him. (2 Imit. 2:2) Sometimes trials come to us from our neighbor, and then humility quickly sets right the differences which have arisen; its charms soften the most bitter of hearts, and appease those which are the most irritated. If, on the contrary, the trial comes from ourselves, humility again quickly sets it right. It teaches us to be ashamed in the presence of God, to cast ourselves into His arms as into the arms of a father, to pray to Him, to love Him, to declare to Him that it is He alone we will love, that we will to love Him with our whole heart and always; and immediately the soul is calmed, serenity and peace reappear, and, thanks to humility, the trial turns to our greater good. Oh, how well then it is to be humble! *Resolutions and spiritual nosegay as above.*

Fourteenth Wednesday after Pentecost

SUMMARY OF TOMORROW'S MEDITATION

 e will meditate tomorrow upon the state which is the most opposed to humility, which is pride, and we shall see; First, what pride is. Second, how we render ourselves guilty of it. We will thence deduce the resolution: first, carefully to watch over our interior in order to keep ourselves on our guard against the inspirations of pride, of self-esteem, and of the desire to be esteemed; second, to hold pride in horror, and every day to endeavor to correct ourselves of it. Our spiritual nosegay shall be the advice of Tobias to his son: "Never suffer pride to reign in thy mind or in thy words; for from it all perdition took its beginning." (Tob. 4:14)

MEDITATION FOR THE MORNING

Let us adore God severely chastising pride in the person of Lucifer and of the bad angels. Hardly had these rebels conceived the first thought of raising themselves above what God had made them, than God casts them down from highest heaven into the lowest depths of hell, and makes them pass in one moment from extreme happiness to extreme misery. Thus is punished one single proud thought. O God, who would not tremble in presence of so terrible a chastisement? (St. Bernard, Serm. liv. in Cant.)

FIRST POINT

✝ *What Pride is*

Pride is an inordinate esteem of our own excellence which is always aspiring to raise itself higher and higher. It is a subtle poison which insinuates itself insensibly into the soul, and corrupts, if it does not destroy, the most sublime virtues. It is a mental malady which makes us lose our mental balance, and leads to insanity, there being no greater madmen than the proud, who feed upon wind and smoke, and lose eternal glory for the glory of a moment. It is a poisoned fountain whence flow forth all kinds of sin, (Ecclus. 11:15) and this evil is more common than we think; for it is pride which, after having been the ruin of the bad angels, is still the cause of every day casting so great a number of men into perdition. It is an execrable evil which tends to nothing less than to dethrone God in the soul by stealing His glory from Him, an evil which the Holy Spirit for this reason strikes with the anathemas of heaven and earth. (Ibid. 10:7) Therefore God takes pleasure in confounding the proud, first in this world, by permitting them to fall into shameful sins; then in the next world, by casting them into the lowest depths of hell, there to be eternally insulted by the devils. Are these the sentiments we entertain in regard to pride? And do we thoroughly understand the horror with which it ought to inspire us?

SECOND POINT

✝ *In what Manner we Render ourselves Guilty of Pride*

We render ourselves guilty of pride in many ways: first, by attaching ourselves to our own ideas and our own will; we prefer our own way of looking at things to that which is held by others, and we are determined to cling to it.

We are independent, we will follow only our own will, and if we are obliged to obey, we are annoyed at having to do so, we murmur, and we do it badly; second, through presumption; we think ourselves to be capable of everything, we have no doubts about it; we cast ourselves rashly in to the most difficult enterprises, and yet at the same time we are pusillanimous and are stopped by the slightest obstacles. Third, by complaisance in ourselves; we are proud of the smallest advantages which we imagine ourselves to possess; we prefer ourselves to others, and in order to give a reason for this preference, we keep our attention fixed solely on their defects, we make but little account of them, we criticize and ridicule them, we find something to blame in all that they do, we approve only what we do ourselves, and we expect that no one should blame us for any of these things. Fourth, by boasting; we speak of ourselves at every opportunity, we praise ourselves on every occasion, we endeavor to make ourselves looked upon as something; we aspire to honors, to dignities, to exalted positions; we believe that we deserve them and do all we can to obtain them. Fifth, by self-sufficiency; we will not take advice from any one; we imagine that we are sufficient to ourselves. Sixth, by hypocrisy; we make an outward show of possessing more piety and virtue more talent and capacity, than we really possess. Let us examine our conscience; are there not in us some of these characteristics of pride? *Resolutions and spiritual nosegay as above.*

Fourteenth Thursday after Pentecost

SUMMARY OF TOMORROW'S MEDITATION

e will meditate tomorrow upon another inordinate vice which is the opposite of humility, which is vanity, and we shall see: first, what vanity is; second, how we render ourselves guilty of it. We will thence deduce the resolution: first, never to speak of ourselves or, to propose to ourselves God alone, His good pleasure, or His glory as the end of all our actions, thoughts, or words. Our spiritual nosegay shall be the words of St. Timothy: "To the only God be honor and glory." (1 Tim. 1:17)

MEDITATION FOR THE MORNING

Let us adore Our Lord reproving the scribes and Pharisees for doing all their actions in order to be seen of men and to be more esteemed. (Matt, 23:5) He strongly counsels the people and His disciples not to imitate them if they desire that their best actions should not be in this world or in the next without recompense. (Ibid. 6:1) Let us admire the aversion He shows towards vainglory, and give Him thanks for testifying to us that He desires us to avoid it.

FIRST POINT

✝ *What Vanity is*

Vanity is not, like pride, an inordinate idea of our own excellence; it is an inordinate desire for honor and praise, even when we know that we do not deserve either. It is a kind of vice which is so great, that in order to procure the object of our desires, we lie to our own conscience. We wish to obtain elevated and brilliant positions, of which we feel ourselves to be perfectly unworthy, and we have recourse to all kinds of means which may enable us to occupy them, to become noticed, praised, and applauded. In order to carry out our desires, we descend to the lowest species of baseness, we turn everything into vanity: vanity in regard to our clothes, which we desire should be rich, splendid, and well made; vanity in the very smallest details respecting our dress, to the extent of making a serious affair of it, and sacrificing to it a great deal of time and a great deal of money, even becoming irritated and imbued with discontent, if fashion, taste, and caprice are not fully satisfied; vanity in regard to furniture, which we desire should be handsome; vanity respecting the table, which we wish should be richly served; vanity in our language, which we endeavor to render clever and to distinguish ourselves by being original in what we say; vanity with regard to our talents: instead of making use of them with a view to the glory of God, we make use of them with a view to our own glorification; (John 12:43) vanity in our conduct and deportment, which reveal affectation and a desire to attract notice; vanity in regard to society: we like to frequent the great and the rich; we blush at having relations with the insignificant and the poor: vanity with respect to our virtue: we are more desirous to induce people to think us virtuous than really to become so; we are assiduous in going to church, but we do not pray when we are there; we frequent the sacraments, but without being changed; there is vanity even in out humility: we say that we are miserable and sinners, that we do not know how to conduct ourselves, that we have no intelligence, no talents, but we should be very angry to be taken at our word; we only desire to insinuate that we are very humble, in the hope that we shall not be taken for what we say that we are; and at the bottom, however false may be the praises which are addressed to us, we are delighted to listen to them, caring less for what we are really and in the presence of God than for what we are in appearance and in the opinion of the world. Alas! Is not this our history? Let us thoroughly sound our heart

SECOND POINT

✝ *How we Render ourselves Guilty of Vanity*

We render ourselves guilty of vanity: first, by all that we have just said; second, by addressing praises to our own selves; we speak of ourselves and of all that we foresee will be to our advantage; we publish the graces bestowed upon us, and also our good works, often in an exaggerated manner and at the expense of truth; third, by speaking of our condition, of our birth, of our fortune, of our employments, and we are careful in revealing the least circumstance which may be the means of our obtaining- esteem; fourth, by praising others in order to oblige them to pay us in return by some tribute of praise; fifth, by bringing the conversation upon public undertakings in which we fancy we have succeeded, and about which no one says a word to us; we make use of stratagems and cleverness to enable ourselves to snatch at praises; we beg our hearers to say wherein we have failed; we say that we are not satisfied with what we have done, and we blame ourselves for not having done better, in order that we may force others to speak advantageously of us; sixth, by ourselves confessing our own faults, when we cannot hide them, for fear lest others should reproach us with them, and we exaggerate them, that others should at any rate say of us that we are very humble. What does our conscience say to us in respect to all these things? *Resolutions and spiritual nosegay as above.*

Fourteenth Friday after Pentecost

SUMMARY OF TOMORROW'S MEDITATION

e will meditate tomorrow upon a third vice which is the opposite of humility, which is ambition, and we shall see: first, how hateful this vice is; second, in how many ways we may render ourselves guilty of it. We will then make the resolution: first, to be content with the position in which Providence has placed us, without attempting to rise any higher; second, to resist the proposals and the urgent endeavors made to us in this sense, at any rate unless we have very clear proofs that what is proposed to us is in the order of God. Our spiritual nosegay shall be the words of St. James: "Do not seek for high places, knowing that you receive the greater judgment." (James 3:1)

MEDITATION FOR THE MORNING

Let us adore the Holy Ghost forbidding us in the Holy Scriptures to seek after domination and grandeur and the immoderate desire to rise above others; that is to say, the passion of ambition. (Ecclus. 7:4) Let us thank Him for such useful advice and ask of Him grace to profit by it.

FIRST POINT

✝ *How Hateful Ambition is*

It is a vice, the Holy Spirit says, which is hateful to God. (Luke 16:15) The children of Zebedee asked that they might be raised above the other apostles, and placed in the first rank. You are blind; "you know not what you ask," (Matt. 20: 22; Mark 10:38) Jesus Christ answered them. The princes of the nations aspire to rule; "My disciples, on the contrary, are great only in proportion as they abase themselves", (Matt. 20:26) At the wedding-feast some who were ambitious sought out the highest places. Do not you do so, He said to His disciples. "When thou art invited, go sit down in the lowest place; because every one that exalteth himself shall be humbled, and he that humbleth himself shall be exalted." (Luke 14:10,11) And Jesus Christ confirmed this doctrine by His example. His whole life preaches nothing else but humility, a hidden life, flight from greatness. When the people desired to make Him king, He took flight as though He were threatened by a great misfortune. (John 6:15) Until He was thirty years of age He lived ignored in a poor dwelling; during His mission He lived a life of poverty, devoid of honor; in His passion He was satiated with opprobrium. If He accepts a crown, it is a crown of thorns; if He receives a scepter, it is a scepter of ignominy. How could those present themselves at His tribunal whose sentiments and conduct are in direct contradiction to such an example? Lastly, what faith teaches us, even reason also tells us. Ambition only renders man unhappy. Amongst its slaves whom do we see? Many unfortunate persons who hope; many dupes who hope no longer; very few who enjoy, after having, in order to arrive at the position they occupy, devoured a thousand deceptions without daring to complain, a thousand estrangements and vexations which nevertheless it was necessary they should seem eagerly to embrace, a thousand caprices and repulses the odiousness of which they were obliged to conceal; and now that they have attained the object of their desires, new annoyances and fresh deceptions await them. Something is always wanting to them. The homage of Mardochai, one single man in the whole empire, was wanting to the proud Aman, and he was unhappy. The vineyard of Naboth was wanting to Achab, king of Israel, and he was inconsolable; he knew no rest until he had made Naboth perish.

And again, when they had obtained what they wanted, they did not cease to be unhappy: "I have been everything that it is possible to be" said a Roman emperor, "and I see that it is all of no use to make a man happy."

SECOND POINT

✝ *In how many Ways we Render ourselves Guilty of Ambition*
    We render ourselves guilty of ambition: first, by passionately desiring another position than the one we occupy, by aspiring to honors which are not our due, or by insisting too vigorously upon such as are due to us; second, by taking ambition as our counselor in our judgment as regards our appreciation of others, to the extent of loving or hating them, favoring or opposing them, according as they show themselves to be for or against us; third, by looking upon those as happy who attain success, and never pausing in our pretensions, excepting in presence of our powerlessness to obtain our desires; fourth, by looking upon no position whatever as being above our merits, and seizing all opportunities that present themselves of procuring distinctions and advancement; fifth, by proposing to ourselves as the principal motive of the majority of our actions a vain honor which flatters our pride; sixth, by aspiring, in the spiritual order, to extraordinary and special graces, without being contented with the measure of light and of grace which it has pleased God to give us. *Resolutions and spiritual nosegay as above.*

Fourteenth Saturday after Pentecost

SUMMARY OF TOMORROW'S MEDITATION

 e will meditate tomorrow upon a fourth vice which is opposed to humility, and which is presumption, and we shall see: first, how unworthy this vice is of a Christian soul; second, in how many ways we render ourselves guilty of it. We will thence deduce the resolution: first, to be confounded in the presence of God at the sight of our miseries, and to reject all complaisance in the good opinion we may be tempted to have of ourselves; second, to confide in God alone, and to mistrust ourselves to the point of avoiding even the very least occasions of sin. Our spiritual nosegay shall be the words of the Holy Ghost: "The greater thou art, the more humble thyself in all things." (Ecclus. 3:20)

MEDITATION FOR THE MORNING

Let us adore Jesus Christ esteeming Himself so little, in so far as He was man, that He looks upon Himself as the opprobrium of the world, as the least of men, (Ps. 21:7) and calls Himself by His prophet a worm of the earth, fit only to be trodden under foot (Ibid.). Let us admire this surprising disposition of the heart of Jesus, and let us render Him all our homage.

FIRST POINT

✝ *How Unworthy Presumption is of a Christian Soul*

Presumption is a vice by which, full of a good opinion of ourselves, we put our confidence in our own strength, in our intelligence, our talents, and our virtue, as if they did not all come from God, the absolute master of all events. This presumption is reproved in all the pages of the Holy Scriptures: here it is said that it is an impiety (Prov. 12: 2); there it is written that it is a folly. (Ibid, 28:26) Elsewhere God curses it: Cursed be he who confides in man (Jer. 17:5), and consequently in himself, since he is nothing but a man. To count upon ourselves and upon our ability, to the exclusion of God, is to misconceive the supreme dominion of God over all things, contrary to the words of Sacred Scripture: "O Lord, Lord, almighty King, all things are in Thy power." (Esth. 3:9) It is giving the lie to the words of Jesus Christ: "Without Me you can do nothing." (John 15:5); it is doing one's self the greatest prejudice, for with confidence in God, instead of presumption, the most feeble of men can do everything. David casts down Goliath; Judith defeats an innumerable army, saying to God: "Hear me, a poor wretch, making supplication to Thee, and presuming of Thy mercy." (Judith 9:17) and her confidence is not confounded. With presumption, on the contrary, the most powerful fail. The army of the Assyrians counted upon its strength, and it was cut in pieces, according to the words of Judith: "Lord, show that Thou forsakest not them that trust in Thee, and that Thou humblest them that presume of themselves and glory in their own strength." (Judith 6:15) It is the law which God has established for all ages, and the first of the apostles submitted to it, as well as the ethers. He swore that he would be faithful to his Master at the peril of his life, but because, presuming upon himself, he confided only in his own strength, he fell in the most terrible manner. Who would not tremble on seeing this pillar fall? If Peter fell, who could presume on himself? (St. Bernard, Serin, vi. de Cena Domini.)

SECOND POINT

✝ *In how many Ways we Render ourselves Guilty of Presumption*

We render ourselves guilty of presumption: first, by believing that we have more intelligence and have a better judgment, and that we are superior in our conduct to others; all which opinions make us take counsel always of our own wisdom, even in the most delicate and difficult kind of matters; second, in imagining that we have sufficient talents to succeed in everything and never distrusting our own weakness; third, in attributing the grace of God to our own merits and imagining ourselves to be better than those who have received less; fourth, in leaving to others the fear of the judgments of God and anxieties in regard to salvation, because we do not attach any importance to our faults, and are proud of not committing certain sins into which others fall; fifth, in preferring ourselves to others, because even if they surpass us in respect to certain talents which we do not possess, we flatter ourselves that we are superior to them through other qualities in which they are deficient; and besides, if they are more perfect than we are, it is not on account of our infidelities, but because of the more abundant graces which have been imparted to them. Full of these false ideas, we are unreasonable in our desires to be treated with the greatest respect, distinction, and preference; we make an idol of ourselves, we only approve what we do ourselves, we have a good opinion only of what we ourselves say, we hardly ever yield to any one, and we make ourselves by our pride and obstinacy disagreeable to others. Let us examine ourselves as to whether we do not fall into one or other of these sins. *Resolutions and spiritual nosegay as above.*

Fifteenth Sunday after Pentecost

THE GOSPEL ACCORDING TO ST. LUKE, 7:1-16,

"At that time Jesus went into a city called Nairn, and there went with Him His disciples and a great multitude. And when He came nigh to the gate of the city, behold, a dead man was carried out, the only son of his mother, and she was a widow, and a great multitude of the city was with her. Whom, when the Lord had seen, being moved with mercy towards her, He said to her: Weep not. And He came near and touched the bier. And they that carried it stood still. And He said: Young man, I say to thee, Arise; and he that was dead sat up and began to speak. And He gave him to his mother. And there came a fear on them all; and they glorified God, saying: A great prophet is risen up among us, and God hath visited His people."

SUMMARY OF TOMORROW'S MEDITATION

he gospel of tomorrow, by recounting to us the funeral procession of a young man who is about to be buried, invites us thereby to meditate upon death. In order to obey this desire of the Church, we will make tomorrow three reflections: First, what is it to die? Second, when and how shall I die? Third, if I should have to die today, what should I wish to have done? We will then make the resolution: first, to detach ourselves from the present moment from all that we shall have to leave at our death; second, to perform each action as though we had to die immediately afterwards. We will retain as our spiritual nosegay the words of St. Bernard: "If thou hadst to die in a moment, wouldst thou do this or that?"

MEDITATION FOR THE MORNING

Let us adore the Holy Ghost inviting us to meditate upon our last end, and assuring us that this meditation will enable us to lead a perfect life, because it will reveal to us what time and eternity are worth, that the world is worth with all its enjoyments, its riches, and its honors; what we must think of the adversities which try us, of the prosperity which tempts us, of the frivolity which renders us dissipated, of the pride which swells us, of the tepidity which makes us drowsy, of the indifference and temerity with which we treat the affair of our salvation. (Ecclus. 7:40) Let us thank the Holy Ghost for so important a counsel.

FIRST POINT

✝ *What is it to Die?*

I shall die; that is to say, first, I shall leave everything without exception; I shall quit my relations, my friends, my family; I shall address to them an eternal farewell; I shall quit my home, my furniture, my possessions, all that belongs to me. I shall leave everything and absolutely. What are the things to which I am most attached? I shall leave them as well as everything else. What a universal abandonment! However, it must be. Alas! What folly to attach one's self here below to what one will have so soon to leave! I have given myself a great deal of trouble to acquire and preserve what I possess, and I must quit everything. Why not separate myself from it beforehand by a complete detachment? I shall die; that is to say, second, my soul will leave my body, and from that time my body will be an object of which my relations and friends will only think of getting rid as soon as possible, an infected corpse capable of poisoning everything if it be not at once buried; it will therefore be put into the ground, and what will there become of the body which at present occupies me so much? What will become of these hands, these feet, this head? How insane, then, I am, to flatter and adorn what will soon be nothing but dust and ashes! How insane I am to expose my soul and my eternity to risk for the sake of my body and its empty enjoyments! Shall I be much thought of by men after my death? Alas! The dead are so little remembered! Who is it that recollects such or such a person whom I have known, whom I have seen die? Oh, of how little value is the esteem of men! I shall die; that is to say, Third, my soul will go and appear before the tribunal of God. O fearful moment! To find myself alone in the presence of God, there to answer for the whole of my life before a God who is supremely just, supremely enlightened, a supreme enemy of sin, and therefore without mercy! To escape this judgment there is but one means; it is to judge myself severely here below, and then I shall not be judged. (1 Cor. 11:31)

SECOND POINT

✝ *When and How shall I Die?*

How long have I still to live? I cannot tell. (1 Kings 20:3) On an average 4,500 men die every hour upon the globe, 75 every minute. What hour, what minute will be mine? The gospel tells us it will be the hour and the moment when I least expect it. (Luke 12:40) God has ordered it thus, so that I may not with any show of reason relax in my preparation during one single day and that I may be always ready (St. Augustine); for if I go to sleep for one single day in a state in which I would not wish to die, perhaps my awaking will be in hell. Not only am I ignorant as to when I shall die, but I am also profoundly ignorant as to how I shall die. Shall I die a sudden death, without having time to prepare myself? There are so many who die in this way. Shall I die of a malady which will take from me my senses and my speech, and consequently the possibility of preparing myself? Shall I die of a slow malady which will make others and myself fancy that I am not in danger and there is no hurry? Shall I die surrounded by persons who, being afraid of alarming me, will not dare to speak to me about sending for a priest? Shall I die, lastly, without confession, without the last sacraments? I know nothing about it, and even should I be able to receive them, physical suffering distracts and absorbs me, and we are capable of but very little; it is therefore folly to count upon the last moments to regulate the most serious of all affairs, the affair of a happy or unhappy eternity. Let us then be ready today, let us be ready always, and do not let us put off anything to an uncertain tomorrow. (Matt. 24:44)

THIRD POINT

✝ *If I had to Die Tonight, what should I Desire to have Done?*

First, am I ready to die? Are my temporal affairs settled and my will properly made? Is my conscience in order? Have I nothing to fear in regard to my confessions, to my communions, the accomplishment of the duties of my position? Second, if I knew that I was to die at the end of today, how well should I spend it, how well should I employ every moment! If I had to die after this prayer, with what attention and fervor should I not pray! If it were to be after this confession, after this communion, after this Mass, after this visit to the Blessed Sacrament, in what a holy manner should I perform all these holy things! Let us here examine ourselves thoroughly and understand what a change would take place in ourselves and in all our conduct after having thoroughly well meditated upon the thought of death. (Ecclus. 41:3) *Resolutions and spiritual nosegay as above.*

FIFTEENTH MONDAY AFTER PENTECOST

SUMMARY OF TOMORROW'S MEDITATION

fter having laid in humility the solid foundation of all the virtues, we will raise upon this foundation the first stones of the building, which are penance and mortification, which are called by the saints the virtues proper to the purgative life, because they tend to cleanse the soul from past vices and bad tendencies in regard to the future. We shall therefore consider tomorrow: first, the necessity of penance; second, its urgency. We will thence deduce the resolution: first, to offer all our actions to God in a spirit of expiation and of penance for our past sins; second, cheerfully to accept in this same spirit all the trials and crosses we may meet with during the day. Our spiritual nosegay shall be the words of Our Lord: "Except you do penance, you shall all perish." (Luke 8:5)

MEDITATION FOR THE MORNING

Let us adore the Son of God, who in order to show us the necessity of penance and the obligation incumbent upon every man to perform it, begins by the preaching of this virtue to announce the gospel, (Mark 1:15) expressly declaring that without it there is no salvation! Let us render to Him a thousand thanksgivings for the knowledge He gives us of this great truth.

FIRST POINT
✝ *The Necessity of Doing Penance*
We have all sinned; we ought therefore to do penance until our death, Tertullian concludes. By receiving baptism, we receive the Spirit of God shed upon Jesus Christ penitent; therefore we are obliged to perform continual penance. There is in all of us a tendency to evil which requires to be combated by penance, without which we should be lost; therefore the future to forestall, as well as the past to repair, obliges us to a penance which will last as long as our life. Even the sins which are pardoned have left in our souls a wound to be healed, a temporal debt to pay in this world or in the other; therefore we ought every day to do penance, and to fear the chastisements with which God threatens those who do not perform it. There is no reason to say that, Our Lord having fully satisfied for us the justice of His Father, we are thereby freed from the obligation of doing penance. Let us believe St. Paul, who says: "I fill up those things that are wanting of the sufferings of Christ in my flesh."(Coloss. 1:24) Let us believe Jesus Christ Himself, who has said: "Except you do penance, you shall all perish." (Luke 8:5) Whence it follows that although the goodness of God is infinite, He will not show mercy to any who have not done penance. We must therefore do penance, and a true penance which shall convert us, and not one of those false kinds of penance of which St. Ambrose complained when he said: "I have known more persons who have preserved their baptismal innocence than I have met with others who have recovered it by perfect penance."

SECOND POINT
✝ *The Urgent Necessity of Performing Penance*
In the same proportion as it is necessary to perform penance, it is of urgent necessity to do so. The Holy Spirit says to us: "Delay not to be converted to the Lord, and defer it not from day to day." (Ecclus. 5:8) It is a bad thing to say, I quite feel that I am not what I ought to be, I do not wish to die in my present state; later on I will reform my life. "And until when will you defer it?" asks St. Augustine. Why tomorrow? Why not this very day reform your life? Do we forget that tomorrow is uncertain, that it is folly to risk our salvation upon a perhaps and to abandon our eternity to chance? How is it we do not understand that it is unworthy to make use of the goodness of God for a pretext to delay

our conversion, alleging that He is too good not to wait for us, as though His goodness and mercy ought not, on the contrary, to be a powerful reason for advancing our penitence rather than delaying it? (Rom. 2:4) We imagine that later on our conversion will be easier, as if, on the contrary, our delays did not render it more difficult by weakening grace, strengthening habits, hardening our hearts, and irritating God against us. (Ibid. 5) At other times we imagine that our conversion is incompatible with our present affairs and our employments, as though the business of our salvation were not the first and most important of all that we can have to do with in this world; as if, also, there were any employments wherein salvation is impossible. Lastly, the devil perhaps tries to make us believe that at the hour of death we shall imitate the good thief; as though we could count upon Our Lord renewing that miracle for us, a miracle which was one of the greatest He ever did, and the only one which occurs in the Scriptures, says St. Bernard. There was one sole man that was thus saved at the last moment; there was one that you may not despair; there was only one that you may not trust to it. (St. Bernard) To trust to it is the last degree of imprudence! *Resolutions and spiritual nosegay as above.*

FIFTEENTH TUESDAY AFTER PENTECOST

SUMMARY OF TOMORROW'S MEDITATION

e will tomorrow consider in our meditation: first, the excellence of the virtue of penance; second, the advantages which true penitents derive from their falls. We will then make the resolution: first, after each action to examine into the defects which have been mingled with it, and to repair them by performing the following action better; second, heartily to accept, and in a spirit of penance, all the crosses we may meet with during the day. Our spiritual nosegay shall be the words of the gospel: "Bring forth fruits worthy of penance." (Luke 3:8)

MEDITATION FOR THE MORNING

Let us adore Jesus Christ, the head and chief of the penitents of the whole Church: penitent in the womb of Mary, where He expiates our crimes; penitent in the crib, where His tears wash away our stains; penitent at Nazareth, where He bears, by a laborious life, the penalty of our sins; penitent at Gethsemane, where He weeps over the iniquities of the world with tears of blood; penitent at the praetorium and on Calvary, where, as the victim of the crimes of the earth, He gives up His body to torments and to death. Let us render to Him our homage in the state to which His love for us reduced Him.

FIRST POINT

✝ *The Excellence of the Virtue of Penance*

Our Lord esteems this virtue so highly that in the gospel He praises it at every opportunity. He preaches it in all places and to all kinds of persons. However holy and innocent He may be in Himself, He wills exclusively to lead an extraordinarily penitent life, that He may enable us to feel the excellence of the virtue of penance and its great merit before God. All the saints, entering into the views of Our Lord, have held penance in special esteem. There is not one of them who has not honored and practiced it; not one who has not lovingly accepted in a spirit of penance all the trials of life, all the opportunities of mortifying and vanquishing themselves. The reason is that, considered in itself, penance is of marvelous excellence. It destroys the empire of the devil in souls, and substitutes for it the reign of Jesus Christ. From being slaves of Satan it makes us children of God; from being guilty it makes us just; after being victims of hell it makes us co-heirs of Jesus Christ and fills heaven and earth with joy; it breaks our chains and gives us the crown of justice; it not only obtains for us the pardon of our faults, but also eternal glory, says St. Cyprian. Are these the lofty sentiments of esteem and love which we feel for penance? Do we not, on the contrary, hold it in such aversion that we look upon a life of penance as being an unhappy life, and consider Lent and other seasons which the Church sets apart for penance as being melancholy and disagreeable? Have we not ridiculed those who make a profession of penance? Have we never thought and said that penance is incompatible with health, and that to perform upon our bodies the severities which holy penitents have practiced would be to commit homicide?

SECOND POINT

✝ *The Advantages which True Penitents Derive from their Falls*

God, by His infinite goodness, makes true penitents find, even in their sins, the greatest advantages in regard to their salvation. (Rom. 8:28; St. Augustine, Solil.33) Their falls render them more humble, by convincing them still more of their weakness and frailty; they inspire them with a distrust of themselves which makes them be on their guard and have recourse more frequently to praying to Our Lord and the Blessed Virgin. They excite them better to fulfill their obligations, to repair their falls, by hastening more quickly along the road of salvation (St. Ambrose, Apolog. David,), to compensate wrong-doing in the past by a multiplicity of good works in the present, in such a manner that there should be a superabundance of justice where formerly there was an abundance of sin, and that they should now do ten times more for the glory of God than they had done against it. (Baruch 4:28) They give them experience which teaches them to take precautions on the side whereby sin has entered into their hearts, like a governor of a city who fortifies the quarter which had once been taken by surprise. Lastly, they work in the soul the penitence of which St. Paul speaks, and which leads to the avoiding with greater vigilance the occasions of sin; to have a greater hatred of ourselves, more zeal for perfection, more fear of displeasing God, and more desire of satisfying His justice. (2 Cor. 7:11) It is thus that what is most worthy of repulsion in us may, if we so will, serve as ladders to raise us to God (St. Augustine, Serm. 76 de Temp.)] and that even our very falls, if we know how to profit by them, may become means of perfection and instruments of our salvation. Each fault that we commit ought to make us avoid many others. For example, I have failed in charity towards my neighbor; I will thence deduce the resolution to be meek and humble towards all. I have yielded to a feeling of self-love; I will thence conclude that I must firmly and constantly labor to be very humble. Thus evil will turn to our good. *Resolutions and spiritual nosegay as above.*

Fifteenth Wednesday after Pentecost

SUMMARY OF TOMORROW'S MEDITATION

e will meditate tomorrow upon the spirit of penance, and we shall see that it consists: first, in the sighs of a heart repenting its past sins and its present wretchedness; second, in the firm determination to reform our life. We will then make the resolution: first, to give ourselves up with all our heart to the spirit of penance, bitterly regretting our sad past life, and humbly sighing over our sins and present wretchedness; second, to make some special acts of penance. Our spiritual nosegay shall be the words of the Psalmist: "My sin is always before me." (Ps. 1:5)

MEDITATION FOR THE MORNING

Let us adore Our Lord Jesus Christ, the most perfect of penitents, who is willing to take upon Himself our sins, to weep over them with tears of blood in the Garden of Olives, and to offer reparation for them to His Father, prostrate on His knees and with His face to the earth. What homage ought we not to render to Him for such great goodness!

FIRST POINT

✝ *The Sighs of our Heart over our Past Faults and our Present Wretchedness*

One of our greatest evils is to hide from ourselves what sinners and miserable creatures we are; it is to have a high opinion of ourselves, whereas we ought to be covered with such shame and confusion at the remembrance of our offences that we ought to blush to appear before God and to live amongst the holy children of the Church, that we ought to look upon the most desert solitudes as the places to which we deserve to be relegated forever; (Ps. 59:8) and, lastly, we ought constantly to bear this shame in ourselves and keep it constantly before our eyes. (Ps. 43:16) The true penitent never ceases to lose sight of his sins and to sigh over them; (Ps. 37:18); he considers himself as a criminal guilty of high treason towards the Divine Majesty, and feels it to be only just that he should be despised and treated with seventy, that all creatures should rise against him, that God Himself should exercise him by means of internal trials, disgust, aridities, abandonments; and he looks upon it as a great favor not to be abandoned by God throughout eternity. Fearing, in spite of all this, not yet to having a sufficient spirit of penitence, he does not cease to ask it of Heaven: "Lord, my God," he says with St. Anselm, "give to my heart a sincere penitence, to my soul a true contrition, to my eyes a fountain of tears." (Or. x.), or with St. Augustine: Woe to me, for I have sinned; my faults make me tremble, and I blush for them in Thy presence; (Conf. 2:10) and full of the desire to expiate his sins, he cheerfully accepts all the penances he may meet with, above all those which are not of his choice, which are contrary to his inclinations, still more those which are attached to his position, lastly, death itself, as the just punishment of his sins. Alas! How many Christians, very different from these true penitents, never enter into themselves, are contented with their state, and never humble and confound themselves either before God or before men, or in the bottom of their conscience! Unhappy those who blind themselves, who neglect penance, and always lead the same kind of life, without ever reproaching themselves. Are we not of that number?

SECOND POINT

✝ *Resolution to Correct Ourselves*

If the first element of penitence is to weep over our sins, the second is to be strongly determined not to fall again into them. The one is inseparable from the other, since a frank detestation of sin necessarily involves the resolve not to commit it any more. There is therefore no kind of penance which is real and acceptable to the divine justice, except that wherein there exists a firm and resolute determination never again to offend God, whatever it may cost us, according to what Tertullian says. In vain shall we make acts of contrition and sacramental confessions, all will be of no use to us, unless at the same time we renounce all self-indulgence in our conduct and the indolence of a purely natural life; if we are not resolved, from the bottom of our hearts, to live in a better manner; to substitute for our avarice charity towards the poor, for our pride the humility which despises self and suffers contempt patiently, for our sensual pleasures the spirit of mortification, the acceptance of sickness or other sufferings, and the austerities inspired by the spirit of penance; lastly, for our whole life of caprice and fancies a life perfectly regulated and usefully employed. Are these our dispositions? In what illusions may we not have indulged on this head! *Resolutions and spiritual nosegay as above.*

Fifteenth Thursday after Pentecost

SUMMARY OF TOMORROW'S MEDITATION

e will meditate tomorrow upon the hatred of sin which is the first effect of penitence, and we shall see: first, what are the motives for hating sin in general; second, the motives for hating even venial sin. We will then make the resolution: first, never to allow ourselves deliberately to commit any venial sin; second, to watch specially over certain sins into which we fall the oftenest, such as sins of the tongue or of the temper. Our spiritual nosegay shall be the words of the patriarch Joseph: "How can I sin against my God?" (Gen. 39:9)

MEDITATION FOR THE MORNING

Let us adore the God of infinite wisdom in His immense hatred of sin; let us love His holiness, which cannot bear even the shadow of sin; let us adore His justice, which everywhere pursues it; let us fear His chastisement, which He does not spare at any time or in any place.

FIRST POINT
✝ *On Hatred of Sin in General*
The true penitent hates all sin as being the inveterate enemy of God. He holds it in horror and detests it as the most execrable thing in the world, as the source of the deluge of miseries with which the whole earth has been inundated since the disobedience of Adam; as the greatest of all evils, since it can be the means of making us lose a blessed eternity; lastly, as an evil which we ought to fear more than the most acute maladies, than tortures and the gibbet, than the most cruel of deaths. It is our duty to be ready to lose and to suffer everything rather than to commit it, to fly it as we would from the pestilence, from all occasions of it; to wage against it at all times and in all circumstances mortal war; to persecute it as men who are full of hatred persecute their enemies wherever they may meet with them; to attack it at its very fountainhead by crucifying the flesh and all its concupiscence; (James 1:15) lastly, to efface the least idea and recollection of it. This is what hatred of sin prescribes; let us beg of God to penetrate our hearts so entirely with these sentiments that we may be able to say with the prophet: "I have hated and abhorred iniquity." (Ps. 118:163)

SECOND POINT
✝ *On the Hatred of Sin even when it is only Venial*
We ought to fear venial sin even more than death: first, because it displeases God, insults Him, does Him an injury, and grieves the Holy Ghost. Now, is not an evil which involves such consequences more serious than all imaginable evils? Second, because God punishes it in the next life by more terrible chastisements than any sufferings which can be inflicted upon us here below, and that more than once He has punished it with death even in the present life. Because of thoughtless curiosity the wife of Lot was suddenly struck down with death; (Gen. 19:26) for hewing gathered a little wood on the Sabbath day, let the guilty man be stoned and let him die, said the Lord, (Num. 15:32-36) a prophet remains a little longer than he ought to have done in the place whither he had been sent, a lion comes out of the forest and devours him; (3 Kings 13:24) David, through secret vanity, numbers his people, and seventy thousand of his subjects fall a prey to pestilence. (2 Kings 24:19-25) We ought to fear venial sin, third, because it stops the course of graces and leads to mortal sin, according to the oracle of the Holy Ghost that "he who contemneth small things shall fall by little and little," (Ecclus. 19:1) and thus a venial sin is often the beginning of reprobation. Fourth, we often look upon as a venial sin what is a mortal sin in the eyes of God; whence we may conclude how we ought to avoid false hood, calumnies, even such as we term slight ones the ridiculing

this person or that, hasty or ill-tempered speeches, and all the other venial sins we so often allow ourselves to commit in conversation; voluntary distractions in prayer, loss of time, negligence in our employments, sensualities in regard to our meals, vanity with respect to our external appearance, human respect about our religious duties. Are these the sentiments we entertain in regard to venial sin? Do we not every day, through love for ourselves or complaisance towards others, often even without scruple, deliberately and wantonly allow ourselves to commit them, under the pretext that we shall not be punished eternally? Lastly, do we hate it to the extent of hindering it, so far as we can, in others, never applauding their defects, and persuading them to avoid the least laxity and the least license in their actions and language? *Resolutions and spiritual nosegay as above.*

FIFTEENTH FRIDAY AFTER PENTECOST

SUMMARY OF TOMORROW'S MEDITATION

e will meditate tomorrow upon the second effect of penitence, which is hatred of self, and we shall see: first, that to hate ourselves is a duty; second, that the accomplishment of this duty is full of sweetness and consolation. Our resolution shall be: first, to be on our guard against the wholly pagan tendency of a self-indulgent and sensual, comfortable and pleasant life; second, to grant nothing during the day to the love of pleasure and the fear of restraint, and in all things to be guided by the sentiment of duty. Our spiritual nosegay shall be the words of the gospel: "He that loveth his life shall lose it, and he that hateth his life in his world keepeth it unto life eternal." (John 12)

MEDITATION FOR THE MORNING

Let us adore Jesus Christ preaching to the world a maxim which until then was unknown, that a man must hate himself, and putting it in practice by the severity with which He treats Himself during His life and at His death. Let us thank Him for this lesson and this example; let us ask Him to enable us to understand it and courage to conform our conduct to it.

FIRST POINT

✝ *To Hate One's Self is a Duty*

In order to understand this, it is sufficient to consider what we are through original corruption. There is in us a principle of indescribable malignity which leads us constantly to evil, passions which urge us on to what is forbidden and remove us from what is commanded. To this element of evil is added a principle of baseness and effeminacy which is devoid of courage to resist these bad tendencies, and, on the contrary, allows itself to be ruled by them. Now, it is evident that in order to save ourselves in such conditions as these, there must be no alliance, no peace or truce made with this evil principle; it must be treated as an enemy, otherwise it will be our ruin. This is what Our Savior meant by these words: He that loves himself loses himself, and he that hates himself is the only one who saves himself. What does hate himself mean? It means that as in the world, and externally to the gospel, we do not grant to an enemy what he desires, and that it is sufficient for him to desire a thing in order that it should be refused, so we must refuse nature the sensualities it desires; that in the same way as we take pleasure in annoying an enemy and doing him all the evil we can, so in like manner we must annoy the flesh, never flattering or sparing it, treating it harshly, using no self-indulgence towards it; that in the same manner as we mistrust an enemy capable of ruining us, we must also mistrust our evil nature, which is always ready to serve the designs of the devil against our salvation; lastly, that in the same way as we endeavor to weaken and overcome an enemy, we must strive to weaken and overcome the flesh, by cutting off the sensual pleasures which are its life and granting to it only what cannot be refused to it. Let us here examine our conscience; do we really hate our flesh, and do we refuse to it what it desires? Do we inflict upon it what is displeasing to it, and is it only with regret that we give it what is necessary? Lastly, do we treat it as an enemy over whom we keep watch, whom we mistrust, whom we are very glad to see badly fed, ill-lodged, badly clothed, despised, repelled, infirm, occupied in low employments?

SECOND POINT

✝ To Hate One's Self is the Sweetest and most Consoling Thing in the World

War against one's self is the means of procuring three great things which fill the soul with sweetness and consolation: first, victory over our passions, and there is therein an inexpressible happiness, for passions render the heart wretched, tear it with remorse, make it vile in its own eyes, cast it into trouble and sorrow. Second, internal peace, the joy of a good conscience, serenity of soul delicious fruits of war against one s self, according to the maxim, "it is through war that we obtain peace." Third, the sweet hope of a happy eternity; whilst he who flatters his body prepares it to be a victim of hell, he who mortifies it prepares it for the glory of risen bodies: a blessed state where the body will be impassible, agile like the spirits, dazzling as the sun. Hence it follows that to hate one's self in the gospel sense is to love one's self with a true love, solid and rightly understood; whilst to flatter one's self in a worldly sense is to hate one's self with a blind, cruel, and very real hatred. *Resolutions and spiritual nosegay as above.*

Fifteenth Saturday after Pentecost

SUMMARY OF TOMORROW'S MEDITATION

fter having meditated upon penitence, we will meditate tomorrow upon mortification, which is the consequence of it, and we will consider: first, the precept of it; second, the practice of it. Our resolution shall be: first, to combat the passion of enjoyment in us, the love of our ease, the search after pleasure, and never to do anything from motives so unworthy of a disciple of the crucified Jesus; second, to make a sacrifice today to Our Lord of something which pleases us, or of some repugnance with which we may meet in the accomplishment of our duties. Our spiritual nosegay shall be the words of Our Lord: "If any man will come after die, let him deny himself." (Matt. 16:24)

MEDITATION FOR THE MORNING

Let us adore Jesus Christ declaring to us in the gospel that He will not admit effeminate, self-indulgent souls into His service, souls which do not look beyond the pleasure of the moment and think only of what will give satisfaction to themselves, sensitive members which are not in their place beneath a head crowned with thorns. He recognizes as His disciples none but strong and generous souls, strong to endure sacrifice, who are able to do themselves violence, attach themselves to the cross with Him, and mortify their evil nature in order that it may bend to duty. Let us offer ourselves to Him in these generous dispositions.

FIRST POINT

✝ *The Precept of Mortification*

Of all the points of Christian morals, none is so often recommended in the gospel as the precept of mortification, that is to say, to labor, by privation, by suffering, and by violence waged against one s self, to repress our evil nature and to combat its tendencies in order that we may keep it always in the path of duty; for the words of Our Lord, ordering us to renounce everything, to renounce ourselves and to bear the cross, cannot signify anything else except that we must mortify ourselves. The reason of this precept is that without mortification there is neither virtue, nor reason, nor happiness. First, no virtue, because in order to be humble we must mortify self-love with its pride, its susceptibilities, and its pretensions; to be meek we must mortify our temper, our hastiness, and our abruptness; to be obedient we must mortify self-will with its repugnance and its attachments, its fancies and its caprices; to be chaste we must mortify the love of pleasure and enjoyment, not flatter the flesh, but crucify it and be always on our guard against its seductions. It is the same with all the other virtues. In the same way that we cannot straighten a crooked limb without binding it up, we cannot bring back the soul to the primitive rectitude of any virtue except by doing violence to it. Second, without mortification there is no reason. It is humiliating to see how without mortification reason is so little reasonable; we find our pleasure, as an animal does, in eating and drinking; we make of it part of the happiness of life; we indulge in it to excess, even to the extent of bodily discomfort and sometimes of losing our senses. Is this reasonable? Without mortification we live upon caprices and fancies; we do constantly what pleases us and not what we ought to do; we turn night into day by delaying to go to bed, and day into night by delaying the hour of rising; we neglect our affairs, the care of our household and our family, the superintendence of our children and our servants, order and economy in household matters, the proportion between what we have and what we spend. Is this reason able? Without mortification we seek nothing but our own self-satisfaction, making pleasure to go before duty, enjoyment before conscience. Is this reasonable? Without mortification we cannot bear anything from others, and we like others to bear everything from us; they must endure our defects, though we will not bear theirs; they must yield to our will without our ever yielding to theirs; they must allow themselves to be ridiculed, reproved, treated by us with haughtiness, and they must be forbidden to do anything of the same kind in regard to us. Is this reasonable?

Finally, every time that we sin, it is because we refuse to mortify ourselves, because we will not deprive ourselves of anything or that we are determined to enjoy something. Now all sin is a fault against reason, because reason tells us to obey God, who commands nothing but what is just and equitable. Third, without mortification there is no happiness: no happiness in the service of God, who withdraws His graces and consolations in the same proportion as we seek enjoyment from creatures and not from Him, or refuse what He demands; no happiness with our neighbor, because we repel him by our want of inclination to render any service which may inconvenience us, by the self-love which seeks what is pleasant without any fear of inconveniencing others, by a temper full of susceptibilities and pretensions, by a liberty of language which cannot restrain a wounding or unkind speech; lastly, no happiness in regard to ourselves: first, because each time that we satisfy the caprices of our own will we feel the pain of remorse which tells us that we have done wrong; second, because whoever has any attachments is angry if attempts are made to deprive him of what he loves, is afflicted if he is obliged to deprive himself of them, and thus he is rendered essentially unhappy.

SECOND POINT
✝ *The Practice of Mortification*

The practice of this virtue ought to be continuous, regulated by wisdom, accompanied by love and joy. First, continuous; because like him who, sailing on an impetuous river, is carried away by the current if he ceases for one single moment to row against it, so the man will inevitably be dragged into the commission of sin who does not energetically combat the evil tendency which leads him to it: for our vitiated nature is continually soliciting us to evil, caring little if we are lost provided that it be satisfied. It is a slave always ready to revolt, which can do nothing but what is evil. All in this sinful nature is dangerous: our eyes, our tongue, our taste, the sense of touch spread over the whole body. Now so many enemies plotting together would in fallibly be our ruin if we were to cease for one single day to mortify them. Second, the practice of mortification ought to be regulated by wisdom; it would be indiscreet zeal to carry to excess mortification which would ruin our health. Health is a gift God has confided to us; we have no right to destroy it. Let us grant what is necessary to the body, but let us have courage to refuse it what is nothing but pleasure and enjoyment. Third, lastly, mortification ought to be accompanied by love and joy; God accepts no sacrifices but such as love offers to Him joyfully, (2 Cor. 9:7) and even man would not bend himself to mortification if love did not render it delicious to him. Love, says the Imitation, renders all that is heavy light, and all that is bitter sweet. (2 Imit. 5:3) The soul which loves knows that sufferings are the best proof of love; and as it has an immense desire to prove to its God that it loves Him, it has also an immense desire to suffer. It knows that sufferings are the food of love, the surest means to make progress, because the heart attaches itself all the more to God in proportion as it is detached from itself and from creatures; and as it has an immense desire to love Him always more and more, so it has always an immense desire to suffer more and more. Hence the cry of St. Teresa, Either suffer or die! Hence in souls which really love God the holy desires which lead them to wards mortification. Let us examine our conscience; what are our dispositions in regard to a subject so important with respect to salvation? *Resolutions and spiritual nosegay as above.*

SIXTEENTH SUNDAY AFTER PENTECOST

THE GOSPEL ACCORDING TO ST. LUKE, 14:1-11

"At that time, when Jesus went into the house of one of the chief of the Pharisees on the Sabbath day to eat bread, they watched Him. And behold there was a certain man before Him that had the dropsy: and Jesus answering, spoke to the lawyers and Pharisees, saying: Is it lawful to heal on the Sabbath day? But they held their peace. But He taking him, healed him, and sent him away. And answering them, He said: Which of you shall have an ass or an ox fall into a pit, and will not immediately draw him out on the Sabbath day? And they could not answer Him to these things. And He spoke a parable also to them that were invited, marking how they chose the first seats at the table, saying to them: When thou art invited to a wedding, sit not down in the first place, lest perhaps one more honorable than thou be invited by him, and he that invited thee and him come and say to thee: Give this man place, and then thou begin with shame to take the lowest place. But when thou art invited, go, sit down in the lowest place, that when he that invited thee cometh, he may say to thee: Friend, go up higher. Then shalt thou have glory before them that sit at table with thee: because every one that exalteth himself shall be humbled, and he that humbleth himself shall be exalted."

SUMMARY OF TOMORROW'S MEDITATION

e will meditate tomorrow upon the gospel for the day, and we shall learn from it: first, the reasons we adduce for mixing with the world; second, the manner in which we ought to conduct ourselves when we enter into it. We will then make the resolution: first, not to frequent the world without having some solid reason based upon utility or propriety for doing so; second, to take with us when we go into society a spirit of reserve and of modesty, of discretion and of charity. Our spiritual nosegay shall be the words of St. John: "Love not the world, nor the things which are in the world." (1 John 2:15)

MEDITATION FOR THE MORNING

Let us adore Jesus Christ in the house of a prince of the Pharisees. Two motives lead Him there charity and zeal: charity, that He may cure a poor man afflicted with the dropsy; zeal, in order that He may give a lesson of humility to all who are in the house. Let us admire His holy motives for this visit, and let us ask of Him grace to have none but holy motives for our visits.

FIRST POINT

✝ *Reasons which we Adduce for Entering into the World*

Four motives may attract us into the world: pleasure, necessity, charity, zeal. To go into the world from pleasure is an imprudence; it is throwing ourselves wantonly into peril; for intercourse with the world is full of danger, it is nothing but dissipation, luxury, vanity, calumny, maxims opposed to the gospel, corruption of the morals, seduction of the senses, complete forgetfulness of salvation and of eternity. Now the Holy Ghost says: "He that loveth danger shall perish in it." (Ecclus. 3:27) To go into the world because our affairs oblige us to do so, or else because our position or motives of propriety render it necessary to do so, is a thing that is permitted, provided we do not go too much be yond the bounds of this necessity, by confounding them with our tastes or our love of pleasure, and provided we mistrust ourselves and practice reserve and modesty, the spirit of charity and discretion; then God will help us not to offend Him. To go into the world from charity, to oblige, assist, console, give pleasure, is a praise worthy thing; and if men blame us, God will recompense us. Lastly, to go into the world from zeal for a good work, to gain to religion a man who is far removed from it, to reconcile enemies, is still better, provided we are armed with the precautions of prudence, of modesty, and of up rightness of intention, which ought always to accompany works of zeal. Let us examine if we frequent the world solely under these conditions.

SECOND POINT

✝ *How we ought to Behave in the World*

First, we must carry with us thither a great deal of reserve and of modesty, for Jesus Christ Himself was blamed for entering into it by the Pharisees, who wanted to make it appear that He was a man who was fond of good cheer and a friend of sinners. (Matt. 11;19) Every one observed, says the gospel, His way of conducting Himself, of eating and of speaking, (Luke 14:1) and this is what happens every day in the world; all observe each other. The good observe, because simplicity, which is the virtue of innocent souls, leads them to observe and to imitate those whom they imagine to be good people; whence it follows that we ought always to be upon our guard, so as to do nothing and say nothing which may do the very least harm. A nothing, an appearance only of something, oftentimes has great consequences following upon it. The wicked also observe; they seek for matter to criticize, to authorize themselves in their sins by our example, to excuse their greatest vices by our smallest defects, and their most criminal omissions by our slightest ones; whence results for us the obligation to conduct ourselves always in such a manner that they shall be reduced, as the enemies of Jesus Christ were, to invent evil against us, or to see it where it does not exist. Second, we must take with us into the world a great spirit of charity. The world is ignorant of this virtue; to amuse itself at the expense of the reputations of others, this is the charm of worldly conversations. It is for us Christians never to let a single word of calumny enter into what we say, and to turn the conversation as much as possible from such subjects. Third, we must carry with us into it the spirit of discretion, which avoids everything that may wound others, all advice good in itself but which would not be appreciated, all positive approbation of what is evil or contrary to the gospel; to do and say all that may be of use, to make religion amiable, to lead others to the practice of virtue and of good works, to console the afflicted, to sustain the weak, to encourage tried souls. *Resolutions and spiritual nosegay as above.*

Sixteenth Monday after Pentecost

SUMMARY OF TOMORROW'S MEDITATION

he first object on which mortification ought to be exercised, the mortification which was the subject of last Saturday's meditation, is our passions. We shall see: first, the necessity of mortifying them; second, the necessity of specially mortifying the ruling sin. Our resolution shall be: first, joyfully to seize all opportunities of mortifying ourselves which we may meet with in the course of the day; second, every day to be faithful to the making of a particular examination upon our ruling passion. Our spiritual nosegay shall be the words of the Imitation: "The measure of your progress shall be the measure of the violence you do yourself." (1 Imit. 25:11)

MEDITATION FOR THE MORNING

Let us adore Our Lord governing with supreme and absolute rule all the movements of the soul which we call passions. He kept them in such strict order and so perfectly under subjection that not one of them ever took reason by surprise nor was allowed to rise within Him excepting under the direction of the Holy Ghost. Let us admire this divine interior where all is so well regulated, and let us derive from it grace to regulate our passions and to mortify them according to the teaching of the apostles: "They that are Christ's have crucified their flesh with the vices and concupiscences." (Gal. 5: 24)

FIRST POINT
✚ *The Necessity of Mortifying the Passions*

Our passions are the most powerful agents the devil can employ for our ruin; we must, therefore, overcome them or be ruined through them. They are, says St. Bernard, irreconcilable enemies; if we do not crush them they will crush us. (Serm. de Ascens.) If, after having crushed them, we cease to watch them and to be on our guard against them, they will spring up again, will renew the attack, and will put our salvation in danger. (St. Bernard, Serm. Ivi. in Cant.) It is therefore necessarily a daily war which we have to wage; a war directed not merely against an isolated passion, but against all the passions which have their germ in our hearts; a war in which we have to employ different kinds of weapons and to use different tactics, according to the variety of the attacks. We must combat voluptuousness by the retrenchment of sensual pleasures, which are as a bait to it, turn away our eyes from creatures calculated to soften the heart, and promptly turn away our mind from the first dangerous thought which presents itself, saying with St. Bernard: "When my God is hanged on a gibbet, can I indulge in pleasure?" We must combat vain desires by the strength of soul which moderates them and contents itself with little. We must combat profane joys by the contempt of passing enjoyments, which a Christian heart ought to consider as too much beneath it to attract its esteem. Hatred is combated by the consideration that God pardons only those who forgive; fear is repelled by the elevated sentiment that a Christian fears nothing except sin; sorrow puts its clouds to flight by the hope of heaven; presumption yields to humility, which confesses its weakness and powerlessness without the aid of God. We combat despair by the consideration of the mercies of God, of the merits of Jesus Christ, and the all-powerful and loving assistance of the most blessed Virgin. We overcome anger by silence, which closes the mouth as long as we are in a state of excitement; by the consideration of the meekness of Jesus Christ and of the opposition which exists between anger and reason. Lastly, we destroy envy by the spirit of Christian charity. Such is the war we must always wage against ourselves, now in refusing what is pleasant, and now in imposing on ourselves what is bitter, happy if by dint of fighting we can arrive at that happy state in which the soul, mistress of vanquished passions, free and unrestrained, lives only under the guidance of the Spirit of God and of His adorable will. He who does not, however, arrive at this point must not be discouraged. He who dies whilst fighting does not the less merit the palm of victory; but he who does not fight will be lost. The more passions we have the less reason we possess. He who takes counsel of passion takes counsel of a fool. Always before acting we must open our mind to reason, our heart to grace, and put ourselves on the side of virtue against temper, and not on the side of temper against virtue.

SECOND POINT
✝ *The Necessity of Combating the Ruling Passion*
Amongst all the passions there is one which is more dangerous than any of the others; it is the ruling passion. We recognize it through its being, as it were, the distinguishing characteristic of each person, a characteristic which everyone remarks, so that they say, for instance, such or such a person is a passionate man, or such a one is vain, another susceptible, and yet another avaricious; and even every individual can discern it in himself by seeing what are the thoughts and sentiments with which he is the most taken up. That then is the passion which it is the most necessary to combat: first, because it is that which gives the impetus to all the rest and which the most exposes our salvation to danger; it is in regard to the other passions what a commander-in-chief is to an army to kill him is to put the whole army to rout; in the same way, to stifle this passion is to ruin all the other passions; second, because we shall in vain put down the other passions; for as long as the ruling passion exists it will be capable of ruining us. Let us examine at what point we have arrived in our war against this passion. First, do we understand it thoroughly? Are we not ignorant of it from want of reflection, through negligence with regard to our salvation? Second, do we combat it every day, either by flight, if it attempt to seduce us by the temptation of pleasure, or by strife, if it attack us with violence? Lastly, let us direct against it our daily particular examination, as St. Ignatius and St. Francis de Sales did, who, by this means, changed a quick and passionate temper into one of imperturbable gentleness. *Resolutions and spiritual nosegay as above.*

SUMMARY OF TOMORROW'S MEMITATION

e will this week continue our meditations upon mortification, and we shall see that we must mortify self-will: first, in what it wills; second, in what it desires. We will thence deduce the resolution: first, to seize with thanksgiving every opportunity which Providence presents to us for mortifying our will and our desires in order to accustom them always to bend beneath the yoke of duty; second, to lead, today, an orderly and well-regulated life, not granting anything to caprice. Our spiritual nosegay shall be the words of Our Lord: "Father, not My will, but Thine be done." (Luke 22:42)

MEDITATION FOR THE MORNING

Let us adore Our Lord giving us throughout the whole of His life a continual example of mortification of His self-will. Never did He do anything but what His heavenly Father willed He should, and in the manner which He willed, and because He willed it. (Matt. 26:39; Mark 14:36; Luke 22:42) Let us thank Him for this beautiful example, and let us ask of Him grace to follow it.

FIRST POINT

✝ *We must Mortify Self-will in what it Wills*

Let us believe with a lively faith that we are not placed in this world to do our own will, but to do the will of God; that we are not here to do our own pleasure or to amass riches, but to do what God demands from us, in the condition and in the place wherein He has placed us. (1 Pet. 4:2; Rom. 12:2) Our will does not belong to us; it belongs to God, as does our whole being; it is His property. If He leaves it in the hands of our own counsel, it is in order that we should offer to Him a free homage of it, honorable to His greatness, meritorious to ourselves, but not to authorize us to dispose of it according to our own liking and to do what pleases us. Jesus Christ Himself followed this rule; never in anything did He seek His own satisfaction. (Rom. 15:3) In accordance with His example, we ought to bend our will in all things to the good pleasure of God. If what His good pleasure demands is in agreement with our own liking, we must abstract from it what belongs to our natural taste, and only think of what is the divine good pleasure; and if what He commands does not please us, we must rejoice to do the will of God with a more assured and perfect purity of intention. Never, then, ought we to say, I do this because I will to do it, or because it pleases me to do it; but rather we must say, I do this because it is in the order of my duties and of the good pleasure of God. To act otherwise is not to act like a Christian; it is to steal away our life from the essential dominion of God over us; it is to lose the merit of our works. To act in conformity with this precept is to live a perfect life; it is to content God, since in all things we follow His good pleasure, of which we have the faithful expression in a good rule of life, which fixes the order of our actions, which marks the time and the manner of them, in such a way that no duty shall be neglected and that all shall be well ordered. It is to content our neighbor, since the divine good pleasure which we follow in all things disposes us to be always amiable towards every one, and never allows our own will to come in contact with the will of another. Lastly, it is to assure to ourselves happiness in this present life, because we will only what God wills, we see in everything the divine will which rules or permits everything, and we feel a delightful pleasure in saying, "I am doing the good pleasure of God."

SECOND POINT
✝ *We must Mortify Self-will in what it Desires*

It would be impossible to express all the evil which desires and the passions they excite cause to the soul: desires which are too lively and too eager; passions too impetuous and too ardent; desires which are ceaselessly multiplied, which, opposed as they are the one to the other, tear and divide the soul, each in its own direction, tending towards objects incapable of satisfying it; passions which are vain and unjust, which are impatient and murmur if they are not quickly satisfied. Today we desire one thing, tomorrow we desire another. We are never content in our place, because we imagine that we should be better in a place where we are not. We seek happiness here and there, in the world, in solitude, and nowhere do we find it, because we seek it in the satisfaction of our desires, instead of going to seek it at its true source, which is mortification of these same desires. Hence, in the world all complain, all speak only of unhappiness. I am born, they say, to be unhappy; I was wretched in such or such a position; I am still so, and I shall be so always. Yes, it will always be thus, because we never give ourselves up to an unruly desire without causing ourselves trouble and anxiety; because disgust and weariness necessarily accompany the man who listens to his caprices; because we never satisfy an unruly will without feeling remorse of conscience, which reproaches us with having yielded to passion; because, lastly, the man who has attachments does not know what interior repose is; he is indignant if attempts are made to deprive him of what he loves; he is afflicted if he thinks that he may be deprived of it, or if he is obliged to deprive himself of it. *Resolutions and spiritual nosegay as above.*

SIXTEENTh WEDNESDAY AFTER PENTECOST

SUMMARY OF TOMORROW'S MEDITATION

e will meditate tomorrow upon mortification of the temper or of the disposition, and we shall see: first, the unhappy consequences of an un-mortified temper or of a bad disposition; second, the advantages of a mortified temper or of a good disposition; third, the means of correcting our disposition. We will then make the resolution: first, often to ask God to reform our disposition; second, never to speak, act, or make a decision in a moment of bad temper, but to take time to reflect before acting or speaking. Our spiritual nosegay shall be the words of the Holy Ghost: Do not follow all your caprices. (Gal. 5:17)

MEDITATION FOR THE MORNING

Let us adore Jesus Christ inviting us by His apostle to allow ourselves to be led in everything by the Spirit of God, (Gal. 5:16) and not by our caprices. Let us thank Him for so important a counsel.

FIRST POINT

✝ *The Unhappy Consequences of an Unmortified Temper or of A Bad Disposition*

A bad disposition is the ruin of charity, the dishonor of virtue, a door open to every kind of evil. First, it is the ruin of charity; dispositions, in fact, differ as much from each other as do faces, and from this want of harmony it results that if we do not mortify them, so as to make them agree together, it is impossible for two persons to live harmoniously together. There will be coldness, bitterness, and discords. Charity is impossible excepting under the condition of bearing what is not sympathetic to us in others, and of diminishing, by doing ourselves violence, what there is in us towards which others have an antipathy. There is no room here for saying, It is my disposition, or, The disposition of such or such a person is antipathic to me. Neither the one nor the other of these excuses will have any value in the sight of God, and thereby dispense us from the law of charity or render our antipathies or our impatience justifiable. Second, a bad disposition is the dishonor of virtue. We sometimes see souls which are good at bottom, but which are at the same time brusque, hard to please, cross-grained, inflicting suffering upon others, or which are effeminate and frivolous, having no energy, nothing regular or consequent in their course of life, in constant and eccentric; which desire that what is good should be done after their own fashion, according to their own ideas and likings; which are fire and flame in regard to all that pleases them, and ice with respect to all which is not according to their taste; which make their decisions not through reason and faith, but through their inclination and temperament; and which leave off the best kind of works as soon as they cease to be in accordance with their tastes. Now, such ways of acting are evidently a dishonor to virtue and a means of putting devotion to discredit. If this be religion, says the world, we might just as well not have any. Third, a bad disposition is a door open to all kinds of sin. A jealous disposition caused the death of Abel, exiled Joseph, persecuted David. An austere disposition made Novatian, Tertullian, Lucifer de Cagliari go astray. A proud and susceptible disposition threw Arius into heresy and Photius into schism. Even when an un-mortified disposition is not carried to these excesses, it spoils everything with which it meddles, it introduces discord into families; instead of correcting it embitters, instead of bringing back it repels, and even sometimes propels children into what is evil by the severity with which they are treated. It acts without order, it speaks without reflection, and a man who is reasonable in regard to everything else is intractable in all that touches his disposition. Let us here examine our conscience; have we no reproaches to address to ourselves on this subject?

SECOND POINT

✝ *The Advantages of a Mortified Disposition or of a Good Character*

First, a good disposition makes a person to be loved. It is impossible not to love a disposition which is always agreeable, always the same, and always sociable, which is always kind, converses amiably, which is humble without cringing, dignified without being haughty, active without being either brusque or petulant, always ready to render a service, to forget wrongs, to suffer from others without making any one suffer. Second, loved by everyone, such a person is still more loved by God, because a good disposition is, as it were, the sum total of all the virtues in practice; it is humility, gentleness, and charity in action; it is patience, abnegation, obedience, presiding over words and actions; finally, it is perfection. Under the inspiration of a good disposition we do everything well, because we always act with calmness and reflection, never being carried away by temper. We do not come imprudently in contact with obstacles, we study the means of obtaining our ends, and with time everything is well arranged, everything well done. Third, a good disposition does honor to religion. The world cannot see a Christian always master of himself, always possessing his soul in peace and patience, without rendering homage to the religion which is the cause of such perfect virtue. It is edified by the spectacle in the same proportion as it is not so by the opposite spectacle.

THIRD POINT

✝ *Means whereby to Correct our Disposition*

First, we must study well whatever may be reprehensible in our disposition. In all dispositions there is something to reform, and we only know the defective side by dint of studying ourselves or of consulting a wise friend. Second, the defect once perceived, we must labor every day to reform it, by acting in a contrary sense, and never ceasing from the strife until we have mastered it. The disposition which is too quick must be moderated; the disposition which is too inert must be aroused and stirred up; the brusque and susceptible tendency must be silenced, and not allowed to speak until the soul is calm and in full possession of itself. St. Francis de Sales had received a hot and passionate temper from nature, St. Ignatius a quick and impatient disposition, St. Vincent de Paul an austere and disagreeable character; but these great saints, by dint of combating their defects, succeeded at last in attaining the good and amiable dispositions which will forever render their memory delicious in the sight of God and of men. Third, we must every day examine ourselves on this subject, and for each failure of which we are guilty impose on ourselves a penance, if it be nothing more than the putting aside a small coin to give to the poor. That will have the advantage of awaking our attention and of enabling us to know, in order to confess them, the exact number of our failures. *Resolutions and spiritual nosegay as above.*

SIXTEENTH THURSDAY AFTER PENTECOST

SUMMARY OF TOMORROW'S MEDITATION

We will meditate tomorrow upon the mortification of the tongue, and we shall see: first, what evil the tongue which does not know how to rule itself commits; second, what good the soul which is wisely ruled does. We will then make the resolution: first, to remember when we speak that God hears all our words, and that we shall have to render a severe account of them; second, never to speak of our neighbor excepting to say what is good of him, or at any rate to say nothing injurious; third, to speak little or to speak in a moderate tone; he who speaks much and loudly speaks without reflection and without wisdom. Our spiritual nosegay shall be the words of the apostle St. James: "If any man think himself to be religious, not bridling his tongue, this mans religion is vain." (James 1:26)

MEDITATION FOR THE MORNING

Let us adore Our Lord revealing to us by the apostle St. James the necessity of governing our tongue, since if it be left to itself it may work so much evil, and if rightly governed it may do so much good. From the tongue, he says, proceed good and evil: with it we bless God, and with it, we curse men who are made in the image of God; by it we are useful to our brethren, and by it we are hurtful to them; by it we take desolation into the heart, and by it we take happiness and joy. (James 3:10) Lastly, the Holy Spirit says in the Book of Proverbs: "Death and life are in the power of the tongue." (Prov. 18:21) Let us thank God for a warning of such importance in regard to our salvation and to the welfare of society.

FIRST POINT

✝ *What Evil the Tongue Does when it is not Properly Ruled*

When the Holy Spirit speaks to us of the evil the tongue does when it is not governed, He seems to exhaust all that language can express: "The tongue" He says, "is a world of iniquity," (James 3:6), it is an "unquiet evil," (Ibid. 8) which carries trouble and unhappiness with it; which divides minds, embitters hearts, engenders hatred and discord. It is a mortal poison, (Ibid. 7) which kills at one and the same time him who speaks and him who listens with an air of approbation, often even him who is spoken of, whether because of the spirit of irritation and vengeance with which it inspires him, whether on account of the loss of his reputation and honor, which he does not know how to bear in a Christian manner. It is a fire of hell, (James 3:6) which does not spare either what is sacred or what is profane, either superiors or equals, which attacks God by blasphemy and impiety, which corrupts souls and excites them to evil. The proof that this picture has nothing exaggerated in it is, first, that sins of the tongue are the most common of all sins and form the habitual subject of nearly all confessions; it is, second, that the tongue serves as an instrument for the most ignoble of passions: for the bad dispositions of those persons who cannot say anything calmly, but are peevish and are angry about the smallest matters; for pride, which desires to make everyone descend to a lower level than the one we ourselves occupy, criticizes everything that is done by others, exaggerates their faults, diminishes their virtues; for envy, which endeavors to darken everything which eclipses it, which thinks others worthy of blame only because they possess certain advantages over us, which cannot hear them praised without weakening approbation by a criticism, or see merit superior to its own without seeking to lower it; for lewdness, which exhales from the heart in licentious speeches; for anger, which gives way to violence; for duplicity, which flatters persons to their face and tears them in pieces behind their backs; for baseness, which shoots its arrows at the absent for lies, which sacrifice truth to the pleasure of being witty or rising above others; for malignity, which casts mockery and ridicule upon others who do not please it; for a bad spirit, which delights in disputes and contentions and always wants its own ideas to prevail. Now all these facts, and a thousand others revealed by daily experience, do they not tell us how necessary it is to mortify our tongue, to moderate our language, and to remember when we speak that God is beside us, that He hears all and registers it in the great Book, and will demand an account of it at the last day, not even excepting idle words? (Matt. 12:36)

SECOND POINT

✝ *What Good a Tongue Wisely Governed can Do*

When a man knows how to govern his tongue he employs it only for things that are good, and says nothing but good things which lead to God and to virtue. "The mouth of the just" says the Holy Spirit, "is a vein of life!" (Prov. 10:11) His tongue is as precious as silver tried in the fire, (Ibid. 20) and wisdom is found upon his lips. (Ibid. 13) Jesus Christ teaches us this by His example, for He never let a word fall from His lips but words of grace, which ravished all His hearers, (Luke 4:22) and after listening to Him they cried out, "Never did man speak like this man." (John 7:46) By the tongue we make God to be known and loved, together with His commandments and counsels; we teach men to love one another, to endure and oblige one another, to turn themselves away from the evil road which leads to perdition and to follow the good road which leads to heaven. (Prov. 10:21) By the tongue we console the afflicted, we dry tears, and we make men bless the religion which inspires such kindness and grace. (Ecclus. 20:13; 6:5) By the tongue we bring together divided hearts, reconcile families, dilate the reign of peace and charity. (Prov. 10:32) By a gentle word we make wise counsels and pious exhortations acceptable. (Prov. 31:26) Oh, what good the tongue does which is well ruled! Let us ask Our Lord thus to govern ours! *Resolutions and spiritual nosegay as above.*

SUMMARY OF TOMORROW'S MEDITATION

e will meditate tomorrow upon the mortification of our own mind, and we will consider its three principal digressions, which are: first, useless thoughts; second, wandering thoughts; third, the temerity of our judgments. We will then make the resolution: first, to apply ourselves solely to the action we have to perform at any moment, and to perform it with the view of pleasing God; second, to send away useless or wandering thoughts as soon as we perceive them; third, to mistrust our own judgment. Our spiritual nosegay shall be the words of the Imitation: "Attend to what you are doing."

MEDITATION FOR THE MORNING

Let us adore the Holy Ghost dwelling in us in order to be the rule of our actions, of our words, and of our thoughts. (1 Cor. 3:16) Let us render our homage to the Divine Spirit, who is willing to lead us, and let us ask Him to enable us always to follow His light instead of the aberrations of our own mind. (Gal. 5:25)

FIRST POINT

✝ *We ought to be on our Guard against Useless Thoughts*

First, they render us unhappy; a wrong which we have felt, an affront which we have received, a loss which we have endured, may have touched us just once; the thought which recurs to the wrong, the affront, or the loss will grieve us, perhaps, a hundred times, and without any useful result. Second, useless thoughts are one of the greatest obstacles to our sanctification. One of the most positive marks of tepidity, says St. Bonaventure, is not to feel the evil which useless thoughts do to the soul. We allow ourselves to give way to curiosity, that is to say, to a certain kind of love of what is novel; we in quire about all that passes, and we want to hear all kinds of news; sometimes we give way to reveries of the imagination, which keep the soul in a state of continual distraction, fill it with a thousand foolish thoughts, occupy it with a hundred chimerical events and designs; sometimes, lastly, we give way to excessive activity, which renders us uneasy and impatient and excites our brain, without our being able to make any progress. It is a little world of which the tumult amuses and dissipates us, where thoughts succeed one another without any order, are confused together and trouble us, render us unfit for prayer, for recollection, for self-examination, for the inspirations of the Holy Ghost, for the practice of virtues, which demand a mind at leisure with itself, a spirit of reflection. Thus day after day passes in distractions, without attention to God, without attention to ourselves, and often the devil profits by it to insinuate into the soul, under cover of use less thoughts, a thousand dangerous ones, in which charity, purity, and all the virtues run the greatest risks. Doubtless it does not depend upon us never to have useless thoughts, since we are leaves carried away by the wind, but what depends upon us is: first, to diminish the evil by less frivolity in our conduct, less curiosity about things we have no need to know, by less useless reading, by more exactitude in keeping the avenues of our senses, and retrenching numerous frivolous conversations; second, to put a stop to useless thoughts as soon as we perceive them, returning sweetly to God by raising our hearts to Him by ejaculatory prayers; third, during the day to have certain marked-out moments for entering into ourselves and recollecting ourselves, following therein the example set by the father of a family who, from time to time, leaves his affairs to return to his home and see whether every one has done his duty, after which he resumes the thread of his occupations.

SECOND POINT

✝ *We ought to be on our Guard against Wandering Thoughts*

Another abuse into which we fall is hardly ever to give up ourselves to what we are doing at the moment, and to preoccupy ourselves now with preceding actions and now with those which will follow. We forget the axiom of the sage: "There is a time for every business." (Eccles. 8:6) We forget above all the example of Jesus Christ, who said, when He was urged to act: "My hour is not yet come." (John 2:4) He did not anticipate it, He did not delay it, He let it come in peace. To be wholly given up to the present action as though we had done nothing before it and as though we should have nothing to do after it, that is great wisdom. We attain to it by means of being firmly determined to combat the preoccupation as soon as we perceive it; but still more by means of purity of intention, disengaged from all attachment and from all human motives. Do you wish, says the author of the Imitation, to possess your souls in peace amidst the most multifarious and the most difficult occupations, see in all things only the most adorable will of God, which is order and wisdom itself, and do not cling to any of your occupations. Be always above them, never below them, always standing upright between eternal and temporary things, having the latter under your feet and your eyes fixed on those which are above. (3 Imit. 38:1)

THIRD POINT

✝ *We ought always to be on our Guard against the Temerity of our own Judgment*

Our own judgment is presumptuous; it thinks it is able to examine everything and to pass sentence on everything, and it does both the one and the other with incredible thoughtlessness. It fancies that it, has no need of advice; it does not ask for any, and rejects that which is given to it, or if it submits, it is only at the end of a discussion, and it is always saying, like St. Thomas, I will not believe any one upon his own word, I will only believe after I have myself seen it. (John 20:25) Looking upon its own imaginations as infallible reasons, and on all its thoughts as oracles, it is so attached to its own ideas that it will never yield; it contests and disputes unceasingly, until others yield to what it asserts. Lastly, it argues about everything, and pronounces judgment upon everything, and passes a supreme sentence on everything, as though there was nothing which it is not competent to decide. Now, who is there who does not see the evil of such a digression, the pride which is at the root of it, and the eternal abysses which are the consequence of it? *Resolutions and spiritual nosegay as above.*

Sixteenth Saturday after Pentecost

SUMMARY OF TOMORROW'S MEDITATION

We will meditate tomorrow upon the mortification of the imagination, and we shall see: first, that our happiness in this world depends upon the government of our imagination and the repression of its wanderings; second, that nothing less than our eternal salvation is implicated in it. We will then make the resolution: first, in the morning, as soon as we awake, to employ our minds with holy thoughts and our hearts with pious affections, in order to prevent the wanderings of our imagination; second, to recollect ourselves at different moments during the day, to see whether we have yielded to our imagination, and to renew our resolution to combat it. Our spiritual nosegay shall be the words of the Holy Ghost: Do not give up your heart to your imaginations. (Ecclus. 34:6)

MEDITATION FOR THE MORNING

Let us adore Jesus Christ in the desert, raised by the devil upon a pinnacle of the temple and transported thence to a high mountain, where the tempter shows Him all the kingdoms of the earth: a striking type of our imagination, which transports us in a moment from one end of the earth to another, preoccupies us with pictures of exterior things, and tries to seduce us by its fantasies. Rebellious to reason, it revolts against the empire which we wish to exercise over it; and even when we are the most determined to combat it, it escapes from us and has already gone all around the world before we ourselves have perceived what it was doing. O Jesus, tempted in the desert, teach us to resist the temptations which our imagination excites in us!

FIRST POINT

✝ *Our Happiness in this World Depends upon the Government of our Imagination and the Repression of its Digressions*

There are no beings more unhappy than are men who have an ungovernable imagination; the past, the present, and the future everything troubles them. The past shows them a humiliation, a reverse, a disagreeable incident which had annoyed them at the time; and immediately the imagination seizes hold of the annoyance which exists no longer, increases, exaggerates it, and makes them feel it again in a hundred-fold degree, and always more keenly, changing the slightest trouble into an overwhelming one and rendering what was only a temporary evil permanent. The present annoys and disgusts them; they imagine they would be better placed anywhere than where they are; that others, who less deserve it, are happier than they. They are never wholly devoted to what they are doing; always their imagination distracts them from it, fatigues them with innumerable fancies and with vain phantoms, or with shame and remorse for their frivolity. The future does not less importune them, now by means of a pretended happiness towards which they eagerly rush, and which soon afterwards they despair of obtaining, and now by the apprehension of trials and imaginary crosses, which make them suffer as much as though they were real. In this way they become unbearable to themselves, always uneasy, and sad, discontented, and inconstant; then their imagination makes them see, in the minds of others, suspicions, contempt, hatred, bad intentions which do not exist, and they are overwhelmed; it inspires them with uneasiness and alarm which have no foundation, and they allow themselves to be cast down. In order to chase away annoyance and trouble, they would like to apply themselves to some serious pursuits, to some solid reading; but their imagination still distracts and absorbs their thoughts; they become disgusted and give up the attempt. Is not all this our history, and how often have we not sacrificed our happiness to vain phantoms?

SECOND POINT

✝ *Our Eternal Salvation Depends upon the Governing of our Imagination and the Repression of its Wanderings*

Who does not know, in fact, that the imagination is the place where all the passions take their birth and their increase and strength, the heart being attracted to an object from love towards it, or turned away from it by hatred, according as the imagination depicts it as being good or evil? Who does not know that when all kinds of objects are allowed to be impressed upon the imagination, there is insinuated into the mind more than can be expressed in words, which not only robs it of devotion and charity, but which exposes the soul to speedy loss? It is from this excess of liberty granted to the imagination that proceed dangerous thoughts, impure images, temptations of all kinds. If the world is so dangerous for those who frequent it, it is not less so, nay, it is even sometimes more so, for those who allow themselves to be introduced into it by means of their imagination, because it is then more seductive; the scenes it presents to the soul are more varied, and make a more immediate impression upon the senses, inflame the desires, awaken the passion which was lying dormant, increase and strengthen that which was ruling. Jerome, in the desert, saw in his imagination all the pomp of Rome; St. Augustine, in his retreat, saw all the pleasures of the world dragging him along, as it were, by his garments, and calling out to him: What! Wouldst thou forsake us forever? What! Wilt thou have nothing more to do with us? Happy those great saints who combated their imagination; otherwise they would have been lost. But if the imagination did not drag us into these states of great disorder, it is at least certain that it would be an obstacle to the acquisition of all virtue. We cannot expect from a soul which is the slave of imagination either the habit of reflection, which enables us to study, to know, and to superintend ourselves, nor the lively faith which supposes a soul given to reflection; nor the charity which supposes the forgetfulness of the faults and wrongs of our neighbor; nor the modesty which proceeds from calmness and the spirit of order ruling within us; nor the humility which closes the eyes to the picture of its own excellence, drawn in the imagination by the hand of self-love; nor the spirit of prayer, which is essentially opposed to the wanderings of the imagination. Let us examine our selves. Have we not taken pleasure in following the digression of our imagination and in busying it with a thousand phantoms? *Resolutions and spiritual nosegay as above.*

SAINTS DAYS

July 19th

ST. VINCENT DE PAUL

FIRST MEDITATION

SUMMARY OF TOMORROW'S MEDITATION

e will meditate during three days upon this incomparable priest, and, reflecting tomorrow on what he was towards God, we shall see: first, what was his faith; second, what was his confidence; third, what was his love. We will then make the resolution: first, often to repeat by day and by night the acts of faith, hope, and charity, in order to perfect ourselves in these three virtues; second, to do and say everything in a spirit of faith and love. Our spiritual nosegay shall be the words of St. Paul: "And there remain faith, hope, and charity; but the greater of these is charity." (1 Cor. 13:13)

MEDITATION FOR THE MORNING

Let us adore Our Savior giving St. Vincent de Paul to the Church to be forever the model of the priest and the most beautiful type of sacerdotal holiness. Let us thank Him for the magnificent present made to His Church and ask of Him grace to profit by it.

FIRST POINT
✝ **What the Faith of St. Vincent de Paul was**

Penetrated, by means of a lively faith, with the infinite greatness of God, this holy priest was filled with the most profound humiliation at the thought of his littleness in presence of the immensity of God; and this self-annihilation

---

showed itself in the whole of his person. It was seen in the humble and reverential manner in which he offered all his prayers, great or small; in his zeal for the decency of churches; in his piety in presence of the tabernacle, which seemed to make him long to abase himself to the very center of the earth, in such a way that nothing more than the sight of him was sufficient to awaken the most dormant faith, and to inspire the most insensible with feelings of piety. It was seen in his pious manner of celebrating the Holy Sacrifice, which made those who assisted at it exclaim with admiration: "My God, here is a priest who knows how to celebrate Mass well; it seems as though he were an angel." Lastly, in the reverential language with which he always spoke of God. "If," he said on one occasion, "the eyes of our mind were but strong enough to penetrate but a little way into the immensity of His supreme excellence, O Jesus, what lofty sentiments we should entertain of it! He is an abyss of perfection, an infinitely holy Being, infinitely pure, infinite in all things, whose supreme greatness ought to keep us always annihilated in His presence." The sentiment of this lofty truth was so deeply rooted in him that it kept him as recollected in public as he was in private, in the street as well as in the house, amidst the tumult of affairs as well as in the calm of prayer. Hence that perfect equanimity of his mind and in the expression of his face in which he was kept by the thought that the eyes of God were fixed upon him; hence the principles of faith which animated all his actions, even the most ordinary amongst them, and which he so strongly recommended to his followers. "It would be better," he said, "to be cast, with the head and hands bound, into a fiery furnace than to perform an action only to please men." It was observed that he used to pause for a moment before speaking or acting: first, to consult God, and to say to Him: "Let my judgment come forth from Thy countenance" (Ps. xvi. 2); second, to ask himself: What would Jesus Christ do or say if He were in my place? And he considered this practice to be one of the greatest importance in Christian life. "The cause of the little progress which some persons make," he said, "is because they act from human motives. In order to become perfect in a short time, we need only follow the light of faith in all things, and lean with all our weight upon it." Let us examine if it be thus that we live.

SECOND POINT
✝ What the Confidence of St. Vincent de Paul in God was

Always confiding in God, spite of the obstacles which his enterprises met with, and spite of the interior trials which he experienced, St. Vincent lived in a constant abandonment to Providence, without ever allowing himself to be cast down or discouraged. He did not neglect any human means, in order that he might not tempt God; and he waited with that heroic confidence which man's reason does not in the least comprehend and which faith alone can give. The more obstacles he had to encounter, the more he hoped, on account of the principle that Providence is never wanting in regard to things undertaken by its orders, and that it puts forth a helping hand to make them succeed when human means fail. On one occasion he was told that the house, exhausted by almsgiving, had nothing wherewith to supply its own needs. "So much the better," he replied. "The time has come when we shall see whether we have confidence in God. My God," he added, raising his eyes and his hands to heaven, "what happiness it is to be obliged to depend upon Thee, like a poor man on the liberality of one who is rich! O Lord, infinitely good! We cast ourselves headlong and with closed eyes into Thy paternal arms with firm and loving confidence."

THIRD POINT
✝ **What the Love of St. Vincent de Paul was for God**

St. Vincent placed the perfection of the love of God in the perfect conformity of all our sentiments and the whole of our will with the will of God. To confound the whole of our will with His adorable will, to find our whole pleasure in it, to have only one and the same will with His, to think anything to be good and amiable which it wills and not to desire anything else, this, according to him, is love in its highest degree; and these also were his dispositions. Whatever were the afflictions which happened to him, he met them with these simple words: It is the good pleasure of God; who would not acquiesce in it joyfully? An act of perfect acquiescence is worth more than a hundred thousand successes." Under the inspiration of this divine goodwill, he endeavored to do everything in the most perfect manner, with the sole object of pleasing God, of spreading everywhere the kingdom of Jesus Christ by missions, conferences, foundation of seminaries, and other holy works, the number of which it would not be possible to estimate.

His greatest sorrow was to see God offended; his greatest desire, to see Him known, loved, and served; his greatest joy, to think of the infinite glory which God possesses in Himself; his greatest anxiety, to obtain as much exterior glory for Him as possible. "My brethren," he said one day to his followers, "do you not feel the sacred fire burn within your breasts?" This divine fire burnt within his to such a degree that sometimes it kept him absorbed whole hours long in the contemplation of the crucifix which he held in his hands. Alas! How far we are from having this great love! Let us humble ourselves and ardently desire to love always more and more. *Resolutions and spiritual nosegay as above.*

July 20Th
ST. VINCENT DE PAUL

SECOND MEDITATION

SUMMARY OF TOMORROW'S MEDITATION

e will consider tomorrow what was towards his neighbor: first, the charity of St. Vincent; second, his meekness; third, his special tenderness with regard to the poor. We will then make the resolution: first, to treat our neighbor, above all those who wound or displease us, with great charity and meekness; second, to entertain a feeling of affection towards the poor, as being the best friends of God, and to help them as far as we can. Our spiritual nosegay shall be the precept of Our Lord: "A new commandment I give unto you, that you love one another, as I have loved you." (John 13:34)

MEDITATION FOR THE MORNING

Let us adore God forming in St. Vincent de Paul a heart so good and charitable, so gentle, so compassionate towards all human miseries, especially the needs of the poor. Let us bless Him for this masterpiece of His grace, and let us ask Him to enable us to participate in the virtues of this amiable heart.

FIRST POINT
✝ **The Charity of St. Vincent de Paul towards his Neighbor**
It is doubtful whether, since the apostles, grace has ever formed a heart more loving and more devoted to his neighbor than was that of this holy priest. His soul overflowed, as it were, with mercy and the divine goodness. He saw in each individual an image and a child of God, a living member, a brother, and a co-heir of Jesus Christ, a temple of the Holy Ghost; and this consideration

inspired him with a respect, an esteem, and a love which cannot be described. Recalling to himself, on the one side, that we ought to love one another as Jesus Christ Himself has loved us, and on the other side, that our divine Savior loved us to such a degree as to come from heaven to earth to subject Himself to our miseries, to suffering, to ignominy, and to death, he loved his neighbor with all the love of which his soul was capable, and even then he was afraid of not loving him sufficiently, and asked for grace to love him more and more. "Oh, if we had," he said, "but a single spark of the sacred fire with which the heart of Jesus burned, should we not do a thousand times more for our brethren than we do now? Those who have true charity in their hearts reveal it by their works; and as it is the property of fire to warm and enlighten, so it is the property of love to communicate itself to all, and to spread itself everywhere." Hence that loving heart which showed itself to all who came to him; that zeal to send his missionaries to solace the unhappy, to instruct the ignorant, to convert sinners, into hospitals and prisons, into fields and upon mountains, into Ireland, Poland, and Italy, Tunis, Algiers, and Madagascar, without allowing himself to be disconcerted by pestilence and the tempests which absorbed his best workmen. Hence that watchfulness over his heart and his words, so that he never complained or spoke evil of any one whatever, and always took in hand the defense of the absent; hence that touching love for his enemies, which enabled him to bear reproach, shame, and troubles, rather than justify himself at their expense. It was sufficient to have shown enmity towards him in order to make him the best of friends, full of kindness and delicate attentions. Is it thus that we love our neighbor?

SECOND POINT

✝ Meekness of St. Vincent de Paul

St. Vincent was born with a bilious and choleric temperament. But, he said, "I prayed to God, and I earnestly entreated Him to take from me this hard and forbidding disposition, and to give me a meek and benign spirit; and through His grace, with the efforts I have made to conquer myself, I am somewhat reformed." And it would not be possible to give expression to the perfection of this reformation. He had a frankness of manner, a serenity of expression, an obliging manner of conversing, which recalled to mind the meekness of Jesus Christ, who willed to have rude and uneducated men for His disciples that He might teach us mutual endurance, and then an apostle who was a traitor, but whom He embraced tenderly, addressing to him the words, My friend, to teach us meekness. O Lord, said the holy priest, after having shown us such an example, Thou hast indeed good reason to say: "Learn of Me, because I am meek of heart." (Matt. 11:29) In order to persuade his followers to imitate so beautiful an example, he was accustomed to say to them: How do you wish to be treated your selves? With meekness doubtless; every one desires that, no one likes to be reproved with bitterness, and be led under the influence of bad humor. Therefore you must repress all impatient movements, the impetuosities of the fire of anger which rises to the face and changes its hue, troubles the soul, and makes us no longer what we were. Cut passion short, in order to recollect yourselves, and unite yourselves with God, saying, Lord, teach me to be meek. Preserve the affability, the serenity of countenance, the cordial manner which gives consolation and confidence, and that ease of manner, that charming simplicity, which seems to give you its heart and to ask for yours. Is it thus that we are meek towards our neighbor?

THIRD POINT

✝ The Special Tenderness of St. Vincent de Paul towards the Poor

We are astonished when we do nothing more than read the enumeration of all that this holy priest did for the poor: the numerous hospitals with Sisters of Charity to serve them; the convocations and the confraternities for helping the poor in their own homes; the institutions for abandoned children and forsaken old people, the redemption of captives, the succors taken to districts which had been a prey to conflagration, to the shipwrecked, to laborers ruined by adverse seasons; Lorraine and the Duchy of Bar, Artois, Maine, Angoumois, Berri, Picardy, and Champagne, fed for more than ten years, during which the ravages of war and famine lasted; more than two thousand poor fed every day in Paris in the midst of the troubles of civil war; more than fourteen thousand assisted elsewhere by his aid, without counting the succors sent to submerged towns. Our littleness could not, of course, attempt to do anything of the kind, but what we can do is at least to imitate the sentiments of this holy priest towards the poor. He was filled with a tender and paternal love for them; he bore them in his entrails, as being the best friends of God and the suffering members of Jesus Christ; their indigence and misery excited all his compassion, to help them was the object of all his thoughts. Alas! he exclaimed, at the approach of winter, whilst uttering deep sighs and shedding tears, this is indeed a very severe season! What will become of the poor? Where will they go? That is my sorrow and the care which weighs me down. Then he gave away all he had, happy at being deemed worthy to use all that there was in his house that he might help the poor. How happy should we be, he once said, to become poor, because of our having exercised charity towards the poor! And if one of us were reduced through charity to beg his bread, to lie down out of doors, perishing with cold, and if someone were to come and say to us: Poor priest, what is it that has reduced you to this state? what happiness to be able to answer: It is charity! Oh, how highly esteemed would such a priest be by God and the angels! Let us here examine our conscience; what relation is there between his sentiments and ours? *Resolutions and spiritual nosegay as above.*

July 21ST

ST. VINCENT DE PAUL

THIRD MEDITATION

SUMMARY OF TOMORROW'S MEDITATION

e will tomorrow continue our meditations upon St. Vincent de Paul, and we shall see that, considered in himself, he was an admirable pattern: first, of humility; second, of mortification; third, of wisdom. We will then make the resolution: first, to be on our guard against the suggestions of self-love in our thoughts, our words, and our acts; second, to mortify ourselves today in what is most contrary to our inclinations. Our spiritual nosegay shall be the words of the Holy Spirit: "He that walketh sincerely walketh confidently." (Prov. 10:9)

MEDITATION FOR THE MORNING

Let us adore Jesus Christ as the great pattern after which St. Vincent de Paul molded himself in regard to all the beautiful virtues which have rendered His memory dear to heaven and earth. Let us beg this holy priest to obtain for us the grace of taking Jesus Christ as our pattern in all things, so that like him we may become humble, mortified, and wise in true Christian wisdom.

FIRST POINT
✝ The Humility of St. Vincent de Paul

This wonderful man, who did more for religion and humanity than did any prince seated upon a throne, never departed from the humble sentiments he entertained in regard to himself. He looked upon the esteem in which he was held as a chastisement for his sins, an insult to his extreme misery, considering himself to be a perverse man capable of everything that is evil, incapable of everything good, a marvel of malice, as he said of himself, more wicked than the devil, who, he said, had not deserved to be in hell as much as he himself had. "What astonishes me," he also said, "is that I should have been allowed until now to remain in the situation where I am, I the most rustic, the most ridiculous, and the most foolish of men, and incapable of saying half a dozen consecutive sentences, and continually showing that I have neither intelligence nor judgment, nor any kind of virtue. I am not a man, but a poor worm which crawls upon the earth without knowing where I am going, and who only seeks to hide himself in Thee, O my God! who art all my desire. I am a poor blind man, who cannot advance a single step in what is good, except Thou holds out the hand of Thy mercy to lead me." So much humility within reflected itself necessarily on the exterior, spite of the efforts which he made to hide it, and to appear, not humble, but contemptible. Hence his care never to justify himself when he was reproved, to endeavor to make his slightest defects of memory or understanding to pass for a want of good sense and of judgment, to proclaim on all occasions the lowliness of his birth, together with anything that might tend to lower him in the esteem of others; hence the feeling which led him with regret to make use of all things, not only of those which are useful and agreeable but even those which are necessary to life; he considered himself to be unworthy of them, and even when sitting down to table he would say, " Miserable man, you have not earned the bread you eat." Hence the rule of his conduct which he had laid down: "If I perform a public action, I will cut off from it all the luster I might be able to put into it, and I will limit myself to what is strictly necessary. Of two thoughts which may present themselves to my mind, I will only show the smallest and most simple, retaining the most beautiful in order to sacrifice it to God in the secret of my heart, through love for Our Lord, who takes delight only in actions and words marked by simplicity." Hence, lastly, the modesty which shone in the whole of his person, in his behavior, his language, his clothing, and even his eyes. All these things made a friend of his say that never had an ambitious man so great a passion for honors, elevation, and esteem, as this holy priest had for abjection, humiliation, and contempt.

SECOND POINT

✝ Mortification of St. Vincent de Paul

The life of St. Vincent displayed nothing very austere as regarded its exterior; it was apparently an ordinary kind of life, but within there was universal mortification; his chamber was of the most simple and unfurnished description, his clothing of the poorest kind, often worn and patched; he wished to have the poorest kind of food given him, and paid no attention to what was put before him. When anything was wanting to him, he rejoiced at being able thereby to honor the poverty and destitution of Jesus Christ; and when the season was severe he would not accept anything calculated to afford him some alleviation. Lastly, nothing more than the restraint visible in his eyes, his speech, and his behavior was requisite in order to show how perfectly mortified he was. At the same time he excelled still more in interior mortification. He was so entirely his own master in all the movements of his soul that no annoyance of any kind could disturb his perfect equanimity. There was always the same calmness within, upon his face the same serenity, in his manner of acting or of speaking the same reserve. Tribulation did not cast him down or joy transport him, or reverses disconcert him, or success inebriate him, because in all things he saw nothing but the will of God, which was always the same to him in whatever disposition he might be. "O my Savior," he often said, "give us grace to do away with ourselves, to hate ourselves that we may love Thee better, to die to ourselves that we may save ourselves," and he gave for it this reason namely, that mortification is so necessary to salvation that if a person who had already one foot in heaven were to leave off the exercise of this virtue only for the space of the moment required for putting his other foot there also, he would run a risk of being lost.

THIRD POINT
✝ The Wisdom of St. Vincent de Paul

True wisdom consists: first, in tending constantly to our end, which is God; second, to tend towards it through the means which are the most efficacious. Now, St. Vincent de Paul did both the one and the other admirably. First, in all things he considered God alone, without human respect, without regard to self-interest, without subterfuge, with a simple mind, a simple heart, a simple intention, language that was always sincere, even though shame might accrue to him from it; this is what the whole of his history attests. Second. He tended to God by means of the most efficacious ways; for it was by following the maxims of the gospel, the example of the Savior, the guidance of the Holy Ghost; it was by allowing himself to be directed by Providence and waiting until it manifested itself without ever attempting to forestall it. He always studied the ways of God, in order to follow them, and was afraid of infusing anything human into them, because, he said, "man always spoils the work of God. It is God," he himself remarked, "who has done all in anything that I have done; all has been begun without my having thought about it, without my even knowing what God had the intention to perform." Let us compare ourselves with this beautiful model. What is the point we have attained in this simplicity of aim, which seeks for nothing but God, and in this wisdom in the choice of means, which consults God rather than the prudence of the flesh? *Resolutions and spiritual nosegay as above.*

JULY 22ND

FEAST OF ST. MARY MAGDALENE

SUMMARY OF TOMORROW'S MEDITATION

e will meditate tomorrow upon the great love which St. Mary Magdalene felt for Jesus Christ, and we shall see that it was: first, a love prompt for sacrifice; second, a humble love; third, a generous love. We will then make the resolution: first, to be determined once for all to entertain a true love for Our Savior, confessing that we have not hitherto loved Him sufficiently; Second, not to refuse to our gracious Savior any of the sacrifices His grace may require from us. Our spiritual nosegay shall be the words of Jesus Christ respecting Mary Magdalene: "Many sins are forgiven her because she hath loved much". (Luke 7:47)

MEDITATION FOR THE MORNING

Let us admire the great mercy of God the Son towards Mary Magdalene. She had greatly sinned; and Jesus Christ, far from repelling her from Him because of her great sins, has compassion on her; His grace goes in search of her in the midst of her wanderings, like the good shepherd who goes in search of the sheep who has wandered from the fold; He calls her, and she comes. O goodness! O love! O infinite mercy! how worthy art thou of all our praise, of all our admiration, of all our love! Let us bless this tenderness of God towards poor sinners, and at the same time let us congratulate Mary Magdalene on her docility to the grace which called her.

FIRST POINT

✝ St. Mary Magdalene Entertained towards Jesus a Love which was Prompt in Making Sacrifices

As soon as the first rays of grace had enlightened the soul of Mary Magdalene and enabled her to see in Jesus her Savior and her God, she hastens immediately in search of Him. She hears that He is at the house of Simon the Pharisee. Does she wait until He has left and she can speak to Him secretly? No, she cannot remain one moment longer in a state of sin, or bear to be an object of hatred to her God. Without any delay, and treading under foot all human respect, she rises; love seems to give her wings, and she flies to the dwelling of Simon the Pharisee, taking with her an alabaster vase, full of exquisite perfumes which had been destined for the satisfaction of her sensuality. She falls at the feet of Jesus, she breaks the vase, and pours the perfume with her tears upon the sacred feet of Jesus, dries them with her hair, and kisses them with the most tender and loving affection, sacrificing at once human respect, the vanity of her hair, and the refinements of her sensuality. She is still in the flower of her age; her days flow on happily according to worldly ideas, in the midst of all that gives pleasure, amusement, and distraction, of all that is the charm of life, that flatters the senses, self-love, and the passion for pleasure. But nothing of that kind stops her; she makes an eternal divorce from the world, that she may attach herself to Jesus, to Jesus alone, to Jesus with her whole heart, and in order to do so she counts all sacrifices as naught. Is it thus that we are prompt in allowing ourselves to be led by grace, prompt in making to God all the sacrifices He asks of us, without ever drawing back in the presence of any human consideration of the repugnance of nature, of self-love, or for the sake of what the world will say? Alas! what delays! what resistance! Let us humble ourselves and be converted on this holy day.

SECOND POINT

✝ St. Mary Magdalene's Love for Jesus was Humble

Mary Magdalene does not pride herself upon the goodness of Jesus towards her; she does not esteem herself any the more because she is more loved, because she is converted, and because her love is greater; she is always filled with the most humble sentiments in regard to herself; she is ashamed at having loved a God so amiable so late; she despises herself, and accepts the contempt of every creature as being her due. She knows that the step she has taken in going to the house of Simon the Pharisee, and presenting herself before a great number of brilliant guests, will render her an object of censure to the whole assembly, the object of public ridicule, and her name a byword in Judea. It does not signify.

Never, in her own opinion, will she receive enough of shame and contempt. On her entrance into Simon's house she prostrates herself on her knees, and then draws near to the Savior, not in front of Him, she deems herself to be unworthy to look at Him, but she keeps behind Him, and kisses, not His adorable face, but His sacred feet (Luke 7:38) and waters them with her tears, bitterly regretting her past life; and the blood of her heart flows from her eyes. Happy tears, which extinguish the fire of concupiscence in her, drown her sins, chase away the demons, and rejoice the angels! Let us hence learn that our love ought always to be accompanied by shame and humility. Let us learn to be content to be at the feet of Jesus, cast down by the feeling of our littleness and our unworthiness, and not be ambitious for the extraordinary graces which God bestows upon elect souls. It is enough to be suffered in His presence, without His raising us to the kiss of His mouth and the holy joys of His divine Spirit.

THIRD POINT

✝ St. Mary Magdalene had a Generous Love for Jesus

Possessed with the love of her good Master, she follows Him as much as she can in His apostolic journeys, to receive the instructions which issue from His adorable mouth and to serve Him in all His needs. When the divine Savior visits her at Bethania, she can think only of Him, occupy herself only with Him, and on her knees before Him she listens to Him with delight; He is everything to her heart. When, at the season of the Passion, He is raised upon the cross, she is there, together with the Blessed Virgin, that she may console Him if she cannot defend Him, and she braves with intrepidity the mockery and the insults of the people. When He has breathed His last sigh, she purchases perfumes to embalm His body, and the same night she hastens with such eagerness to perform this pious duty that she reaches the tomb before the rising of the sun.(John 20:1) The apostles come in their turn, and not finding Jesus there, they return; but Mary remains; love keeps her there; (John 20:11) and, inconsolable as she is, she asks men and angels for her good Master. "They have taken away my Lord," she says; "tell me where they have laid Him, that I may go and take Him away." (John 20:13,15) Could there be a love more generous? Lastly, Jesus shows Himself to her; she casts herself at His feet, and will not be separated from Him anymore; but Jesus desires her to go and announce His resurrection to the apostles, and she sacrifices the sweetness of her interview to obedience. After Pentecost her generous love does more still; she sets out with Lazarus, her brother, and Martha, her sister, to evangelize the Gauls; she evangelizes them by her words and still more by her example, leading a life of mortification and penance, lying upon the bare ground, passing a portion of the day and night in prayer, having as her asylum nothing but a grotto in a rock, which is known at the present day by the name of Sainte Baume. May such generous love as hers confound our cowardice, which always wishes to enjoy without ever suffering, to live at its ease and never have any annoyance. No, that is not to love! *Resolutions and spiritual nosegay as above.*

JULY 25th

FEAST OF ST. JAMES THE GREATER

SUMMARY OF TOMORROW'S MEDITATION

e will meditate tomorrow upon St. James, and we shall remark in him two very different kinds of ambitions: one vicious, the other honorable and holy. We will then make the resolution: first, not to listen to self-love, which leads us to put ourselves forward and to endeavor to raise ourselves; second, to have no other ambition here below but that of suffering, living and dying like Jesus Christ and for Jesus Christ. Our spiritual nosegay shall be the words of the Psalmist: "How inebriating, how delightful, is the chalice which God presents to us, that we may drink out of it!" (Ps. 22:5)

MEDITATION FOR THE MORNING

Let us adore Our Lord calling to the apostolate St. James the Greater, the elder brother of St. John the Evangelist, the son of Zebedee and of Salome, and favoring him on several occasions, especially on Tabor, where He made him to be a witness of His transfiguration. Let us thank Our Lord for all that He did on behalf of this apostle, and let us receive instruction from studying the good and the evil which characterized the life of this happy disciple.

FIRST POINT
✝ The Vicious Ambition of St. James

It was a belief universally spread in the Jewish nation that the Messias would found a temporal kingdom upon earth. The mother of James had often conversed with him and St. John, his brother, about it; and, in accordance with the inspirations of maternal love when the future of her beloved children is in question, she went with them to Jesus Christ and said to Him: Master, command that my two sons here present shall sit in Thy kingdom one on Thy right hand, the other on Thy left. And the Savior made to these two disciples, of whom their mother was only the organ, this beautiful answer, which is well worthy our meditation: "You know not what you ask." (Matt. 20:22) How true these words are! No, my God, he who desires to be raised to a lofty position does not know what he asks: first, because to desire to quit one's position is not reasonable; such a pretension, if it were to become general, would upset the whole of society; second, because every one of us ought to respect the order of Providence; we should be wanting towards God if we attempted to leave it, and we cannot count upon His assistance excepting when we are in the position in which He wills we should be; third, because it is an error to imagine that we should be better elsewhere than where we are; such an idea only engenders unhappiness and discontent; fourth, because where positions are more elevated, the responsibility is greater, self-love stronger, pride more lofty, dangers more numerous; fifth, because to place our ambition upon things here below is not worthy of man; we must raise our aspirations higher and elevate them up to heaven. My son, said King Philip to Alexander, my kingdom is too small for you; extend your great heart further. And we, Christians, we ought to say to ourselves: Earth is too low for us; do not let us attach a heart made for heaven to lower things. My son, said St. Ignatius to Xavier, who was in love with the world, be ambitious if you will, but do not have an ambition so low that it contents itself with perishable honors; aspire only to the immortal honors of Paradise; love glory if you will, but let it be the glory which does not pass away like smoke, the solid glory of the kingdom of heaven. Let us here examine our hearts; are these sentiments ours?

SECOND POINT
✝ The Holy and Honorable Ambition of St. James

Jesus Christ, raising the thoughts of His apostles from an earthly kingdom to the kingdom of heaven, said to them: In order to reach My kingdom you must drink of the chalice of suffering and of bitterness that I must drink of Myself; are you able to do it? "Yes, Lord," they replied, "we can"; (Matt. 20:22) and from that time forward a new and holy ambition took hold of them, that of being poor and following a God who was poor, to accompany Him in His journeys, to labor during the day, to watch and pray during the night, and constantly to bear the cross; to forget themselves, to despise themselves, and to sacrifice anything for the gospel. The life of St. James, in fact, as St. Epiphanus tells us, was most austere, and his zeal for the conversion of Jews and infidels knew no bounds. He was the first of the apostles to give his life for Jesus Christ, the first among them who dyed the holy city with his blood. He converted his executioner by embracing him; and his death, being the occasion of the dispersion of the apostles, was the means of spreading the preaching of the gospel over the earth. O holy ambition! thou wert satisfied! Thou didst drink of the chalice down to its last drop, and, like the Psalmist, thou didst delight in its savor, saying with him: How beautiful is my chalice, how inebriating it is! (Ps. 22:5) Let us learn from hence where to place our ambition. *Resolutions and spiritual nosegay as above.*

JULY 31ST

FEAST OF ST. IGNATIUS

SUMMARY OF TOMORROW'S MEDITATION

e will meditate tomorrow upon St. Ignatius, and we shall see with what zeal he labored: first, to sanctify himself; second, to sanctify others. We will then make the resolution: first, to examine into all the attachments which may still remain in our hearts and generously to break them off; second, to watch over our intentions, that we may do nothing from habit or routine or from human motives, but refer all to the greater glory of God; third, to lead our neighbor to what is good by means of our example, and when we are able by our words. Our spiritual nosegay shall be the motto of St. Ignatius: "All to the greater glory of God."

MEDITATION FOR THE MORNING

Let us adore Jesus Christ bringing the fire from heaven to earth, and with it kindling the heart of St. Ignatius (Luke 12:49). Let us admire the wonderful change which He worked in this great saint, and let us beg of Him to change us in the same manner.

FIRST POINT

✟ Zeal of St. Ignatius in Sanctifying Himself

Whoever aspires to holiness must destroy in himself nature vitiated by original sin, and fill himself with holy love. This is what St. Ignatius understood in an admirable manner. First, he destroyed nature in himself. When he was one day reading the Lives of the Saints, grace said to his heart: Do like the saints whose lives you are reading; leave the world, its hopes, its possessions, and its glories, but above all bid farewell to yourself. At that very moment he quit the world, which until then had been his idol; he renounced the love of his senses, which until then he had flattered by a life of pleasures and enjoyments; he condemned himself to the privations and severities of penance, exchanged his luxurious garments for the rags of the poor, and, shut up in the grotto of Manresa, without any other bed than the bare ground, without any other food than bread and water, he crucified his flesh by severe discipline. If, later on, he spared his body these austerities that he might employ his strength for the greater glory of God, he counterbalanced them by the austere modesty which, by regulating the behavior, the deportment, and the eyes, preserves the soul in a state of holy recollection. At the same time he renounces his inclinations; from the magnificence and the refinement of the court, he passes into hospitals, devotes himself to the care of all kinds of human miseries, even the most disgusting, and makes himself the servant of all, he who, until then, had been accustomed to command and to speak as a master. He renounces his temper; he who had been hasty and choleric by nature, still more choleric and more likely to be carried away by anger in his profession as a soldier, becomes gentle as a lamb and patient like Jesus Christ, even when he was being subjected to the most shameful kind of treatment, the sole thought of which would formerly have made him shudder, but which now was his delight and the object of his desires. He renounces his self-love; not content with hiding the splendor of his birth beneath the commonest kind of clothing, the charm of his courtesy under a negligent exterior, the talents he possessed under an affected stupidity, he receives, as a piece of good fortune, contempts and insults, and exults when he is put into chains like a criminal. Lastly, he renounces all attachments, to the extent of being able to say, "I see nothing on earth the loss of which could trouble the peace of my soul." Second. His heart, thus emptied of all that is not God, fills itself to such a degree with God, that he breathes henceforth nothing here below except holy love. All creatures recall God to him so perfectly that nothing more than the sight of a flower throws him into ecstasy, and thus all things considered outside God seem to him to be insipid. At the same time it seems to him as though he did not even yet love enough, and he asks God for His love, sacrificing to Him everything else for the sake of so great a possession. He is heard and answered; new flames of love consume him, make him fall into a swoon, draw from his eyes torrents of tears, keep him in an habitual union with God, in an abandonment without reserve to the divine rule, in so great a horror of displeasing God in the very slightest degree that it seems to him that in hell his greatest torment would be to see God was not loved there; lastly, he exercises constant attention to do everything, to say everything, and to think everything for the greater glory of God.

SECOND POINT
✝ Zeal of St. Ignatius in Sanctifying Others

It is not enough for me only, he said, to serve the Lord; all hearts must be brought to love Him, all tongues to bless Him. From the depths of his grotto at Manresa he sees a world to be reformed, another world to be evangelized: Europe, which is losing the faith, America and the Indies, which do not as yet possess it; and embracing the whole of the universe in his zeal, he begins by composing and spreading the book of the Spiritual Exercises, which has converted more souls than it contains letters; then he comes to Paris to mix with children and to pursue his studies, which had been neglected until then, but which are necessary to his designs. There he founds the Society of Jesus, the center of so many doctors and apostles, of so many evangelists and martyrs. The general of this new army, he sends these soldiers of Jesus Christ into all parts of the world; and he, whilst governing this great body from the centre of Catholicity, catechizes little ones and the poor, brings back sinners, embraces all kind of good works, and is so full of devotedness that on one occasion he threw himself into a frozen pond that he might touch a soul which was on the point of being lost, even to the point of losing his eternal salvation had it been necessary; for, he said, I would rather remain on earth uncertain of my salvation than enter at that moment into Paradise, if I could thereby convert one single soul. Could there possibly be more zeal for sanctification of his neighbor? Alas! what do we do in comparison? Resolutions and spiritual nosegay as above

August 4th

FEAST OF ST. DOMINIC

SUMMARY OF TOMORROW'S MEDITATION

e will make our next meditation upon St. Dominic, whose feast we shall celebrate tomorrow. We shall admire in this great saint three different kinds of apostolate: the apostolate of prayer, the apostolate of example, and the apostolate of preaching. We will then make the resolution: first, to pray with more fervor for the conversion of sinners and the needs of the Church and of our own country; second, never to set anything but a good example towards others, so that they may be led to God. Our spiritual nose gay shall be the words of St. James: "Pray one for another that you may be saved; for the prayer of a just man availeth much." (James 5:16)

MEDITATION FOR THE MORNING

Let us adore Jesus Christ, who is always attentive to the needs of the Church, raising up St. Dominic in the thirteenth century to defend her against the ravages of the heresy which desolated the south of France, and to preach against the bad passions which covered the world with scandals. Let us admire the fidelity of St. Dominic in responding to his vocation. Not only did he re-establish faith and morals wherever he went, but he founded a society of apostles who were destined throughout all coming ages to bear the gospel to the extremities of the earth. Let us consider above all the triple apostolate by means of which he performed all these great works: the apostolate of prayer, the apostolate of example, and the apostolate of preaching. Let us bless Jesus Christ for so much good done to the Church by St. Dominic; let us congratulate St. Dominic upon it, who himself was the apostle and the founder of a society of apostles.

FIRST POINT

✝ St. Dominic was one of the most Beautiful Examples of the Apostolate of Prayer

The apostolate of prayer consists in calling down the blessing of Heaven, by means of fervent prayers, upon sinners to be converted, upon the evils by which the Church is attacked, in order to repair them, upon all kinds of calamities, that they may be averted, upon all kinds of good works to be founded and pursued. This apostolate has four remarkable characteristics: first, it is possible to all, since all can pray; second, it is protected from all danger of self-love, since all passes in secret between God and the soul: third, it is the necessary condition of all success, since without the intervention of God human works cannot produce any fruit; fourth, it is a certain means of success, since prayer which is well performed is all-powerful over the heart of God, and often certain conversions, of which the world gives the honor to a preacher, are really only the work performed by an unknown pious soul who prays in secret Filled with these holy thoughts, St. Dominic made of the whole of his life a life of prayer. From his earliest youth he prayed during the day, he prayed during the night. Raised to the priesthood and named canon of the cathedral of Osma, he devoted himself still more fervently to the apostolate of prayer, and he was seen in his stall at his chapter praying with the modesty and the fervor of an angel. Sent by his bishop to the south of France that he might defend religion, menaced by the heretics, and not being able to make himself heard by them, he had recourse to his usual weapons: he prays and makes the faithful pray by means of the recitation of the Rosary. Everything yields to this new kind of apostolate; heresy gives up its arms; order, peace, and happiness are renewed in the desolated provinces. Dominic, delighted with so good a result, dreams of erecting into a religious order the apostolic men who aided him. The Holy See at first refuses its approbation. Dominic prays; the Holy See thereupon erects the new Order; and numerous subjects are procured for it. From Rome, where he had obtained a victory destined to be so fruitful, the new founder goes into different towns and villages, there to preach the gospel, but always under the safeguard of prayer. In his journeys he walks alone, separated from his companions, that he may converse with God more at his ease. Arrived at the gates of the town, he falls on his knees, praying God not to send thunder upon the town wherein he is about to penetrate. Having entered the town, his first visit is to the churches, there to adore God who inhabits them, and to recommend to Him his ministry. This is how St. Dominic accomplished the apostolate of prayer. How do we fulfill it ourselves? Do we often pray for the conversion of sinners, for the Church, for our country, for the whole of society, for the success of holy works?

SECOND POINT

✝ St. Dominic was an Apostle through the Apostolate of Example

We may all be apostles without preaching: a good example is a sermon; and it was one of the means whereby St. Dominic converted so many souls. From whatever point of view we may regard him, down to the smallest details of his public or private life, in his manner of acting, of speaking, and of praying, even in his deportment, his repasts, and his clothing, everywhere he was seen to be a holy man who had nothing earthly about him, a man without any other passion save that of the glory of God and the salvation of souls, who, notwithstanding an illustrious birth and the possession of great riches, loved poverty to such an extent as to make himself a beggar for the sake of Jesus Christ, and to choose for his own use the poorest tunic of the community, after having distributed amongst the poor, before entering into religion, not only his possessions, but even his books, annotated with a great deal of labor by his own hand. We see in him a penitent who had no other bed than a plank or the bare ground, no other undergarment than a coarse hair-shirt which tore his innocent flesh. He was, lastly, admired as a religious so humble that he received opprobrium and insults as things that were due to him; so modest in his behavior, that his face, as though it were shining with a ray of the divine majesty, inspired every one with profound veneration; so recollected, above all in prayer, that no one could behold him without being astonished. He was always full of reverence in presence of the greatness of God; sometimes his eyes were cast down and his body motionless; at other times his arms were stretched out in admiration like a man who is in an ecstasy, And all these things taken together were an eloquent sermon, which touched and converted souls. Behold a man of God! They said, and no one could resist such an example. Let us here examine ourselves; is it thus that we exercise the apostolate of example? Does everything in us, in the house, at church, in society, everywhere where we are, edify others?

THIRD POINT

✝ St. Dominic Exercised the Apostolate of Preaching

The first condition for performing this kind of apostolate with success is to burn with the sacred fire of zeal, in such a manner that the mouth really speaks out of the abundance of the heart. Now such was St. Dominic in an eminent degree; and God was pleased to reveal this several times to the world, sometimes by making a halo of glory appear above his head, sometimes by raising his body from the ground, as if the flame, which tends always to rise, had endeavored to take to Paradise his pure body and holy soul. Every day this true apostle wept over the sins of the world, and made the accents of his charity, like a cry of distress, ascend to heaven. "O Lord," he would exclaim, "have pity on these poor sinners; what will become of them if they are not converted? " Then, possessed by a holy passion for the glory of God and the salvation of souls, he appeared in the pulpit like Moses descending from Sinai, and from his mouth flowed words full of fire which converted hearts. When he descended from the pulpit he went into the houses of the people, into the fields, along the roads, by the bedside of the sick, speaking to all of God and of salvation. He sometimes met with perverse and wicked men who responded to his zeal by insults, threw mud at him, and spat in his face; but he continued his apostolate in spite of them. They threatened to kill him. "Ah!" he exclaimed, "I do not deserve so beautiful a death!" and he pursued the course of his preaching in Italy, France, and Spain. He was an indefatigable apostle, and yet it seemed to him as though he had done nothing yet; and in order to increase the little he did in his own opinion, he created the Order of Friar Preachers, who were to go throughout the whole world bearing with them the Cross and the Gospel. What is our zeal for God and for souls compared with that of St. Dominic? *Resolutions and spiritual nosegay as above.*

AUGUST 10ᵀʰ

FEAST OF ST. LAWRENCE

SUMMARY OF TOMORROW'S MEDITATION

e will meditate tomorrow upon this illustrious martyr, and we shall see: first, what St. Lawrence did for Jesus Christ; second, what we ought to do, following his example. We will then make the resolution: first, to encourage ourselves to increase daily in divine love, which alone can give us courage to perform our duty in all circumstances; second, to be ready to die rather than offend God, and to suffer all the trials of life in a spirit of martyrdom; third, to declare ourselves openly to be on the side of religion and the Church, without regard to human respect. Our spiritual nose gay shall be the words of Our Lord in the gospel: "He that shall be ashamed of Me and My words; of him the Son of man shall be ashamed when He shall come in His majesty and that of His Father." (Luke 9:24)

MEDITATION FOR THE MORNING

Let us adore the power of grace communicating to St. Lawrence superhuman courage to do and suffer all that he did and suffered for Jesus Christ. Let us offer to God our praises and thanksgivings for it, saying with the Psalmist: "God is wonderful in His saints." (Ps. 57:36)

FIRST POINT

✝ What St. Lawrence Did for Jesus Christ

St. Lawrence, one of the most illustrious martyrs of Rome, was filling the position of deacon to St. Sixtus the Pope, when, on August 2, 258, the holy Pontiff was arrested and led to martyrdom. Afflicted at not dying with his Bishop for Jesus Christ, he went to him: Where art thou going, my father, without thy son? he said to him with tears and sighs, thou who didst never ascend the altar without him? In what have I had the unhappiness to displease thee? Try me, holy father, try me, and see whether thou wast deceived in the choice thou didst make of me; if, charged by thee with the dispensation of the blood of Jesus Christ, I am cowardly enough to refuse Him mine. These words recall to us the custom of the time, which was for the deacon to distribute holy communion to the faithful at the same time as alms to the poor. The holy old man, in order to console this fervent levite, tells him that in three days he will follow him by a still more dazzling and forever memorable martyrdom. St. Lawrence, receiving this answer as a certain prediction of his martyrdom, hastens to distribute amongst the poor what he had in his hands of the possessions of the Church, selling even the sacred vessels and giving away the price of them. The pagan judge, not less miserly than he was cruel, asks him where are the treasures of the Church. "Behold them," replies St. Lawrence, pointing out to him the poor whom he had collected together; "these are the greatest riches of the Church." Irritated by this answer, which frustrated his cupidity, the judge ordered that his body should be lacerated with scourges, and then had him stretched upon a gridiron under which were coals, hot enough to burn him, but only sufficiently hot to burn him slowly and make him suffer his martyrdom all the longer. St. Lawrence, with his heart full of joy, stretches himself on this terrible couch; he remains there with a serene countenance, blessing God, and when one side is burned he invites the tyrant to have him turned on the other side. Ah, said St. Leo, it was because the fire of divine love burning within him was more ardent than the fire which burnt his outside. O love! How admirable thou art! O sacred fire! Consume us. St. Lawrence is invincible under suffering because thou didst fill him; whilst we, we are so cowardly that the least difficulty stops us, because we do not love enough.

SECOND POINT

✝ What we ought to Do for Jesus Christ, following the Example Set for us by St. Lawrence

We ought first to detach ourselves from everything, even as this holy deacon did, giving to the poor all that he possessed. Do we do for the poor all that we ought? Do we love them like St. Lawrence, and do we provide for their needs in proportion to our means? Are we not of those who hoard up treasures, and, like the wicked rich man, leave the poor in need of what is necessary to them? Not content with giving his possessions to God in the person of the poor, St. Lawrence gives Him his blood by martyrdom. We are not called to such great happiness, but at least we can live in a spirit of martyrdom; that is to say, of being ready to die rather than to offend God; to mortify our flesh and our passions; to suffer in patience the miseries of this life, the trials incident to our position, injuries, calumnies, persecutions; in everything to take the cause of religion, to preach it by our example as well as by our words; not to make any account of human respect, and never to blush at what is our duty. It is thus that we may be martyrs in the peace of the Church, and this martyrdom is a precept obligatory on all Christians. Let us examine how we acquit ourselves of it. *Resolutions and spiritual nosegay as above.*

August 15th

THE ASSUMPTION OF THE BLESSED VIRGIN

SUMMARY OF TOMORROW'S MEDITATION

e will meditate tomorrow upon the three mysteries which we honor on this blessed day: first, the death of the Blessed Virgin; second, her glorious resurrection; third, her triumphant assumption and her coronation in heaven. We will then make the resolution: first, to express tomorrow, and during the whole octave, frequent desires to go to heaven, and contemplate Jesus in His glory and Mary on her throne; second, to preserve ourselves, by means of, watching over our interior and exterior senses, in the eminent purity suitable to a body called to the glory of the resurrection; third, to excite in ourselves humility, by considering of what value this virtue was to Mary on the day of her assumption. Our spiritual nose gay shall be the words of the Psalmist: "O God, the Queen is at Thy right hand." (Ps. 44:10)

MEDITATION FOR THE MORNING

Let us adore Our Lord glorifying Mary, His mother, by a holy death, a glorious resurrection, a triumphant assumption, followed by her enthronement in heaven and her coronation as queen of heaven and of earth. Let us thank God, and let us congratulate Mary on so many inexpressible favors.

FIRST POINT

✝ Edifying Death of the Blessed Virgin

The death of Mary was neither an effect of sickness, nor of failing nature, nor a penalty of sin, since the Blessed Virgin had never sinned; it was, on the contrary, a pure effect of the love with which her heart was inflamed (St. Bernard). From the day of the ascension she had never ceased to languish here below with love. (Cant. 2:5) She longed with all her heart for her reunion with her Divine Son, and every moment whilst the separation lasted was martyrdom to her. At last the strength of her love reached such a height as to break the chains which attached her soul to her body, and her holy soul flew to heaven upon a cloud of holy desires. Happy the souls which, detached from earth, have no other desires at heart than to die, that they may see and possess God eternally. These were the desires of the patriarchs, who kept the eyes of their hearts constantly fixed upon their heavenly home; (Heb. 10:13) the desires of David, who, regarding himself as a stranger here below, aspired continually after heaven; (Ps. 119:6; 44:3; 16:15) the desires of St. Paul, who wrote to the Philippians that he longed that his body should be dissolved, so that his soul, springing forth from its prison, should go and be reunited to Jesus Christ; (Philipp. 1:23) the desires of the martyr St. Ignatius, who wrote to the Romans: "I aspire to one thing only, and it is to enjoy Jesus Christ;" of the great doctor St. Augustine, who said: "Whoever does not sigh here below as a traveler shall not rejoice in heaven as a citizen;" of St. Francis of Assisi, who was called the man who looked at heaven; of St. Ignatius, who, during whole nights, when looking at a beautiful sky, uttered the cry of love: "How vile the earth seems to me when I look at heaven!" Those are not Christians who do not desire heaven, and who would willingly do without it if they could be assured in its place of enjoying the pleasures and honors of the world; those are not so either who desire death only from spite and despair, ennui, and disgust at life. Oh, why do they not accept, in a Christian spirit, the troubles of this world? Then they might desire the end of it, provided that it was with submission to the will of God. Let us examine our dispositions on this point.

SECOND POINT
✝ Resurrection of the Blessed Virgin

Divine love had despoiled Mary of her mortal robe; holy purity clothed her with the royal mantle of immortality. It was not suitable that so pure a body should be subjected to the putrefaction of the tomb, which is a chastisement reserved for the flesh of sin. Thus it was that Jesus Christ raised His mother to eternal glory, that He enveloped her with splendor which the Holy Spirit compares, now to the sun, now to the brilliant evening star. (Cant. 6:9) Let us here admire the love of God for chaste bodies and pure hearts, and also how well they understand the love of their body who keep it innocent, and how ill, on the other hand, those understand it who, for the sake of sensual gratifications unworthy of an immortal soul, deprive it of so much glory and condemn it to eternal punishment. O holy purity, with what splendors dost thou clothe the body of Mary! How well thou deservest all our esteem, all our love, and with what zeal ought we to preserve thee as the most precious of all treasures!

THIRD POINT

✝ The Assumption and Coronation of the Blessed Virgin

Such is the law laid down by God: the more we humble ourselves on earth, the more shall we be exalted in heaven.(Luke 14:11) Now, Mary humbled herself below all creatures; she who was queen in her quality of the mother of God takes the title of a servant; she who was purer than the angels assimilates herself to ordinary women on the day of her purification in the temple; she who was the daughter of kings lowers herself to such an extent as to pass for a poor laboring woman, a woman of the people. It was her due therefore to be raised above every creature, since she had placed herself below all; and this is what God did on the day of the assumption. Gloriously assumed, she rises triumphantly above the clouds, the angels come to meet her, they sing her glory, crying out: "Who is this that cometh up from the desert?" (Cant. 8:5) The prophets and patriarchs receive her with transports on her entrance into heaven; Moses acclaims the Star of Jacob which he had predicted; Isaias, the Virgin Mother whom he had announced; Ezechiel, the Gate of the East; David, the Queen who stands on the right hand of the King; (Ps. 44:10) and in the midst of these songs of gladness, Mary repeats her divine song: "My soul doth magnify the Lord." (Luke 1:46) And yet this is only the commencement; God, enthroning Mary on the throne of glory which has been prepared for her, encircles her fore-head with the royal crown, to show to angels and men that she is queen of heaven and of earth. O my Mother, my Queen, and my Sovereign! I salute thee in the ocean of glory in which thou wilt appear to me on that great day; I consecrate myself to thee and place myself under thy beloved scepter. Be in very truth my patroness and my mother, and by thy prayers make order and peace, religion, the love of God and of the Church, reign everywhere. *Resolutions and spiritual nosegay as above.*

August 20ᵀʰ

FEAST OF ST. BERNARD

SUMMARY OF TOMORROW'S MEDITATION

e will meditate tomorrow upon this illustrious doctor of the Church, and we will consider: first, that he was great by his union with God; second, by his works; third, still more by his humility. We will then make the resolution: first, to give up leading the thoughtless life which is so hurtful to our souls, and to enter upon a life of recollection and prayer; second, always to have very humble sentiments in regard to our souls. Our spiritual nosegay shall be the eulogium of Moses applied to St. Bernard: "Beloved of God and men: whose memory is in benediction." (Ecclus. 45:1)

MEDITATION FOR THE MORNING

Let us adore Jesus Christ, who, always attentive to the needs of His Church, sends her at each epoch saints appropriate to the circumstances, and who, in the twelfth century, in order to apply a remedy to the calamities inflicted upon the Church, specially sent her St. Bernard, a saint who was at one and the same time a doctor endowed with the science of the saints and with the understanding of the divine Scriptures, an apostle by means of his preaching of the gospel, a martyr by the mortification of his senses, a confessor by the eminence of his virtues, a prophet through his predictions of the future, a worker of miracles, a patriarch by the diffusion of his Order, an angel by the purity of his body. Let us thank Our Lord for having given the Church such a saint and to all coming ages such a model.

FIRST POINT

✝ St. Bernard was Great through his Union with God

St. Bernard was aware from his earliest youth that his soul was made for something higher than the world; and in consequence, closing his heart to all terrestrial attachments, and wholly opening it to the love of Jesus and of Mary, he raised himself by means of this double love as by a ladder, even as he himself expresses it, above all that passes away, and said farewell to the world, taking with him, as though triumphantly, into the solitude of Citeaux, his father, his uncle, his brothers, and thirty young men from among the number of his friends, to whom he had communicated the heavenly fire by which he was himself consumed. Leading there a celestial life, under favor of perpetual silence, he kept his soul continually united to God by prayer and disengaged from the senses by fasting and labor. God recompensed so much love by raising him to the most intimate communications with Himself, to the highest contemplations, sometimes even to holy ecstasies, which were for this holy religious a foretaste as it were of Paradise. Therefore the hour for prayer never came, in his opinion, frequently enough, and the time during which he was engaged in it always seemed too short. In comparison with this great saint, how little and degraded are worldly men who live only for earthly things, absorbing an immortal soul in dissipation and in the miserable enjoyments of this world! How poor we are ourselves in regard to the little recollection which we possess, how little do we know of union with God and of the spirit of prayer!

SECOND POINT
✝ St. Bernard was Great in his Works
This marvelous union with God did not hinder St. Bernard from giving himself up to the labors of an active life. He wrote immortal works, admirable epistles to the bishops, the incomparable book, "De Consideratione" to Pope Eugene; and this man, who, according to the expression he made use of, had had nothing but oak trees and beeches for his masters, becomes the doctor of the Church, the oracle consulted by the wisest prelates, the mouthpiece of Sovereign Pontiffs, the scourge of heretics, the living treasure of ecclesiastical science. Then, passing from a life of solitude to the functions of the apostolate, in order to withdraw the Christian world from the chaos of iniquities in which it was buried, he traverses Europe, regulating the Church in regard to both morals and doctrine; makes the truth to be listened to by kings and great men, acts the part of an arbitrator in all differences that arise, draws up the canons and decrees of the councils of Pisa, of Troyes, of Etampes, and of Rheims; draws up the symbols of faith; triumphs in Languedoc over Henry the Heresiarch, in Guienne over William, Duke of Aquitaine; brings about the condemnation of Gilbert de la Poree and of Peter Abelard; stops scandals, abolishes schism and heresy, extinguishes hatreds between princes who are at variance. What man has ever done more great works? And by what means did he perform them? It is a marvelous history. Doubtless, his rare merit contributed greatly to it, but at the same time the principal secret of his success was his incomparable

sweetness, which charmed all those who came near him, and changed wolves into lambs. Let us be confounded and ashamed in the presence of so many great works, we who do so little for God; let us above all be ashamed that we are so far from having the sweetness of St. Bernard.

THIRD POINT
✝ St. Bernard was still Greater by his Humility
To be profoundly humble in the midst of the tumult of praises, of splendor, and of honors, is the masterpiece of true goodness; and it is therein that St. Bernard is admirable. He is praised for his virtues and his miracles, and he begs for pity on his poor soul; he knows himself better, he says, than those who judge him from appearances. He blushes that he should be revered, not what he is, but what he seems to be, and he asks God that his baseness may be so well known that people should be ashamed of having praised a man who so little deserved to be praised. Who will enable me, he said again, to be as much humiliated in the presence of men for the defects which exist in me, as I am praised for the virtues which I do not possess? O Lord, he adds, my monstrous life, my miserable conscience cry out towards Thee; I am neither a monk nor a courtier, neither a priest nor a layman; I am a monstrous composite of all these states; I am the chimera of my century! O prodigious humility! What a lesson for us who have so little, and who, instead of abasing ourselves, seek only to be raised! *Resolutions and spiritual nosegay as above.*

𝔸UGUST 21ST

FEAST OF ST. CHANTAL

SUMMARY OF TOMORROW'S MEDITATION

 e will meditate tomorrow on the virtues of St. Chantal, whose feast we are celebrating, and we shall see: first, how dead she was to herself; second, how she lived for God alone. We will then make the resolution: first, to break with every attachment which has no relation to God, especially attachment to self-love, to self-will, and to our own comfort; second, to desire and to will God alone. Our spiritual nosegay shall be the words of the Saint: "God alone is everything to my heart."

MEDITATION FOR THE MORNING

Let us adore the power of grace which caused all the vicious inclinations of our evil nature no longer to exist in St. Chantal, and in their stead made God and His pure love alone reign within her. Let us admire this marvelous transformation, and let us bless Our Lord, whose grace worked this miracle.

FIRST POINT

✝ How St. Chantal was Dead to Herself

The first step to make in Christian life is to die to one's self. "You are dead" wrote St. Paul to the faithful at Colossa. (Coloss. 3:3) "Mortify yourself in everything to the utmost," wrote St. Francis de Sales to St. Chantal "and let all die within you, in order that God may live therein." Docile to the advice of her saintly director, our saint became really dead to herself. Dead to her self-will, although she was still in the world, the whole of her life was subjected to a rule which left nothing to caprice; her rising as well as her lying down, her spiritual exercises as well as the care of her household, the employment of every moment as well as the way of doing each single thing, all was done regularly. From the earliest season of her widowhood, being more her own mistress, she would not make any other use of her greater freedom than to bend it under obedience to a director whom she consulted about everything. Desire nothing, ask nothing, refuse nothing—such was henceforth the rule of her conduct. Dead to self-love, she knew nothing of self-esteem, despising herself profoundly, and looking on herself as the lowest of the daughters of the Visitation. Far from desiring the esteem of others, she had a supreme horror of it; contempt made her rejoice, humiliations were her happiness, susceptibility and pretentiousness were unknown to her. Dead to the love of riches and of earthly possessions, she delighted in poverty, not even keeping a watch for her own use, not even a relic; and old and patched habits were estimable in her eyes as being consecrated by holy poverty. Dead to the pleasures of the senses, and even to the sensible delights of piety, she joyfully embraced privations because they are disagreeable to the senses; suffering, because it crucifies them; sickness, because it afflicts them. She blessed God in interior abandonments as well as in consolations, in darkness as well as in light. She arrived at the point of being able to say that if the glory and felicity of Paradise had the power of separating her from God, she would not take a single step to obtain them; for, she added, I desire nothing but God in this world and in the next "a sublime and universal death to self, well suited to confound us and to make us feel the necessity of entering upon a new life."

SECOND POINT
✝ **How St. Chantal Lived for God Alone**

Entirely possessed by divine love, St. Chantal did nothing and said nothing except with a view to God and for God. In her it was a strong and vigorous love, which joyfully embraced all kinds of sacrifices, even to the point of passing, spite of the anguish of her most maternal heart, over the body of a son who offered an obstacle to her vocation; a hardy and invincible love, which entered upon the greatest enterprises for the glory of God and the salvation of souls; a love which could not be shaken by reverses, which was always abandoned to Providence, without any self-seeking; a love which was humble to the extent of a total annihilation of self, that God alone might be exalted; a love which was so joyous in anguish that it was a delight to it to feel bitterness and abandonment interiorly, and exteriorly contempt and contradiction; a love, lastly, which kept her in such a state of perfect abandonment to the guidance of God, that she was really like the child who, giving its hand to its mother, allows itself to be led everywhere by her and to do all that she wills. Hence the vow by which she engages to do what is most perfect in everything; hence her seeing God in her neighbor, whoever he might be: in the poor and the sick, even in people full of faults, who, on that very account, became the objects of her most tender sympathies, so that it was a joy to her to render good for evil, to bear anything, to forgive everything, and to love always, spite of everything. What an admirable model, and how far we are from it! *Resolutions and spiritual nosegay as above.*

Λugust 24ᵀʰ

FEAST OF ST. BARTHOLOMEW, APOSTLE

SUMMARY OF TOMORROW'S MEDITATION

e will meditate tomorrow upon this holy apostle, who, after having preached the gospel in the East, sealed his preaching in Armenia with his blood by the most cruel of martyrdoms, for, according to several historians, he was first flayed alive and then crucified. His martyrdom will give us an opportunity to meditate upon two great truths; that is to say: first, that we ought to despoil ourselves of that portion of us which sin has vitiated and which St. Paul calls the old man; second, that this spoliation ought to be entire and without any reserve. We will then make the resolution: first, to study today what it is to which our heart most clings here below, and to make a generous sacrifice of it to God; second, often to repeat the words of St. Francis de Sales: "If I knew that there was in my heart the least fiber which was not wholly steeped in the love of my God, I would tear it out immediately." Our spiritual nosegay shall be the words of St. Paul: "Strip yourselves of the old man, and put on the new." (Coloss. 3:9, 10)

MEDITATION FOR THE MORNING

Let us adore Our Lord Jesus Christ teaching us: first, by the mouth of St. Paul, that we must put off the old man and clothe ourselves with the new; second, by the example afforded us by St. Bartholomew, that this spoliation ought to be entire and without reserve, seeing that this holy apostle was deprived of his skin from the crown of his head to the sole of his foot, and was crucified. Let us thank Jesus Christ for this double lesson, and let us glorify St. Bartholomew, who had the courage to suffer so much for his Master.

FIRST POINT

✝ **The Martyrdom of St. Bartholomew Teaches us not to Cling to Anything Here Below**

St. Bartholomew, after having quitted everything to follow Jesus Christ, devoted himself to the fatigues and to the dangers of the apostolate, that he might go and evangelize the different countries of Asia; and in his evangelical journeys he enjoyed the triple honor of converting many souls, of being persecuted like his good Master, and, lastly, of being condemned by an impious king to be flayed alive and then crucified. St. Bartholomew submitted lovingly to this last torture, the very idea of which makes us shudder, and felt that, even at such a price as that, it was not buying heaven at too great a cost. Let us represent to ourselves the apostle suffering this horrible martyrdom with the calmness of the most heroic patience, and without uttering a murmur or a complaint. Oh, what good right he has to say to us in this state: "Put off the old man," that is to say, your vitiated nature in Adam, the thousand attachments which form an obstacle to grace and prevent you from belonging wholly to God; despoil yourselves, above all, of certain attachments to which you cling the most. For to what does man cling more than to the skin which covers him? And yet the apostle says to us: I despoiled myself of it for love of my Master. I know what it costs, and I do not ask you for as much as that I only ask you to despoil yourselves of that passionate seeking after your own comfort and after pleasure, which maintains you in an effeminate, sensual life, unworthy of a disciple of the cross; to despoil yourselves of the self-love and pride which make you susceptible, jealous, pretentious, and which will lead you farther into evil than you have any idea of, for it is written, pride is the source of all sin; to despoil yourselves, lastly, of self-love and the caprices which make you lead an ill-regulated life, which are hurtful to the peace of your homes, to a cordial intercourse, to the pleasant relations of charity. Let us listen from the bottom of our hearts to the teaching of St. Bartholomew, and let us be docile to it.

SECOND POINT

✝ **The Martyrdom of St. Bartholomew Teaches us to Give Ourselves to God Entirely and without Reserve**

After having been flayed, St. Bartholomew appeared before heaven as a victim ready for the sacrifice, who waits for nothing but the stroke of death. He was crucified in accordance with the barbarous custom imported from Persia into Armenia. The holy martyr, after having sacrificed his body to suffering, sacrifices even his very life. He expires, gives up his holy soul to the Lord, feeling happy to teach us thereby: first, that we must have no reserves in regard to the sacrifice and the spoliation which God requires from us. There are men who would willingly give their money, but on condition of keeping their sensuality or their pride; others would willingly give their time and their services, but on condition of keeping their money. God will have none of these reserves; Jesus Christ told us so plainly on Calvary; St. Bartholomew repeats it on his cross. The holy apostle teaches us, second, that the sacrifice once made, it must be continued until death. God forbids us from taking back what has once been sacrificed to Him; it would be tantamount to introducing theft into the holocaust, which is a thing He detests, and which His example condemns; for the whole life of Jesus Christ was nothing but a cross and a martyrdom. (2 Imit. 12:7) Ours ought to resemble it; every Christian life ought to be a life of sacrifice and of holocaust. Let us examine if ours is such. *Resolutions and spiritual nosegay as above.*

Αugust 25th

FEAST OF ST. LOUIS, KING OF FRANCE

SUMMARY OF TOMORROW'S MEDITATION

e will meditate tomorrow, in the person of St. Louis, upon one of the most beautiful masterpieces of grace, and we shall see that religion made of this prince: first, a great king; second, a great Christian. We will then make the resolution: first, to act, to speak, and to think in a spirit of faith, with a view to God and His glory; second, always to treat our neighbor in a spirit of charity, forgetting ourselves for the good of others. Our spiritual nosegay shall be the beautiful eulogium pronounced upon St. Louis by one of his historians: "He endeavored always to please Jesus Christ, as the sole King of all hearts."

MEDITATION FOR THE MORNING

Let us adore Our Lord Jesus Christ forming by His grace, in the person of St. Louis, a finished model of the most sublime virtue, and thereby showing to all Christians that a man may be a great saint everywhere at court, in the midst of its dangers, as well as in a cloister, in the midst of all the means of salvation; that we can be saints in all conditions in the midst of the embarrassments of affairs, of tumults, and of dissipation, as well as in the silence of solitude and far from the preoccupations of human affairs. Let us thank Our Lord for this great lesson, and propose to ourselves to profit by it abundantly.

FIRST POINT

✝ Religion Made a Great King of St. Louis

By a great king is to be understood not only a powerful monarch who makes everyone surrounding him tremble, but rather a prince eminent in justice, in goodness, in wisdom, in bravery, in dignity of character. Now, by means of religion St. Louis was all this. First, he was eminent in regard to justice; he never undertook or did anything which was not just. He refused the empire offered him to the prejudice of Frederic, because in his eyes nothing was great but that which was upright; and he would not have bought a kingdom, of no matter what extent, at the price of a lie. To render justice to all was, in his eyes, the first of his duties, even in the case of the Saracens, who were guilty of so much injustice towards him. Second, he was eminent in regard to kindness. He aspired to nothing so much as to relieve all who were suffering, and he looked upon himself as the provider of the poor and the steward of Jesus Christ; he raised taxes only in order to be able to give more aid to the indigent, and it was said of him that, like Jesus Christ, his hands were pierced, so that they retained nothing and gave all, even their own blood. Every day he received at his table three poor old men, whom he served with his own hands. On feast days he served as many as two hundred, for, he said, it is our duty to honor Christ in His poor, and if the poor gain heaven by penance, the rich ought to gain it by charity. Third, he was eminent in wisdom. He reconciles the most powerful monarchs, he is successful over foreign armies, he stifles domestic seditions, he unites several provinces to the crown, and no reign has ever been longer or more stable than his, lasting as it did forty-four years; and no line has ever been more fortunate than his, which gave so many kings to France. Fourth, he was eminent in bravery. In the crusades which he undertook to conquer an empire for Jesus Christ beyond the seas, he was the first to advance, sword in hand, against the Saracens. On all occasions he gave proof of intrepid courage, and if he lost two flourishing armies, the treasures and the noblest blood of France, if he lost his labors, his sweats, his liberty, whilst waiting till he lost his life, he never allowed his great soul to be cast down. He was able to keep his kingdom intact, without any of its provinces being detached from it, spite of so long an absence, and he did not lose a single ray of his glory. Fifth, he was eminent in the dignity which marked his character. Humble as the most hidden amongst monks, without any haughtiness of speech, without ostentation in his deportment, without luxury in his clothing, without disdain in the expression of his eyes, without anything affected in his conversation, he knew how to show his greatness when it was necessary to do so, and to rise by generosity above all the powers of the world, above even the Saracens, his conquerors, who were astonished to find in him rather a master than a captive, and who desired to have him for their king. Let us admire the manner in which religion ennobles and elevates characters, how it makes men great and truly honorable, to the point of making even their enemies respect them.

SECOND POINT
✝ Religion Made a Great Christian of St. Louis
Faithful to the lessons of Queen Blanche, his mother, who had said to him, "My son, I would rather see you dead than see you commit one mortal sin," St. Louis did not allow himself to be rendered effeminate by the pleasures of the court, or seduced by the baits of voluptuousness. God alone was everything to him; he breathed only for His service and His glory, the defense of the faith, the abolition of vice, the triumph of virtue, the salvation of his people; and in order to attain this end, he prayed during the day, he prayed during the night, reciting the breviary and assisting daily at two Masses with the fervor of the most perfect religious. He was as mortified as an anchorite; he fasted every Friday, he constantly wore a hair-shirt, he wounded his body with an iron discipline. He was as zealous as an apostle; he made use of all possible means for converting sinners, he sent away actors, he threatened blasphemers with severe penalties, he encouraged all the religious Orders devoted to the preaching of the gospel, he neglected no means whatever of making God known, loved, and served; he labored every day to advance in the perfect life, he was recollected in the midst of the dissipation of the world, mortified amongst pleasures, humble at the summit of earthly greatness. Could there be a more beautiful model? Let us endeavor from this very day to draw near to it by means of recollection, mortification, and humility. *Resolutions and spiritual nosegay as above.*

August 28th

FEAST OF ST. AUGUSTINE

SUMMARY OF TOMORROW'S MEDITATION

We will consider St. Augustine in our meditation tomorrow: first, as an illustrious penitent; second, as a great bishop. We will then make the resolution: first, to apply ourselves, like Augustine, to repair our past life, by a penitence which shall endure until death; second, often to utter acts of love towards God, and to seize upon every opportunity that offers itself to devote ourselves to His glory and the good of our neighbor. Our spiritual nosegay shall be the words of the Apostle, which are so suitable to St. Augustine: "By the grace of God I am what I am, and His grace in me hath not been void." (I. Cor. 15:10)

MEDITATION FOR THE MORNING

Let us adore Our Lord Jesus Christ giving to the Church, in the person of St. Augustine, so illustrious a penitent, so eminent a saint, so admirable a doctor, the oracle of the councils, the light of the Church, the father of fathers, the doctor of doctors. Let us glorify God for the power of His grace, which worked such a miracle, and let us congratulate St. Augustine, who was not only able to say, "By the grace of God I am what I am" but who was also able to add, "His grace in me hath not been void."

FIRST POINT

✝ St. Augustine an Illustrious Penitent

Never was seen a penitent more touched, more humble, more grateful. First, more touched, for his tears began to flow from the beginning of his conversion: "There rose within me," he said, "a tempest, which was followed by an abundant rain of tears," and he resolved to bury himself alive in some solitary place, there to weep over his faults even to his last sigh. As the order of Providence was opposed to this design, Augustine found means for uniting with the labors of the episcopate the penance of the most austere anchorite. His whole life was a continual course of journeys, of watchings, of fastings, and of crosses; and esteeming these expiations as in sufficient in proportion to the greatness and number of his faults, when he felt that he was about to die he had, the penitential psalms placed on the walls of his room, and recited them with a great abundance of sighs, until he breathed his last. Second, there never was a more humble penitent. In his book of Confessions he reveals the most shameful of his sins to the whole world, and bears his shame in the face of all men and before all ages. Forever and ever it will be known that Augustine had given way to indecency and debauchery, and this public and permanent confession he made whilst he was living in the world, seated upon one of the thrones of the Church, surrounded by heretics and envious men, whose contempt he accepted as a thing due to him. Third, never was penitent more grateful. His writings breathe nothing but love of the mercies of the Lord towards him; and in order to recount them, neither his pen nor his tongue is sufficient for his heart; he gives vent to bursts of admiration, to thanksgivings, to effusions of love. "O Beauty, ever ancient and ever new," he cries out, "too late have I loved Thee! Unhappy days in which I did not love Thee! O Fire whichever burnest, and art never consumed; O Love, ever fervent, which knowest neither interruption nor relaxation, inflame me, set me all on fire, that I may love Thee with my whole strength, and that there may be nothing in me which is not love. It seems to me that I love Thee, O my God, but desire to love Thee more and more." What a brazier, what a furnace of love O great saint, make some sparks of this great fire which devoured thee fall upon my heart.

SECOND POINT

✝ St. Augustine a Great Bishop

A bishop is marked by two great characteristics: zeal for evangelizing the people and charity in succoring the unhappy. Now St Augustine possessed these two characteristics in the very highest degree. First, he had zeal for evangelizing the people. Burning with a desire to make Jesus Christ known and loved, not only by the whole world, but by all ages, he applied himself with his whole strength to the study of the Holy Scriptures; he became an abyss of divine science; then shedding the plenitude of it upon the people, he fed them abundantly with the bread of the word. He united to these eloquent sermons an immense number of learned writings, which were dispersed abroad with the mission of bringing back to the truth pagans and philosophers, Arians and Manicheans, Donatists and Priscillianists, Pelagians and Semi-Pelagians. No error escapes his zeal; he specially pursues the heresy of Pelagius in its last retrenchments; he reveals to the world the most hidden mysteries of grace, in immortal works which will remain a focus of light for the universal Church throughout all ages. Second, to zeal for evangelizing and instructing he unites charity in solacing the unhappy. He for gets himself, gives all that he has, and arrived at the point of death, he cannot make a testament, says his historian, because he had distributed all he had to the poor and had nothing more to leave. Could there be more beautiful devotion? Let us bring our life to a nearer resemblance to that of this great saint, and let us judge ourselves. *Resolutions and spiritual nosegay as above.*

SEPTEMBER 8ᵀʰ

THE NATIVITY OF THE BLESSED VIRGIN

SUMMARY OF TOMORROW'S MEDITATION

omorrow the Church will celebrate the anniversary of the birth of Mary; and in order better to understand the splendors of this beautiful feast we will consider: first, what a beautiful day it was for God; second, what a beautiful day it was for Mary; Third, what a beautiful day it was for the whole human race. We will then make the resolution: first, to renew our devotion towards the Blessed Virgin; second, to be born again to a better life, more fervent and more worthy of a child of Mary. Our spiritual nosegay shall be the prayer of the Church: "Show thyself to be our mother."

MEDITATION FOR THE MORNING

Let us thank God for the inestimable gift He made to the earth in giving birth to Mary, our mother, our advocate, our mediatrix, the mother of our Redeemer. We can never thank Him enough for so great a blessing.

FIRST POINT
✝ The Birth of Mary was a Beautiful Day for God

On this day, in fact, there appeared upon earth the greatest marvel on which the sun ever shone, a creature who was at one and the same time the cherished daughter of the Father, the future mother of the Word, and destined to become the beloved spouse of the Holy Ghost; a creature who was a little infant, and already surpassing in greatness and in dignity, not only all creatures who have ever existed or whoever will exist, but also all possible creatures, since these creatures could never be anything but the servants of God, while Mary O immeasurable difference! Is the daughter, the mother, and the spouse; a creature enriched with all the gifts of holiness, with all the supernatural virtues which belong to the condition of a creature; a creature who is the masterpiece of the power of the Father, of the wisdom of the Son, of the love of the Holy Ghost, seeing that it was incumbent on the Father, the Son, and the Holy Ghost to make a person linked with them by such intimate relations all that it was possible to be; a creature, consequently, whom they looked at with love, whom they admired with delight, in whom they took the pleasure which the workman feels in his master piece. O Mary, in thy little cradle I love to contemplate thee as being the paradise of God upon earth, as beautiful above expression and without the shadow of a spot. Thou art still only an infant, and already thou art the object of the complaisance of the Most Holy Trinity. Oh, what happiness is thine! To please God is the greatest of all kinds of happiness; and this happiness, O my mother, thou hast enjoyed from the day of thy birth! This happiness I can also enjoy myself in a certain degree by means of the sanctity of my life, by the purity of my intentions in all things; for, O my God, in order to please Thee, it is sufficient to have the will to do so! O consoling thought!

SECOND POINT
✝ The Birth of Mary was a Beautiful Day for Herself

What a joy it was for her heart to see herself by the aid of her reason, which was perfectly developed, as being the object of the tender affection of St. Anne, her mother, and presented by her to the Most Holy Trinity as the most beautiful present that earth could give to heaven, and lovingly received by the Three Divine Persons! What joy for her to unite herself with all the pious sentiments of her holy mother, and to offer her whole being to the great God, living in order to be wholly His, living and breathing only for Him, and not having a single pulsation of her heart which is not directed towards Him! What joy to see heaven give such a magnificent reply to her offering, and inundate her with an immense holiness, which incomparably surpasses the holiness of all the blessed spirits! What joy to see herself saluted by the Most Holy Trinity, when addressing her in the words of the Canticle it says: Thou art all fair, O My love, and there is not a spot in thee." (Cant. 4:7) "One is My dove, My perfect one is but one;" (Cant. 6:8) saluted at the same time by all the angels, who exclaim, How lovely she is, this flower which has come to blossom on earth; she is filled with delights. (Cant. 8:5) She is "as the morning rising, fair as the moon, bright as the sun." (Cant. 6:9) Amidst so many causes of joy, the newborn infant utters in the bottom of her heart the words which later on she will repeat with her pure lips: "My soul doth magnify the Lord, and my spirit hath rejoiced in God my Savior." (Luke 1:46, 47) Let us unite ourselves with the joys of the Blessed Virgin, let us bless God for them, let us congratulate Mary, and let us learn from her to place all our joys in the Lord, and not to desire any others. In God alone is true joy, the joy which does not leave any remorse in its train, the joy which completely satisfies the heart, and is for it a foretaste of Paradise. Let us leave to the world the false joys which are a source of dissipation, which seduce, which corrupt, and which are incompatible with true and solid virtue.

THIRD POINT

✝ The Birth of Mary was a Beautiful Day for the whole Human Race

It was, indeed, a day of glory for the world, of happiness, of hope, and of ineffable edification. First, a day of glory; for what honor was it not for human nature that a child of Adam should be destined to become the mother and the spouse of a God! Who would have imagined such grandeur in a simple creature, and what thanksgiving ought we not to render to God for it? Second, a day of happiness; for what happiness for the world was not the apparition of the star which was the precursor of the Sun of justice, the birth of her whom Heaven had chosen to be the mediator and the advocate of men in the presence of divine justice! Third, a day of hope; for this holy child will one day be our mother and will co-operate in the designs of love and mercy which God entertains in regard to us. Fourth, a day of ineffable edification; for what does she do in her cradle? She prays for herself and for us. She prays for herself, for she must first of all sanctify herself and advance every day from virtue to virtue; she prays for us, because she knows that her mission is to save the world and to co-operate in all the designs of God respecting the salvation of men. Is it thus that we fulfill our mission upon earth? Do we labor to sanctify ourselves and to sanctify others? *Resolutions and spiritual nosegay as above.*

September 14ᵗʰ

THE EXALTATION OF THE HOLY CROSS

SUMMARY OF TOMORROW'S MEDITATION

e will meditate tomorrow on the feast of the day; and in order to excite ourselves to love the Cross and to exalt it in our hearts, we will consider: first, how Jesus Christ loved and glorified it; second, how ill it would become us not to love and glorify it. Our resolution shall be: first, cheerfully to accept any cross which may present itself to us, and never again to become impatient or be cast down by contrarieties and affliction; second, to receive all the trials of life as particles of the Cross of Jesus Christ, and therefore to cherish and honor them, saying with the Apostle: "My glory is in the Cross." (Gal. 6:14) These words will serve as our spiritual nosegay.

MEDITATION FOR THE MORNING

Let us thank Our Lord for having so marvelously exalted His holy Cross: first, through the piety of the Emperor Heraclius, who, after having taken it out of the hands of the infidels, carried it himself and placed it once more upon Calvary. Second, through the devotion of the Church, which celebrates annually this beautiful triumph in the feast of the Exaltation of the Holy Cross. Let us beg of Him to exalt this Cross in our hearts by inspiring us with more esteem and love for it.

FIRST POINT

✝ How Jesus Christ Loved and Glorified His Cross

Nature does not love the Cross; even the mere sight of it makes it shudder. Jesus Christ, in order to correct this wrong disposition, showed Himself during His whole life to be a friend to the Cross; He constantly desired it, (Luke 12:50) and on the day which was to be the last of His life He lovingly embraced it; He took it on His shoulders, He Himself bore it to Calvary, He allowed Himself to be nailed upon it, and He died in its arms as on His bed of honor. Could He have better shown us how He loved it, consequently how amiable it is, since

Eternal Wisdom cannot but greatly love what is superlatively amiable? After this first homage rendered to the Cross, He glorified it by means of the great things of which He made it the instrument. By the

Cross, in fact, our sins are expiated and we are reinstated in grace; after having been the enemies of God through sin, we become His best friends; in the Cross we find the principle of Christian life, the teaching of all the virtues, the foundation of all our merits in this world and of our glory in eternity; the Cross is for us the warrant of the love of the Father, the characteristic and the seal of the predestinate. (Rom. 8:17) Who at the sight of so much glory would not esteem and love the Cross? Who would not feel it to be good, beautiful, honorable, and precious? (Office of St. Andrew.)

SECOND POINT
✝ How Wrong it would be of us not to Love and Glorify the Cross
First, it would be doing an injury to the Cross; for it is not only by kissing or by embracing the crucifix that we honor the Cross, but much rather by receiving patiently and lovingly the thousand little trifles of life which are as so many particles of the Cross of the Savior. If we fly from trouble, if we become impatient in the midst of annoyances, if we seek for content in pleasure and in ministering to our own comforts, it is a proof that we do not hold the Cross in esteem, that we do not desire it, and that it would give us pleasure if it would depart far away from us; it is consequently to dishonor it, to despise it, and to treat it as refuse. At the last day it will come to judge the world, (Matt. 24:30) and then the friends of the Cross will be as happy as those will be miserable who dishonor it, and who will have none of it. Second, not to love the Cross is to insure our unhappiness even in this present life; for trials are inseparable from life here below, and if we do not resign ourselves and bear them patiently, if we give ourselves up to sorrow, to vexation, to heaviness, trials thus ill endured are incomparably more painful and the misery of them increased a hundred-fold. Looking at the matter from another point of view, we are unhappy even in the midst of what is pleasant, because all things here below being mingled with what tends to make us sad and discontented, he who does not love the Cross will never taste true joy and will be unhappy even in prosperity. Nor must it be forgotten that during the whole of our life, if we desire to be saved, we must mortify our temper, bring our passions into subjection, crucify our senses, resist temptations, fly from evil and do what is good. Now all these things are possible only on condition of striving and fighting against self. Now where there is no love of the Cross we become weary of these difficulties and these

combats; we become melancholy, sad, and disgusted; we are unhappy. Ah! Why do we not frankly love the Cross? We should then turn even these very troubles into causes of joy we should consider ourselves happy to be allowed to share the Cross of Jesus Christ and to drink of His chalice. Let us be confounded before God for having until now so little loved the Cross, and let us ask of Him grace to love it henceforth. *Resolutions and spiritual nosegay as above.*

See the meditations on the saints at the end of the fifth volume for meditations on St. Matthew (September 21); St. Michael (September 26), the first Sunday in October, and the Holy Guardian Angels. (October 2nd)

HAMON, A. J. M. BQ

Meditations for All the Days of the Year.

Reprinted by Valora Media 2011

Made in the USA
Middletown, DE
28 June 2023

34052854R00139